WAGERING THE LAND

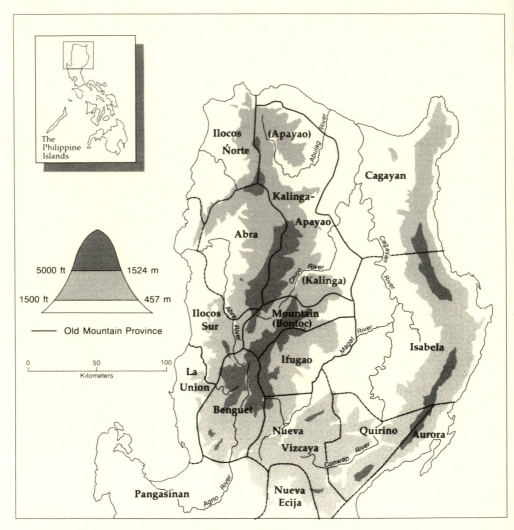

The
Philippine
Islands

5000 ft — 1524 m

1500 ft — 457 m

—— Old Mountain Province

0   50   100
Kilometers

Ilocos
Norte

(Apayao)

Cagayan

Kalinga-
Apayao

Abra

(Kalinga)

Ilocos
Sur

Mountain
(Bontoc)

Isabela

Ifugao

La
Union

Benguet

Nueva
Vizcaya

Quirino

Aurora

Pangasinan

Nueva
Ecija

Map 1. *Northern Luzon: Topography and Provincial Boundaries.*

WAGERING THE LAND

RITUAL, CAPITAL, AND ENVIRONMENTAL DEGRADATION IN THE CORDILLERA OF NORTHERN LUZON, 1900-1986

MARTIN W. LEWIS

UNIVERSITY OF CALIFORNIA PRESS

Berkeley · Los Angeles · Oxford

The author thanks the Association of American
Geographers for permission to reprint much of chapter 4
and maps 1, 2, 3, 4, 6, 7, 8, and 9 from *Annals of the
Association of American Geographers* © 1989.

University of California Press
Berkeley and Los Angeles, California

University of California Press
Oxford, England

Library of Congress Cataloging-in-Publication Data

Lewis, Martin W.
    Wagering the land : ritual, capital, and environmental
degradation in the Cordillera of northern Luzon,
1900–1986 / Martin W. Lewis.
        p. cm.
    Includes bibliographical references (p.   ) and index.
    ISBN 0-520-07272-3 (cloth : alk. paper)
    1. Man—Influence on nature—Philippines—Buguias.
2. Agricultural   ecology—Philippines—Buguias.   3. Tropical vegetable industry—Philippines—Buguias.   4. Agriculture—Economic aspects— Philippines—Buguias.
5. Agriculture—Social aspects—Philippines—Buguias.
6. Rites and ceremonies—Philippines— Buguias.
7. Buguias (Philippines)—Politics and government.   8. Buguias (Philippines)—Religous life and
customs.   I. Title.
GF852.P6L48   1992
333.76'09599'1—dc20   91-12307
                                                    CIP

Printed in the United States of America

1 2 3 4 5 6 7 8 9

Contents

Illustrations

Acknowledgments

I have often had occasion to think that I was fortunate to have attended graduate school in geography at Berkeley when I did. The 1980s saw the traditional concerns of the department, human-environmental relations culturally and historically framed, co-existing—however uneasily—with a vigorous movement toward social theory. Had I enrolled any earlier or later, I doubt that I would have received an education sufficiently broad to have allowed me to write this work.

My debts at Berkeley are numerous. James Parsons's utter delight in landscape will ever be an inspiration, as will Bernard Nietschmann's intellectual courage and iconoclastic visions. To Michael Watts I owe a grounding in political economy; to Robert Reed and to anthropologist James Anderson, many thanks for introducing me to things Philippine. Fellow graduate students from Berkeley played a formative role as well; great appreciation goes to Paul Starrs, Karl Zimmerer, and especially, Karen Wigen.

The geography department at George Washington University has offered an ideal environment in which to prepare the manuscript. Don Vermeer consistently provided support and encouragement, while Deborah Hart furnished intellectual companionship. Monica Jordan was ever helpful. I would also like to thank Joel Kuipers of the G.W. anthropology department for many stimulating observations.

Numerous Cordilleran scholars have substantially contributed to this work. My most perceptive critic has been William Henry Scott, whose scholarship on the Philippine highlands has set the standard of the field. Harold Conklin enthusiastically pushed my inquiries forward in several important directions; to him I owe my deepest appreciation. Special thanks also go to Gerard Finin and Patricia Afable for generously sharing their works in progress. In Benguet, Bridget Hamada-Pawid offered suggestions and advice that proved essential for the completion of fieldwork. All of the scholars associated with the Cordilleran Studies Center of the University of the Philippines, Baguio, provided great assistance for which I am most grateful. My debt to the Cordillera's local intellectuals—those perceptive observers of their own societies unschooled within academia—is too vast to be recorded here. (Their contributions are discussed in the introductory chapter.)

Financial support for fieldwork was generously provided by a Fulbright Fellowship. Archival work in the United States was funded by a University of California Graduate Humanities Research Grant. A Junior Faculty Incentive Grant from George Washington University allowed me to complete the manuscript. Many thanks to Ellen White for the cartographic work. And finally, this book would not have been possible without the continued support of Kathryn and James Lodato, and of Nell and Wayne Lewis. To the latter I am indebted beyond reckoning.

M. W. L.

1

Introduction

ABATAN, BUGUIAS, APRIL 15, 1986

Five long hours by bus from the highland resort city of Baguio lies the unremarkable town of Abatan, a cluster of colorless storefronts of corrugated iron. Perched on a narrow ridge between the headwaters of the Agno and Abra rivers, the huddled buildings of this unpretentious town belie its importance as the marketing headquarters of the northern Benguet vegetable district, centered here in the municipality of Buguias. Where the ridge drops sharply away on both sides, metal sheeting gives way to terraced gardens of cabbages and potatoes extending hundreds of meters down the mountain slopes.

Abatan on most days presents a stark townscape, but a traveler passing through on April 15, 1986, would have witnessed a remarkable sight. On that day, dozens of vegetable trucks packed with villagers converged from miles around on the center of town. Some five thousand persons, representing over forty villages, had come to receive meat and rice beer, to dance and sing, and, most importantly, to worship their ancestors. Of the many prestige feasts celebrated in the Buguias region every year, this event was extraordinary. The celebrants had laid out a repast worth over 300,000 pesos, or $15,000 U.S., including twenty-seven water buffalo and cattle, scores of hogs, heaps of rice, and countless jugs of rice beer. The purpose of the staggering expense was to enlist supernatural assistance for accumulating further wealth.

THE TRANSFORMATION
OF BUGUIAS LIVELIHOOD

Only fifty years ago, the ridge on which Abatan sits was covered with thick forests of pine and oak. On the lower slopes of the adjacent Agno Valley, herds of cattle, water buffalo, and hogs roamed

1

free in a landscape dotted with small hamlets, irrigated rice plots, and sweet-potato fields. But fierce battles at the end of World War II ravaged herds and fields, demolishing in the process an extensive local trade network that had underwritten social power and wealth. The old ways were never to revive. Within ten years, most residents of Buguias municipality were fully committed to market gardening.

For a time, temperate vegetables provided a measure of real prosperity. Considered a showcase of rural development during the 1960s, the area's landscape still signals the relative wealth of its inhabitants. Houses here are more solid, and clothing more ample, than in almost any lowland area of the Philippine archipelago, a fact not completely explained away by the cool highland climate. Numerous trucks of all sizes similarly testify to past profits, just as the insecticide and fungicide advertisements plastered over the public buildings bespeak a high-yield, chemical-intensive agriculture.

The wealth derived from vegetables also allowed the Buguias people to perpetuate a tradition of redistributive feasting. In earlier days, extravagant animal sacrifice typified religious practice throughout the southern highlands. During the 1830s the would-be conquistador Guillermo Galvey counted some 1,300 hog and water-buffalo skulls on a single house in the village of Kapangan (Scott 1974:214). Yet Kapangan, located on the far fringe of the vegetable district, has not seen a sizable feast in decades. By the 1980s, it was only the market-gardening villages that could finance lavish celebrations. Subsistence-oriented communities, which retained the more environmentally benign indigenous forms of cultivation, greatly curtailed their redistributive feasts after the war, in some instances abandoning the indigenous religion altogether. Benguet's modern center of Paganism—a term used by adherents and their Christian challengers alike—is the thoroughly commercialized village of Buguias Central, focus of this study.[1]

Today, Buguias's prosperity looks increasingly tenuous. Large-scale operators, vegetable traders, and chemical merchants continue to reap substantial profits, but the highland vegetable district as a whole saw its agriculture stagnate and its living standards decline as the Philippine economy stalled and sputtered through the

1970s and 1980s. Most growers have fallen deeply into debt, not uncommonly receiving less now for a given crop than they have to pay for seeds and chemicals. Nor does vegetable agriculture appear to be ecologically sustainable. Biocides and fertilizers have polluted local water supplies, erosion steadily denudes the steeper slopes, and deforested watersheds yield ever-diminishing stream flows.

Yet despite growing ecological peril and economic uncertainty, the people of Buguias remain committed to the gamble that is market gardening. Although they live under a constant threat of market collapse, farm families hope for the unpredictable upturns, wagering their crops—and increasingly their environment—on the day when they may reap the coveted "jackpot" harvest. For gambling is a fundamental precept of life in Buguias, albeit not exactly gambling as we conceive it. Many of the manifestations are familiar: boys of five and six wager their pocket money on the flip of a coin; young men frequent the cardhouses, cockpits, and casino of Baguio City; even elders bet compulsively at rummy. But most Buguias people do not consider fate to be blind; rather, they believe that risk can be manipulated through ritual. Like their grandparents before them, most contemporary villagers attempt to ensure the success of their most chancy undertakings through placating their ancestors and feasting their neighbors. It is the resulting nexus of economy, ecology, and religion, with its unusual concatenation of capitalist transformation, cultural persistence, and environmental degradation, that forms the core of this work.

COMMERCIALIZATION
AND LOCAL CHANGE

COMMERCIAL AGRICULTURE AND
ENVIRONMENTAL DEGRADATION

The environmental destruction accompanying the spread of commercial agriculture along the margins of the global economy is now well documented by geographers and anthropologists. Areas previously marked by sustainable subsistence cultivation soon exhibit such symptoms as rapid soil erosion, deforestation, and pesticide contamination (Nietschmann 1979; Blaikie 1985; Grossman 1984; Grant 1987). Damage most commonly results when impoverished growers are forced to retreat to ever more marginal lands (Blaikie and Brookfield 1987). In Buguias, however, it is primarily the most prosperous farmers—those wealthy enough to hire bulldozers to flatten hilltops and to construct private roads—who precipitate erosion and deforest the slopes. Wealthy growers expanding into the fertile eastern cloud forests also destroy watershed vital for the entire valley, and increasingly outcompete the growers in the older, exhausted districts. But all villagers, rich and poor alike, degrade their lands, especially by unleashing biocides and fertilizers into the streams of the region.

This devastation does not stem from cultivators' ignorance or mismanagement. Benguet vegetable culture is in many respects intricately fitted to the local landscape, with each crop cultivated in the precise microhabitat to which it is best adapted. Moreover, most gardeners are aware of the dangers of chemical contamination and denuded slopes. But the commercial system in which they are imbricated leaves them few alternatives. With a long-term decline in profits and a notoriously capricious vegetable market, growers must feverishly intensify production in a desperate attempt to avoid losing ground during poor seasons (what Bernstein [1977] calls the "simple reproduction squeeze"). And the prospect of unpredictable price jumps propels them in the same direction; the lure of a jackpot harvest brings an even higher pitch of activity during the perilous typhoon season, a time marked by accelerated erosion and periodic market windfalls.

The environmental and social pressures of market-oriented agriculture in the global periphery can be extraordinarily destructive; in the worst cases, as Watts has shown for Nigeria, the "horrors and moodiness of the market" (1983:xxiii) can bring famine and mass starvation. But the vegetable districts of northern Luzon have *as yet* seen only the early warnings of an ecological and economic debacle. The vegetable farmers today remain the envy of both subsistence growers in the mountains and impoverished peasants in the lowlands. Nor has the market's individualizing force brought cultural dissolution as it so often does. In fact, far from destroying local culture, commercial development has greatly enhanced its central feature, the redistributive prestige feast. But the very continuation of communal feasting has actually become an accomplice to the environmental breakdown.

COMMERCIALIZATION AND
REDISTRIBUTIVE FEASTS

While Buguias's environmental destruction replicates a sadly familiar pattern, its elaboration of communal feasting in conjunction with commercial gardening is unusual. Such rituals need not vanish as a community becomes tied to larger economic circuits; indeed, the most famous redistributive rite, the potlatch of northwest North America, flowered after trade links were established with European merchants (Belshaw 1965:28). Yet a long-standing scholarly tradition holds that such feasts, and communal ties in general, wither away once a society is incorporated into the world economy. Bodley (1975:167), for example, argues as follows:

> Integration is not possible unless tribal cultures are made to surrender their autonomy and self reliance. When these are replaced by dependence on . . . the world market economy, a whole series of changes will follow until virtually all of the unique features of tribal cultures have been replaced by their contrasting counterparts in industrial civilization.

A pivotal agent of such change is usually said to be an emergent capitalist class, if not a generalized capitalist mentality, that resists ceremonial and other social outlays. As Grossman (1984:10–11) writes:

> Villagers also want to free themselves from traditional social obligations that they believe hinder capital accumulation. Their individualistic behavior is manifested in a variety of realms: the extent of sharing, reciprocity, and cooperation in cash-earning activities is less than in traditional subsistence-oriented endeavors. . . .

And even when ceremonial exchange does persist under expanding market relations, "ritual inflation" (in which wealthy individuals devote ever-larger sums to display while the poor are disenfranchised) may undermine its stability, if not the entire social order (Grossman 1984:23; Volkman 1985:7; Hefner 1983:683). In a similar argument, James Scott (1976) links the spread of commercial relations with the downfall of a communitarian ethos in mainland Southeast Asia. In the precolonial states of this region, he argues, peasant politics were centered around a "subsistence ethic" that united each community within a "moral economy" and militated against risk-taking and profit-seeking behavior. With colonial rule, however, "the commercialization of the agrarian economy was steadily stripping away most of the traditional forms of social insurance" (Scott 1976:10).

During the heyday of modernization theory in the 1950s and 1960s, most scholars applauded the market's ability to displace traditional cultural forms. Religion in general was thought to fetter development (see von der Mehden 1986:5), and many observers predicted that competitive economics would destroy communal institutions, leading eventually to "detribalization" (see de Souza and Porter 1974). Present-day writers tend to view cultural breakdown in the wake of commercialization as ethnocide rather than progress, but they have inherited the assumption of its inevitability. The two schools' analysis of the occasional survival of communal feasting bears this out. What constituted for modernization theorists an irrational stumbling block has become for scholars of the underdevelopment camp a bulwark against capital, the key to cultural persistence, and a core around which to organize political resistance.

Voss (1983) has recently extended the anticommercial version of this thesis to the Cordillera of northern Luzon. He argues that redistributive rites are declining in commercialized areas, but that their survival limits capitalist penetration elsewhere. Specifically, he holds that in Sagada "the maintenance of such non-commercialized relations as redistributive feasting . . . has been instrumental in limiting class differentiation" and in molding market economics into a socially benign form, whereas in the Buguias region, he claims, socially atomized and fully capitalistic producers have reduced their ceremonial expenditures to a minimum (1983:14–15, 225–230).

Voss is probably correct in regard to Sagada, the primary locus of his research, but I would argue that he misrepresents feasting in Buguias. In Buguias not only are public feasts much more common than in Sagada, but more importantly, they are strongly reinforced by agricultural commercialization. Farmers who successfully accumulate must also feast their neighbors. This should not surprise us. It has long been acknowledged that "redistribution" is usually a misnomer for what happens in prestige feasts; as Wolf (1982:98) writes, "Feasting with the general participation of all can go hand in hand with the privileged accumulation of strategic goods by the elite." Yet conventional academic wisdom has not taken this point to heart. Commercialization does often leave cultural wreckage in its path, but as Buguias shows, such is not invariably the case (for examples other than Buguias, see Parker [1988] and Fisher [1986]).

In Buguias, public and private interests are tightly fused. The celebrants of the community's grandest feasts are its most successful entrepreneurs, individuals who invest in business expansion as well as in communal rites. And with few exceptions, those who have renounced, often on economic grounds, the old religion they call Paganism have been unable to translate their savings into prosperity. Pagan ideology expressly endorses commercial ventures, reserving its highest accolades for the "progressive" individuals who work hard, adopt new technologies, invest in productive enterprises, and lend money for gain—so long as they also honor their ancestors and feast their neighbors.

THEORETICAL UNDERPINNINGS

The conceptual framework adopted here derives in part from "regional political ecology," a recent movement formed through the marriage of the environmental concerns of cultural ecology and the developmental focus of political economy. In this emerging literature, social conflict and land degradation tend to be emphasized over the communal harmony and environmental adaptation highlighted by earlier scholars. (See, in geography, Grossman 1984; Blaikie and Brookfield 1987; Bassett 1988; Zimmerer 1988; Hecht and Cockburn 1989; and Turner 1989. In anthropology, see Schmink and Wood 1987; and Sheridan 1988). Inspiration is also found in traditional cultural geography, which approaches the human modification of local environments as deeply rooted historical processes, molded in part through the cultural perceptions of human agents. Culture is viewed here not as an autonomous, "superorganic" entity (see Duncan 1980), but rather as inextricably bound

up with politics and economics, continually reconstituted and reshaped through subtle interplay between individuals and social
groups.

The underpinnings of the "political" side of political ecology derive largely from radical development studies. This tradition has
been fruitful in illuminating specific economic processes behind
local environmental change in the modern era, which must in most
instances be analyzed within the context of global capitalism. But it
has also biased the field against recognizing that "precapitalist" societies, and certainly "socialist" ones, often evince similar processes of land degradation. Blaikie and Brookfield (1987) offer one
corrective in the novel tactic of collegial disputation, one writer arguing from a Marxist background and the other countering from a
behavioralist stance throughout a coauthored text. Although writing in a dialogic mode is not an option for the solo author, I have
allowed a degree of theoretical agnosticism into this text by (loosely)
employing both Weberian and Marxian notions, tending toward
the latter when analyzing the economy, and veering toward the
former when considering religious issues. Both traditions offer
powerful lenses that can profitably be trained on social and ecological change in Buguias; to take either one alone is to risk limiting
inquiry and obscuring those processes that defy expectations.

One of the fundamental premises of this study is that social,
cultural, economic, and ecological change must be analyzed in
dense empirical detail. Here I am especially inspired by Stephen
Toulmin, whose richly eloquent *Cosmopolis* (1990) thoroughly undermines the modernist agenda of "universal, general, and time-
less" theorization and instead leads the way into a more humane
appreciation of "the oral, the particular, the local, and the timely"
(1990:186)—all conceived within a fluid ecological perspective.
Thus, while employing a variety of theoretical constructs, I have
avoided couching the findings within any "grand theory." My
ethnographic sensibility leads me to seek "explanation[s] of exceptions and indeterminants rather than regularities" (Marcus and
Fischer 1986:8); by the same token, as a geographer I am wary of
"spatial over-aggregation" (Corbridge 1986). Broadly similar patterns often emerge where modern economic processes transform
ritual and ecological practices, but a useful heuristic for directing
the questions must not become a limiting template for interpreting

findings. Commercialization has often dissolved communal bonds, but its failure to do so in Buguias does not necessarily mean that we have found an aberrant exception. In practice, this means being willing to revise radically one's preconceptions. I argue from experience here; having arrived in Buguias with a deep Polanyian (see Polanyi 1957) skepticism regarding "precapitalist" markets, I was only gradually, and painfully, disabused of this romantic notion as I delved into the commercial history of Buguias.

FIELD METHODS

In probing the paradoxes implicit in interpreting "the other," Marcus and Fischer (1986) conclude that fieldwork is essentially dialogic, a fact that they argue should be acknowledged by incorporating the voices of the studied not as informants but as collaborators. Such an approach, they claim, can open doors to indigenous "epistemologies, rhetorics, aesthetic criteria, and sensibilities" (1986:48).

This project followed Marcus and Fischer's dictum in important ways. From the day I arrived in Buguias with Karen Wigen, my wife and fellow geographer, research was not only facilitated but actually guided by a local couple, Lorenzo and Bonificia Payaket. The Payakets took keen if often amused interest in all of our questions, repeatedly suggesting new avenues of inquiry. In particular, although we entered the field with no intention of studying religion, they insisted on introducing us to indigenous priests. Their message was simple: to understand Buguias you must understand religion. Eventually we deferred.

After a few weeks in Buguias, a basic routine was established. Each evening, two or more of us would meet to determine the next day's explorations, the Payakets suggesting local experts with whom we could consult on a given topic. The following morning, we would walk to where the chosen individuals lived and interview them, often through the agency of field guides. In the early months our inquiry was limited to the village of Buguias Central. Gradually we began to venture farther afield, eventually making foot and bus journeys of several days to visit each settlement prominent in Buguias's history.

After returning home we would again confer with the Payakets, who would judge the reliability of our findings, suggest individuals who could either corroborate or give conflicting accounts, critique our field maps, and add observations of their own. These evening discussions can only be described as seminars. The sessions grew particularly lively when the Payakets brought with them individuals expert in the subjects at hand. But all conversations eventually wandered freely, leading in many unexpected directions. Nor did we limit ourselves to empirical findings; our evolving interpretations also formed a conversational mainstay.

Through these alternating interviews and evening discussions we gradually elicited the outline of Buguias's history presented here. Although I have also consulted the standard sources of historical scholarship (colonial documents, travelers' accounts and diaries, early scholarly reports, and newspaper articles), these rarely elucidate the most important local developments. Since Buguias was and is a predominantly oral culture, living memory is the primary source for reconstructing the community's past. In seeking standards of reliability, I follow Rosaldo's (1980) lead; where numerous individuals reiterate the same story, without contradictions, I have accepted it as most likely true. Where consensus is not obtainable, conflicting versions are retained with no attempt to choose among them.

Any interpretation is by nature partial, as much allegory as analysis. As such, the story told here remains to the last only one among several possible "true fictions" (Clifford 1986) that could have been wrought from the ethnographic materials pertaining to Buguias. If my time in Buguias proved conceptually liberating, it did not, however, divest me of all prior ideological baggage. Moreover, the individuals with whom I worked have undoubtedly inscribed on the text their own prejudices and programs as well, seeking to project their community in a specific light. The author bears final responsibility for any errors compounded through the numerous tissues of interpretation that constitute the work.

IDENTIFYING BUGUIAS IN THE
ETHNOGRAPHIC LANDSCAPE

The indigenous inhabitants of the Cordillera, collectively referred to as Igorots (a term some groups find offensive), were never hispanicized, and they retain a limited cultural autonomy to this day.

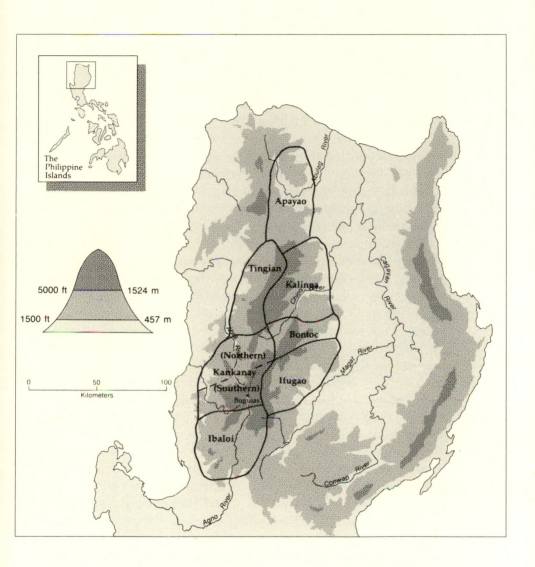

Map 2. *The Standard Ethnographic Map of the Cordillera of Northern Luzon.*

Western ethnographers have divided these highland peoples into seven or eight major groupings, once considered tribes, now usually termed ethnolinguistic groups (LeBar 1975, Keesing 1962; see map 2). But the categories employed here reflect a convoluted history of academic misconceptions (for an indigenous scholar's assessment of the standard ethnographic classification, see Magannon 1988).

In the nineteenth century, Spanish and German observers partitioned the Cordillera by entirely different schemes; these may have been less accurate but they were no more misconceived than those later perpetrated by the Americans. The American ethnographic map originated with the outrageously sloppy scholarship of Dean C. Worcester, self-styled white deity of the archipelago's non-Christians (see Hutterer 1978). Finding the Spanish and German classifications cumbersome, Worcester (1906) took it upon himself to define new groups among the highlanders. Unfortunately, he seriously misunderstood the foreign-language sources he was criticizing.[2] In classifying the various Cordilleran peoples, Worcester ultimately relied on visually distinctive cultural features casually observed by himself and his friends.[3]

Competent ethnographers later modified Worcester's system. In Benguet, Moss (1920a, 1920b) successfully insisted that the linguistic groups called Kankana-ey (or Kankanay) and Nabaloi (or Ibaloi), long recognized by all able observers, deserved separate "tribal" status. But Worcester's overall scheme prevailed, distorting subsequent ethnographic perceptions. Some of his so-called tribes, such as the Kalinga, were but melanges of dissimilar cultural groups (some of which have since coalesced to a degree); other more coherent groupings, most notably the Kalanguya (or Kallahan), received no recognition at all, simply because neither Worcester nor any colonial anthropologist happened to visit them.[4] Recently linguists have begun to devise a more accurate classification system, but many geographic subtleties continue to elude cultural taxonomists (see, for example, Wurm and Hattori 1983; for the best work on southern Cordilleran linguistic and cultural groupings, see Afable 1989).

The case of Buguias reveals the inadequacies of the standard classificatory scheme. The community lies in the interstice of three linguistic or cultural groups; two of these, the Ibaloi and the Southern Kankana-ey, are now recognized, but the third, the Kalanguya (or Kallahan), remains virtually ethnographically invisible (see map 3). Although Buguias was probably an Ibaloi settlement originally, its residents today are most closely related (genealogically) to

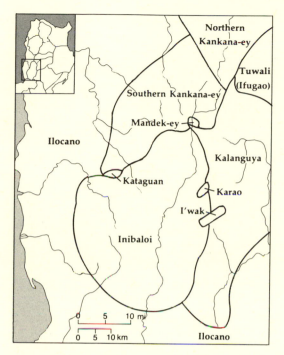

Map 3.   *The Languages and Dialects of the Southern Cordillera.* Mandek-ey, or I-Buguias, is at present spoken only in the southernmost hamlets of Buguias Village.

the Kalanguya; the village dialect (called Mandek-ey, or I-Buguias), while containing elements of all three neighboring tongues, is also most closely affiliated with Kalanguya. Over the past sixty years, however, Kankana-ey has penetrated southward into the village, and today Mandek-ey survives only in the southernmost hamlets of Buguias. As a result, outsiders generally classify Buguias as a Southern Kankana-ey community.

The geographic referent of the term "Buguias" is also equivocal. It originally referred to a single territorially based village, in some respects an indigenous microstate. Like other sizable Cordilleran villages, Buguias was accorded a vague political status under the Spanish colonial regime; gradually this solidified, and today Buguias forms a *barangay*, the smallest political territory in the Philippines. The modern barangay, called Buguias Central, corresponds

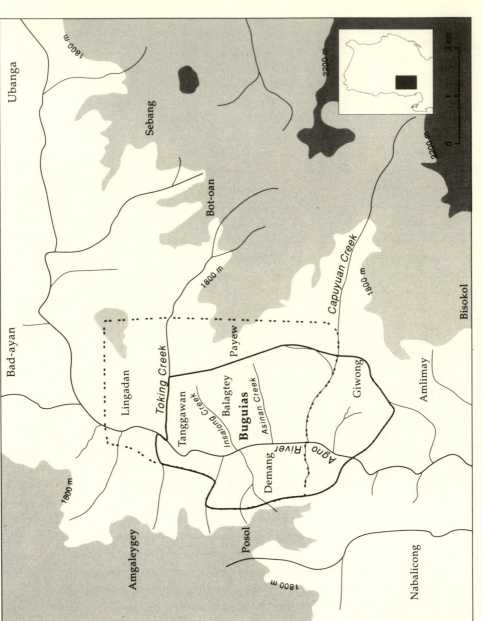

Map 4. *Buguias Village.* The dashed line encloses the modern *barangay* of Buguias Central; the solid line encloses the traditional village, or *ili*, of Buguias. The traditional village was divided into four constituent units (Tanggawan, Balagtey, Giwong, and Demang) during the American period. These smaller *ili* function today

imperfectly to the old village, since over the years some hamlets have been grafted to the original community while others have been deleted from it (see map 4). Only in the ritual realm does the old communal structure survive, and even here it was significantly transformed when the village elders, sometime in the American era, split the old village into four constituent sacerdotal units.

But "Buguias" also refers to an area larger than the barangay, or village, of that name. The southern Cordilleran peoples have long classified their neighbors according to several partly overlapping ethnographic systems, based respectively on language, environment, and proximity to large, older settlements. Since Buguias has long been an important community, its name is applied to a region extending well beyond the boundaries of the village itself. To their Cordilleran neighbors, "the Buguias people" includes not only the inhabitants of Buguias village but also the residents of surrounding communities—individuals who would identify themselves as being from Buguias when visiting distant places.

Roughly corresponding to this region is Buguias municipality in the imposed political hierarchy (see map 5). Both the Spanish and the American colonialists administered sections of the southern Cordillera through the larger villages, first designated *rancherias*, later townships, then municipal districts, and finally municipalities. Since the Americans continually sought to economize by consolidating these units, municipal boundaries remained unstable. Early in the century, for example, "greater" Buguias annexed its northern neighbor, Lo-o. Even under the postcolonial Philippine regime, Cordilleran municipal boundaries have shifted as municipalities have vied for several tax-rich border zones. At the same time, villages within the same municipality have sometimes contended for the seat of local government, further reworking geographical alignments. Buguias municipality, in fact, has for some years been administered not from Buguias Central but from the more accessible crossroads community of Abatan.

In this work, "Buguias" will refer both to the indigenous ritual village (now divided into four units) and to the modern barangay. Although the boundaries of these two divisions are not exactly coincident, ambiguity is minimal. When the larger regional unit is intended, it will be designated either as Buguias municipality or as greater Buguias.

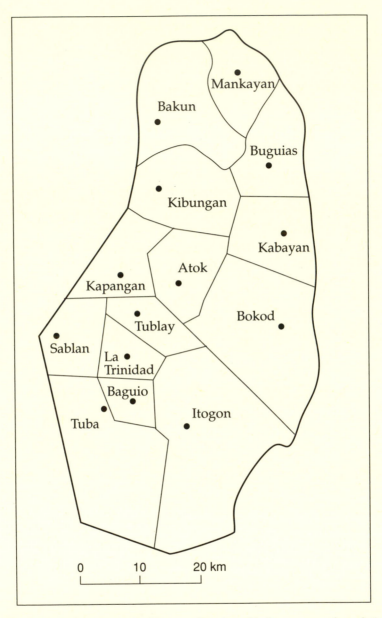

Map 5.   *The Municipalities of Benguet Province.* (Refer to map 1 for relative location.) The city of Baguio forms an enclave, independent from the surrounding province.

OVERVIEW

This work comprises two intertwined allegories. The first concerns the persistence of a society and the continued florescence of a culture, the inverse of a long dominant theme. The second tells a more familiar and more tragic tale: while this culture has so far abided the engulfing global economy, its very foundation is at risk. Buguias's commercial gambit may simply prove to be a brilliant disaster.

The story opens with a view of the landscape of Buguias as it appeared in the time of American rule. The initial chapter outlines subsistence production, an environmentally benign agricultural system that nevertheless radically transformed the landscape of Buguias. The following chapter explores the contours of social life, which were marked by distinct class stratification but tempered by frequent interclass mobility. A look at the ritual system, in which consumption climaxed, rounds out the picture of prewar Buguias as a self-contained community. The discussion then broadens out to consider the wider networks within which the Buguias people operated. Chapter 5 maps first the geography of trade, and then the penetration of imperial power. This completes Part I, a largely synchronic cut at prewar life.

World War II constituted a radical discontinuity in Buguias history, and with an interstitial discussion chronicling the war's devastation, the narrative takes a more diachronic turn. The story of the postwar era in Part II opens with the drama of reconstruction. The first two chapters of this second part cover the vegetable boom years from 1946 to 1973; the remainder of the work focuses on the era of stagnation and turmoil beginning in 1973 and continuing to the late 1980s. Topically, the discussion thus progresses from the successful rise of the new agroecological and economic order to its darker underside, the social tensions and environmental traumas that are increasingly revealed. The work concludes with an analysis of religion, the focal point of current ideological, economic, and political contention.

PART I

PREWAR BUGUIAS

2

Food, Fuel, and Fiber:
*Human Environmental Relations
in Prewar Buguias*

INTRODUCTION

A view of Buguias from the air in the 1920s would have revealed
a complex landscape of interwoven plant communities. On the
highest reaches of the eastern slope, outliers of the dense, oak-
dominated cloud forest (or *kalasan*) protruded below the misty
ridgeline of the Cordillera. Downslope, the oaks gave way to single-
species pine stands, forming a true forest on the higher and steeper
slopes and thinning out at lower elevations. Near the upper hamlets of the village, pines crowned a savannah community of short
grasses, yielding on steeper sites to cane-grass swards. Still farther
downslope, the pines dropped out altogether, leaving only pasture
grasses on the lowest slopes.

Within this broad zonal pattern, variations of soil, relief, and
long-standing agricultural practice created a vegetational mosaic.
The shady northern faces of steep side canyons supported diverse
hardwood thickets, while on their sunny southern exposures grew
a jumble of brush, pine, and coarse grasses. Scattered throughout
the landscape, but particularly in the lower reaches, were sharply
bounded cultivated plots. Most contained tangles of sweet-potato
vines, a select few were flooded and planted to rice, and small
plots surrounding the village's several score dwellings supported
diverse assemblages of herbs and fruit-bearing trees.

This landscape was a cultural artifact, continually reshaped
through the labor of the Buguias people as they wrested their livelihood from the land. In provisioning themselves, the Buguias people
transformed their homeland, altering both its physical substrate
and its biotic communities. Through cultivating and pasturing they
worked their greatest ecological transformations. But the residents

of Buguias also gleaned a harvest of wild edible plants and animals, as well as vital nonfood plant products (including fibers, woods, and medicines). All microhabitats of Buguias thus contributed to human livelihood, and all were remolded in turn by human activities.

But if the Buguias people transformed their landscape, the human impact varied widely in extent and duration. Sites found suitable for terracing were entirely remade; others, such as ravines, were only casually tapped for wild produce. The territory of Buguias was thus loosely divided into separate geographical zones, each subjected to different kinds of human pressures.

The fundamental division enclosed the cultivated from the "wild." Both cropped and non-cropped lands were further subdivided according to the plant associations they supported. Agricultural plots were of three distinct named types: dry fields (devoted largely to sweet potatoes), flooded rice terraces, and door-yard gardens. Less exact divisions marked the uncultivated lands, as many species (the insular pine, for example), could grow in virtually any area; yet even here, distinct plant associations emerged in part through human interference. These various plant communities, both wild and cultivated, might aptly be called *subsistence sectors* (what Wadell [1972] refers to as "agricultural subsystems"), highlighting at once their role in provisioning the human community and their spatial boundedness.

The areal configuration of subsistence sectors was never static. In the long view, fields and pastures expanded steadily. New dry fields could be carved from woodland, meadow, or canebrake; hillsides were slowly terraced; and new pastures sprouted from the charred soils of former woodlands. In specific instances, the direction of change could be reversed. A rice field might yield to cane or brush, for example, if its supply of water suddenly diminished.

The following chapter reconstructs Buguias subsistence as it existed in the 1920s and 1930s, the earliest period accessible through living memory. Deeper historical background is examined through archival sources where possible. The first section details each of the three major agricultural sectors: dry fields, door-yard gardens, and rice terraces. The next two sections outline the products of uncultivated lands. Here subsistence was less rigidly constrained by sector; domestic animals, for example, could often wander through vast uncultivated areas. These discussions are thus organized along product rather than sectoral lines, first considering domestic stock, and then moving to undomesticated plants and animals. The fourth section examines first human agency in the formation and mainte- nance of distinct communities of uncultivated plants, and then turns to the processes of agricultural intensification at work in the prewar era.

AGRICULTURAL FIELDS

Dry Fields: Uma and Puwal

The core of livelihood in prewar Buguias was a distinctive form of dry-field cultivation called *uma*, derived from swidden practices. Like its slash-and-burn antecedents, uma agriculture entailed cut- ting and burning woody vegetation prior to planting, and in earlier periods all Buguias dry fields had probably exhibited the common features of long-fallow swidden horticulture. By the beginning of the twentieth century, however, the interval between cropping cycles had been shortened sufficiently that most dry fields in cen- tral Buguias were cultivated for much longer periods than they were fallowed. In the *puwal* variant, slashing and burning no longer preceded planting. Both umas and puwals were intensively culti- vated plots, adapted in many respects to a savannah rather than to a woodland environment.

Sweet potatoes, the staple of both people and domestic hogs, dominated the dry fields. Tubers were consumed in such quantity as to completely color the memory of prewar subsistence; this was the time, the Buguias people say, "when we ate only sweet pota- toes." The common people typically dined on boiled sweet-potato tubers seasoned with sweet-potato vinegar, garnished with sweet- potato leaves, and perhaps completed with a dessert of sweet- potato syrup. In seasons of tuber scarcity, dried sweet-potato chips, either reconstituted in soup or pounded and cooked with millet, sufficed. Subsidiary dry-field crops, including several kinds of beans, peanuts, sesame seeds, maize, panicum millet, sorghum, and Job's tears, provided seasonal supplements, but were never abundant in most households. Among the poor, mealtimes were indeed a matter of "*tugi angey*" (or "sweet potatoes only").

Buguias dry fields could thrive only on select sites. Slopes had to be gentle for soil fertility maintenance. Clay-rich soils were always favored, for lighter earth would not retain adequate moisture for dry-season (December through April) growth. The natural terraces above the Agno River formed ideal sites, but many had long been appropriated for rice terraces. The gentle and irregular eastern slope of the village afforded the most numerous suitable locations. Here the favored sites were U-shaped hillside indentations formed by slope failure. The flattish deposit of deep soil at the slump foot could support sweet potatoes throughout the year, while the adjacent scarps produced superior tubers in the soggy wet season. In areas of suitable soil and slope, however, uma fields could form a continuous band of cultivation.

In the heart of every Buguias dry field lay the sweet-potato patch, monocropped for fear that other plants would stymie the all-important staple. The generally heavier-feeding subsidiary crops were relegated to the field edges, or occasionally to central strips. Typically surrounding the nucleus were rings of sorghum, panicum millet, maize, and various pulses. Annuals, such as maize, sorghum, and millet (often interplanted with kidney beans) were favored for central strips, since they would not interfere with the long-term sweet potato rotational schedule. In the wettest months (July through September), larger field segments normally planted to sweet potatoes might be devoted to millet or peanuts. (Some growers, fearing rat predation, would distance their millet crop from brushy surrounding growth by planting it in the center of the field.) Seed of the perennial *baltong* bean (*Vigna sinensis*) were sown among stumps or rock outcrops where they would not interfere with sweet-potato cultivation, while brushy *kudis* beans (*Cajanus cajanus*) often occupied drier slopes on field margins.

Buguias women cultivated approximately a dozen varieties of sweet potatoes. Some women intercropped multiple cultivars; others preferred segregation. Generally, those with large fields (.5 hectares or more) cultivated monovarietal patches, which allowed easier management since each cultivar matured at a different rate. The specific varieties planted, whether in mixed or segregated patches, depended in part on the partialities of household members, as each variety had a distinct taste and texture.

Buguias women planted sweet potatoes thrice annually, and harvested each planting up to three times before the vines reached exhaustion at the end of one year. The first planting, in April or May, either anticipated or coincided with the first rains. By October this planting's initial tubers, though fibrous and of poor quality, were ready for harvest. February marked a second harvest interval, and the final one occurred in May. The dry-season tubers were of higher quality, but as the vines aged, quality declined. A second planting in September or early October produced a superior initial crop; the young vines flourished with the copious rains and the tubers could mature as the soil dried. This planting's harvests occurred in January, again in May, and finally in August. December, marking the start of the dry season, brought the final and least productive planting; success then was possible only in the most moisture-retentive fields. Yet this crop too could produce through the entire year; only in the poorest fields was year-round cultivation impossible. Here harvests would be completed early in the dry season, the remaining foliage burned, and the uma fallowed until the arrival of the rains.

The multiple plantings of differentially maturing sweet-potato varieties coupled with (partial) seasonal rotation with other crops and complicated by the differing physical attributes of each field, required a fine-tuned seasonal labor schedule. Uma work was also highly skilled; even the harvest was demanding, since individual tubers had to be removed at their most palatable stage without damaging the vines. Only carefully tended plants could produce through an entire year. From December to March, the prime harvest, Buguias women sliced and sun-dried the surplus, which would form the mainstay in the lean season following the early rains.

The typical uma was cropped for five to ten years, at which point declining yields forced a two- to three-year fallow. This long cropping period was possible only through continual labor. Weeding was the most arduous task; Buguias women would dig several feet into the ground to remove the tenacious roots of *ga-on* (*Imperata cylindrica*) in particular. Weed foliage obtained both within and from the edges of the uma was buried in the field along with the old, uprooted vines, thus helping to replenish the soil.

Intensive dry-field cultivation required gentle slopes and deep soil, but new fields were sometimes relegated to substandard sites. Steeper plots could be upgraded by leveling; stone-walled semi-terraces minimized erosion while maximizing dry-season moisture retention. Unlike rice terraces, such dry terraces needed some slope, since a flat field would waterlog in the rainy season, resulting in tuber rot. These semiterraces were comparatively easy to construct; often little more than a few carefully placed boulders sufficed.

The nutrients added to the uma from field-margin weeds, downward-moving soil (notable in slump-foot cultivation), and legume root nodules were insufficient to offset harvest losses. Over time, tuber size diminished while insects and pathogens multiplied. Exhausted fields were then left to natural succession. Typical invaders included the ubiquitous bracken fern, several exotic composites (*Tithonia maxima* and *Eupatorium adenophorum*), and the cane grass *Miscanthus sinensis*. After a few years these fallowed umas were cut, burned, and replanted. Abandoned fields on drier sites or in pasture areas were, in contrast, invaded by sod-forming grasses (especially *Themeda triandra* and *Imperata cylindrica*), after which they were characteristically opened to cattle. These tenacious fire-adapted grasses precluded further recourse to the techniques of uma. Rather, if the site were to be recultivated the sod had to be overturned, a practice known as puwal cultivation.

In making a puwal, the cultivator would invert sections of sod with iron-tipped poles. If turned to a depth of some 30 centimeters at the end of the dry season, the grasses would be killed and the soil both aerated and enriched by decaying leaves, roots, and manure. Newly made puwal fields could be quite fertile, encouraging the conversion of prime pastures, even those never previously cultivated. After soil preparation, the puwal was cultivated much like the uma.

Recultivation of the fallowed dry fields was relatively easy; the mandatory fences were already in place (although, if wooden, they would need repair), and, at least with umas, the light successional vegetation could easily be cleared. Newly married couples, however, often had to create new fields. These could be either uma or puwal, depending on the site chosen. Any pine standing on the site would be salvaged for wood, but other woody plants would be burned *in situ* for soil enrichment.

Door-yard Gardens

Haphazard plantings around the houselot constituted the second subsistence sector, the door-yard garden (*ba-eng*). Some gardens produced large quantities of vegetables, fruits, and even cash crops, but most were small affairs. Yet the garden did hold two advantages over the uma: manure-enriched soils and easy access.

Tobacco and potatoes, considered too demanding for dry-field cultivation, often grew alongside the nutrient-rich pigpens. Hog manure was also periodically distributed through the rest of the garden.[1] It could be used to fertilize sweet potatoes only if thoroughly composted (Purseglove 1968, v. 1:85), a difficulty that, combined with the burden of hauling, precluded manure use in the dry fields. But even fresh dung benefited most door-yard crops. Several varieties of taro grown for the piggery were especially favored in the garden because of their shade tolerance and vigorous response to casual manure application.

Condiments (*Capsicum* peppers, onions, ginger, garlic, and sugar cane), and vegetables (lima and other beans, squash), were grown in the door-yard garden mainly for convenience. As new vegetables, such as bitter-gourd, eggplant, and *sayote* (chayote), appeared during the American period, gardens became more diverse. Sayote quickly emerged as the standby vegetable of all social classes; this perennial produces ample quantities of edible leaves, stems, and fruits, and its large tubers can serve as a famine reserve. Only the larger gardens were dominated by fruit trees (such as mangoes and avocados), since frequent household relocation constrained arboriculture. Poorer households thus rarely grew more than a few banana stalks.

The most valuable door-yard crop was coffee. Introduced in the late Spanish period, coffee cultivation spread rapidly among the elite, who found the beans a valuable trade item as well as a beverage source. Having planted sizable orchards of *arabica* trees, wealthy individuals soon lost their inclination to relocate their homes periodically. As coffee drinking and trading spread, poorer couples too planted smaller orchards. But in the final years of the Spanish period, blight struck, damaging especially those orchards located on clay soils. Coffee production henceforth would be concentrated in the gardens of a few wealthy households situated on rich loam.

POND FIELDS: TARO AND RICE

The irrigated or pond-field terrace, an artificial wetland seasonally planted to rice and, occasionally, to taro, formed the third agricultural sector of prewar Buguias. Among many Cordilleran groups (including the Ifugao, the Bontoc, the southern Kalinga, the Northern Kankana-ey, and the Ibaloi of Kabayan and Nagey), pond fields were a significant, if not dominant, element of the agricultural landscape. In the Buguias region, however, rice was a subsidiary crop, albeit vital as the source of rice beer. Buguias residents seldom ate unfermented rice, and on the rare occasions when they did, they usually mixed it with millet or dried sweet potatoes.

The first pond-field terraces in Buguias may have been designed for taro.[2] This most versatile of crops grew unirrigated in dry fields and door-yard gardens, but it produced larger, if poorer tasting, tubers when cultivated in water. In prewar Buguias, taro grew in several aqueous niches: along irrigation canals, in natural seeps, around small ponds, on the edges of rice terraces, and in small terraces of its own. A vastly greater expanse of pond-field land, however, was devoted solely to rice.

Rice beer in prewar Buguias was a necessary ritual intoxicant. Virtually all couples occasionally brewed beer, but only the wealthy owned pond fields; poorer individuals purchased rice or worked in the paddies of wealthier relatives. Even couples possessing extensive terraces (up to several hectares) fermented the bulk of their harvests. The sweet and yeasty beer dregs, however, made a treat especially beloved of small children.

Buguias's pond-field system gradually expanded through the late Spanish and early American periods. Natural river terraces, reasonably level and low enough in the valley to be dependably watered, formed ideal building sites. Some lower terraces could be irrigated directly from the Agno River, but the necessary diversion works would be demolished annually in typhoon floods. More manageable water sources were the non-entrenched, perennial side streams and the natural seeps. But by the American period, continued pond-field expansion necessitated the excavation of canals—some several kilometers long—to tap the larger eastern tributary streams.

Labor in the rice fields was arduous. Leveling and churning the muck had originally been done entirely by hand, although by the later American period some individuals had harnessed water buffalo for the task. Seedbeds, started in November or December, were ready for transplanting by January, although fields watered from the community's several hot springs could be planted a month or more later. By April, the enlarging grains required the constant vigilance of old men and children to ward off birds and other pests. In July, hastened by the impending typhoon season, the fields were reaped. After harvest they remained flooded, thus receiving nutrients from typhoon-eroded sediments. The only other fertility supplements consisted of *Tithonia* leaves and water-buffalo manure, the latter deposited casually when the animals worked the fields or wallowed in them during the off-season.

Compared to other Cordilleran peoples, the Buguias villagers planted few varieties of rice. Each of the two major types, glutinous *diket* and nonsticky, red *kintoman*, boasted no more than three or four distinct strains. The growing conditions of each variety were considered roughly equivalent, although one slowly maturing cultivar had to be transplanted by December. Glutinous and nonsticky grains were usually mixed for eating and for the making of beer. The Buguias people knew of many different varieties planted by other Cordilleran peoples, and some of these they recognized as superior. But although they not uncommonly planted experimental fields, few new varieties proved successful. Especially desired was a lowland strain that would produce a crop in the cloudy wet season, but no planting ever proved successful.

Buguias residents continually enlarged their pond-field system through the American period. Wealthy traders and livestock breeders initiated most new construction, which they usually contracted out to the expert terrace engineers from Ifugao and Bontoc subprovinces. (The latter workers were acclaimed for their ability to lever large river boulders into terrace walls, while the former were noted for their skilled masonry with smaller stones.) Most

Buguias people thought that terraces built by local residents lacked the durability of those constructed by outside workers.

ANIMAL HUSBANDRY

Domestic animals provided the people of prewar Buguias with ample meat, but little else. Leather strips served as ropes and whole hides as sleeping mats, but even cattle skins were often patiently chewed and swallowed. A few individuals plowed with water buffalo, and the elite sometimes rode horses, but animal power was inconsequential overall. Meat was vital, however, and people labored to fashion a landscape that could yield abundant supplies. Houselot animals, such as hogs, foraged in uncultivated areas but depended primarily on agricultural produce. Cattle, horses, and buffalo, however, subsisted solely on the fodder of the human-created and maintained savannah.

HOUSELOT ANIMALS: HOGS AND CHICKENS

Hogs, raised by all families, foraged daily in the open pasture-lands. At night they returned through fenced runways to their pens, situated below each house. In the grasslands and pine savannahs they rooted for worms and grubs, fungus, and wild tubers. Those in the higher reaches of Buguias could roam as far as the kalasan, or cloud forest, well-stocked with acorns, fungus, and especially earthworms. On returning each evening they were fed boiled sweet potatoes and sweet-potato peels, pounded rice hulls and bran, kitchen garbage, and human waste. Both under- and over-sized tubers were relegated to the swine; in most households, well over half of the crop went to the piggery. Hogs flourished in the rainy season, but during the annual drought the earth hardened and wild foods grew scarce, and the weakened animals suffered frequently from skin diseases.

In the American period a few individuals began raising lowland hogs, valued chiefly for their ability to gain weight on the raw sweet potatoes that the so-called native hog could scarcely digest. These animals were not ritually acceptable, however, precluding them from replacing the indigenous stock. Kikuyu grass, purportedly brought to Buguias by a teacher, was also introduced in this period. The thick stolons of this aggressive exotic, which flourished in moist microhabitats, provided a fine year-round hog feed.

Other houselot animals occupied niches similar to that of swine. The average family owned some twenty chickens, while the wealthy might possess as many as two hundred. Chickens returned each night to roost in predator-secure pens or in trees, and foraged daily in the nearby pastures. All households kept dogs, primarily for their meat, feeding them bones, scraps, and, of course, sweet potatoes. And finally, a few individuals raised pigeons, ducks, and even geese.

Pasture Animals: Cattle, Water Buffalo, and Horses

Unlike hogs and chickens, pasture animals were the responsibility of men. The average man in prewar Buguias devoted most of his labor to pasturing horses, water buffalo, and especially cattle. Water buffalo, the only ritually sanctioned pasture animal, were prestigious but not numerous. They reproduced poorly in the cool environment, and surviving calves, completely helpless for three days, often succumbed to disease or were trampled by bulls. Horses were valued primarily for their meat, although a few wealthy men kept riding mounts. But horses did not thrive as well as cattle on the Buguias grazing regime, and were thus relatively rare. Goats were raised in even smaller numbers.

Cattle, horses, and buffalo remained at pasture day and night. They subsisted largely on the native forage, supplemented occasionally with old sweet-potato vines. The few corrals generally held stock only prior to transporting or butchering. During typhoons, men herded their animals into protected areas, sometimes putting them in crude shelters built on the leeward side of hills. Otherwise livestock wandered untended, although conscientious graziers checked daily to ensure that none had wandered away or "fallen off the mountain."

Cattle were provided salt every few days, although several small herds in eastern Buguias obtained salt directly from local springs. Men could assemble their stock by blowing a water-buffalo horn, each instrument having a distinct sound that the animals could distinguish. Buguias cowboys assisted with births and watched after the young, especially the buffalo calves. Breeding received casual attention, although healthy bulls with propitiously placed cowlicks were favored as studs. Branding occurred only at the insistence of the American authorities.[3] Men easily recognized their own animals, and disputes arose only over calves delivered unattended in distant pastures.

Pasture Management

The so-called native cow of Benguet is a small, slowly maturing animal, optimally butchered at four years of age. Like the native hog, it is a fussy eater; several forbs unpalatable to the natives are readily eaten by introduced zebu crosses and so-called mestizo hybrids. But the Buguias pastoralists carefully managed their pastures to provide the grasses on which their stock thrived.

Themeda triandra (red oat grass), usually in association with *Andropogon annulatus* and *Imperata cylindrica,* dominated the savannah landscape of prewar Buguias (see Penafiel 1979). On the higher slopes and ridges scattered pines crowned the pastures, but only the more remote upper canyons supported trees thick enough to shade out the grass. Western range managers consider *Themeda* a mediocre if not poor feed, but to the Buguias pastoralists it was ideal.[4] *Themeda* responds well to fire (Crowder and Chheda 1982: 297), their primary range-management tool, and withstands reasonably heavy and continual grazing.

Buguias pastures grew lush in the wet season, but produced a watery low-protein forage. As protein increased in the early dry season, cattle fattened. December thus marked the optimum time for butchering and selling. Forage quality again diminished as pastures desiccated in February and March; fires might then be lit to stimulate new growth. In the late dry season many small springs would lapse, depriving cattle of several pasture zones. By March stock sometimes had to be hand-fed with cane-grass leaves, brought in from inaccessible ravines and slopes.

The savannah landscape of prewar Buguias was an anthropogenic environment, created and maintained by human intervention. Only continual labor could prevent reversion to woody growth. As burning allowed easy management, many pastures were annually torched, and even the more remote pine woods were occasionally singed. But fire alone would not eliminate all undesired plants; in intensively managed pastures the Buguias people dug weeds by hand. Weed infestations intensified after the invasion, circa 1916, of the Mexican composite *Eupatorium adenophorum*.[5] *Eupatorium*, thriving in all microhabitats from dry, rocky slopes to boggy seeps, soon ranked as the foremost pest. Each plant had to be uprooted and burned, a task performed in prime pastures once or twice every year.

Grazing pressure itself helped maintain the savannah. In areas too steep for cattle but still occasionally burned, the cane grass *Miscanthus sinensis* dominated. *Miscanthus* decreases quickly if continually grazed, as its highly placed growth nodes are easily destroyed (Numata 1974:135). Cane swards could still survive, however, in remote and seldom-grazed pastures.

Although most pastures were held in common, few were overgrazed. Buguias men knew well the carrying capacities of their prime pastures, and if these were exceeded community pressure fell on the offending individual. Some persons believed in naturally—or supernaturally—enforced stocking limits. One story recounted how the ancestors had established the limit of a certain pasture at ten animals; after a greedy man added two more, the correct ratio was restored when the new animals simply "fell off the mountain." Carrying capacity estimations in prime pastures were made for roughly discrete areas, separated by natural barriers (steep slopes and ravines) and sometimes by fences. Distant grazing lands were more loosely monitored. Cattle could not even reach certain remote grasslands unless trails were first cut across intervening slopes. This was risky, as well as labor-consuming, since animals periodically slipped from even the best-graded passages. But stock could sometimes range far from central Buguias, finding greener fields perhaps, but also adding to the cowboys' burdens.

An elaborate fence network marked off cultivated areas from the open pastures. Cattle, hogs, and water buffalo continually threatened and occasionally devastated umas, pond fields, and dooryard gardens. Even chickens could destroy rice-seed beds. Old men remember that making fences and maintaining them were their most arduous tasks. The kind of fence chosen for a given field depended on the materials at hand, the desired level of permanence, and the specific animal threat. Durable stone walls were favored for larger home gardens, more intensively cultivated umas, and rice terraces. For most dry fields, pine fences, sometimes reinforced with hardwood brush, sufficed. Owing to wet-season rot, such fences demanded constant repair. Where wood was not easily accessible, Buguias men usually built sod walls with facing ditches. On the steepest slopes, living fences of agave functioned well with little maintenance. Complex fence networks of pine, stone, and bamboo protected houselot gardens, especially vulnerable to residential swine.

THE HARVEST OF UNCULTIVATED LANDS

Uncultivated plants and wild animals also helped support the people of prewar Buguias. Gathered plants and hunted animals, while never forming staples, provided incidental protein and vitamins as well as welcome culinary variation. The production of fuel, fiber, and building materials from uncultivated lands, however, was absolutely essential.

HUNTING, FISHING, AND
INSECT GATHERING

The hunting of deer and wild hogs, the only large game, demanded skill, patience, and sometimes daring. Although neither creature inhabited central Buguias, deer roamed the more remote pine forests and savannahs, and wild hogs populated the higher oak woodlands. A few expert spear-wielding hunters followed trained dogs in pursuit of game, but most men preferred sedentary techniques. Some excavated pitfall traps alongside animal trails, rendering them deadly with sharpened sticks. The easiest method of deer capture was to burn an area of brush and then hide nearby until the animals arrived to lick the mineral-rich ash. Few men were versed in the more elaborate hunting techniques, but those who were could provide ample meat for their families and their neighbors.

Smaller mammals, such as civets and rats, were both abundant and troublesome. Civets raided houselot gardens, eating even coffee berries and occasionally killing chickens, while rats feasted on most crops. Hunting these animals thus protected other food sources and provided meat as well. Snares were usually employed, but young men enjoyed small-game hunting at night using dogs as trackers and pine torches for illumination.

Birds, ranging from large waders to tiny perchers, provided special delicacies. Buguias villagers caught migratory birds in season and residents the year round. Specialized snares were employed for different species at different times of the year; passive nooses sufficed in favorite roosts, while bent-stick spring traps snagged the warier species. The most plump and plentiful of the avian prey were the quail of the pasturelands, the snipes of the rice fields, and the wild chickens of the higher forests.

Most persons enjoyed fishing. The plentiful sculpins were sometimes netted by women, but were more often trapped by young men who would divert a river channel, thereby exposing all manner of life in the desiccated bed. Men and boys captured meaty eels with nets, hooks, and in river diversions. In rice fields and irrigation ditches, mud fish provided children with easy prey. Amphibians were plentiful in select seasons: tadpoles crowded the riverbed in March and April, and adult frogs could be captured at night, having first been blinded by torch light, in November and December.

Favored invertebrates spiced the seasonal fare as well. Fatty termites were funneled into water pots as they emerged for nuptial flights following the first rains. In the early years of this century an even greater bonanza occasionally appeared in the form of locust swarms. Buguias residents followed the insects for many miles, sometimes returning with several bushels to be dried and consumed at leisure. Lowland locust eradication programs sponsored by the U.S. were little appreciated in Buguias. More regular if less abundant invertebrate morsels included the mole crickets of the rice fields, the three varieties of rice-field snails, and the various river-dwelling water bugs. A few old men specialized in honey gathering, discerning hive locations by patiently observing the flights of bees. Honey itself was a delicacy, but wax was even more appreciated as a fiber coating.

The pursuit of wild creatures, other than deer and hogs, was—and still is—primarily an activity of young, unmarried men. Buguias bachelors still spend hours diverting streams for a meager catch of tadpoles, sculpins, and water bugs. This is not "optimal foraging" so much as simple entertainment. In the prewar period, poorer villagers found intensification of sweet-potato patches much more rewarding than hunting or fishing. But wild meat—some of it, such as tadpole flesh, very strong of taste—did provide welcome variation to an otherwise bland diet.

Wild Plant Foods

Prewar Buguias was endowed with several wild fruits and vegetables. Brambleberries and huckleberries were abundant in pastures and woodland clearings, and wild guavas grew thick in several dry grasslands. Children gathered most fruit, consuming the bulk forthwith but usually bringing some home for their families. The foremost wild vegetable was *Solanum nigrum*, a weed of abandoned dry fields. Buguias residents collected wild tomatoes and *Capsicum* peppers (both exotics), as well as watercress. They regarded mushrooms highly and sought them diligently, gathering over twenty different varieties, some in sufficient quantity for drying. But perhaps the most essential wild "food" plant was the cosmopolitan weed *Bidens pilosa*, which formed the base of *bubud*, the yeast cake used in making rice beer.

Only in famines were wild foods essential. A delay of the southwest monsoon could bring food shortages, and real hunger would ensue if drought persisted, as it once did, until July. A prolonged typhoon could also spoil the sweet-potato crop, thus depleting the essential food stock. Even a rat infestation could cause a food deficiency. During times of severe want, the Buguias people consumed the tubers of a drought-adapted pasture legume and the pithy centers of *Miscanthus* canes. In the harsh famine at the end of World War II, some individuals retreated to the oak forest to gather acorns. The standby food of hard times, however, was taro. Wild taro, common in higher elevation seeps, was edible if leached, and several varieties of cultivated taro survived well through the worst storms and droughts.

Non-food Products

The most significant use of wild plants was for nonfood products. Several wild legumes and the semiwild (and exotic) agave yielded fibers for rope and thread. In the early American period, poorer residents pounded the bark of several different trees into fabrics suitable for loincloths and skirts. Bark clothing disappeared only in the 1930s, when it was universally replaced by cotton cloth. Wild grasses served as thatch, and a variety of vines fastened house rafters and fences. Connected bamboo lengths formed water conduits, and individual sections functioned as canteens. Artisans carved hardwood, obtained from small groves in stream depressions, into bowls, handles, and durable tools. And finally, the versatile *Miscanthus* cane served in all manner of light construction.

But pine wood overshadowed all other hinterland products. Straight-bole trees, found on favored northern exposures, provided lumber. Hand-split pine planks sufficed for house construction in the early period, but by the 1920s boards sawn by itinerant Northern Kankana-ey workers were commonplace. Most fences (planks and posts) were pine, and hollowed pine logs formed conduits over stream crossings in the larger irrigation systems. Pine wood also fueled the hearths and heated the homes of prewar Buguias. The villagers usually derived their firewood from the more gnarled trees of the rocky slopes and southern exposures. Smoldering fires gave warmth when temperatures dipped to near freezing in December and January and helped counter the wet season's damp. Finally, metalworks were fueled by charcoal, derived largely from pine branches and bark.

The most valuable pine product was perhaps *saleng*, the resinous heartwood of old or prematurely injured trees. Saleng provided illumination: torches for outside activities, and slender "candles" for the home. The Buguias people also treasured such wood for its resistance to rot; only saleng posts could support a house for more than a few rainy seasons, or serve at all in fencing.

The inhabitants of prewar Buguias did not consider wood procuring to be an especially onerous chore. Pines were still plentiful and large, and a variety of labor-saving techniques were employed. Men and older boys usually secured a year's supply of fuel in the dry season; left to desiccate in the field the wood would lose roughly half of its weight before being carried. On steep slopes logs were shunted down gravel shoots to more accessible sites, if necessary affixed to boulders for extra weight. Trees closer to settlements were more casually, and gradually, harvested by boys who would climb them to lop off branches for fuel.

VEGETATIONAL CHANGE AND AGRICULTURAL INTENSIFICATION

Since human subsistence in prewar Buguias relied on wild as well as cultivated lands, one may question just how "natural" the uncultivated lands of Buguias were. And since people continually intervened in natural processes, we must also ask whether the reconfigurations they wrought were truly sustainable. The steady growth of human numbers in particular suggests that we must be cautious in proclaiming the prewar subsistence system as ultimately ecologically benign.

VEGETATIONAL CHANGE: THE KOWAL THESIS

Norman Kowal (1966) argues that prior to the advent of swidden cultivation and associated burning, the Cordillera was entirely wooded. Lowland "rainforest" grew below 1,200 meters, the zone between 1,200 and 1,600 meters supported a "submontane" forest of mixed hardwoods (containing pine only on rocky outcroppings and slide scars), and above 1,600 meters grew the true oak-dominated montane forest, called the *kalasan* in Buguias. Following human disturbance, this series was replaced by one containing *Imperata* grassland in the lowest reaches, *Themeda* grassland from approximately 1,000 to 1,400 meters, pine savannah (botanically identical with the *Themeda* grasslands except for the addition of scattered pines) between 1,200 and 2,000 meters (the original hardwoods surviving in stream depressions), and montane oak forest above 2,000 meters. Jacobs (1972) argues that on the very highest level, the summit of Mount Pulog, fires caused by humans (associated with camp sites rather than swiddens) allowed a grassland dominated by dwarf bamboo to replace the oak association.

Oral environmental histories gathered in several Benguet municipalities support Kowal's thesis. Throughout the province, even in now treeless areas, settlement stories tell of wandering hunters building their homes in "jungle" areas. Without further empirical

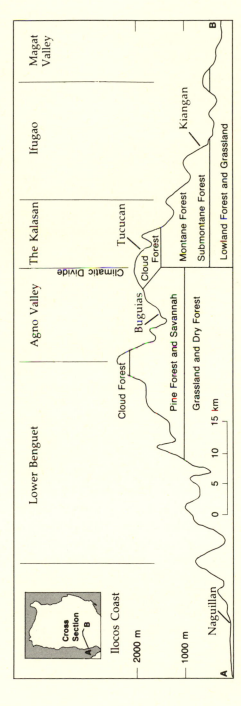

Figure 1. *The Buguias Environment: A Cross Section through the Southern Cordillera.* Vegetation zones modified from Kowal (1966).

work (palynological analysis, for example), any discussion of vegetational change under human pressure must remain tentative. The following pages thus outline the more likely pathways of anthropogenic vegetation change in prewar Buguias.

VEGETATIONAL CHANGE IN BUGUIAS

In present-day Buguias, montane hardwoods occupy only the northern exposures of steep side canyons. According to Kowal's model, hardwoods would have dominated the prefire landscape of Buguias, with pine restricted to dry and rocky sites. Such pockets of seasonal aridity are widespread in this area, however, and many steep southern exposures may never have supported montane forests. Although Buguias lies only sixteen degrees north of the equator, slope aspect is significant since drought occurs when the sun is well within the southern hemisphere. Furthermore, fire, which universally favors pine, can be sparked by the lightning that sometimes accompanies the year's first storms. Thus the vegetation of Buguias in earlier times was probably a mosaic of pine savannah and montane forest.

The early agriculturalists probably chose sites in the fertile montane forests for their first swiddens. With long initial fallow, forest vegetation would have been able to regenerate, but with intensification, *Miscanthus* cane would have spread. Indeed, in both the Ifugao culture region and in the Bot-oan area immediately east of Buguias, *Miscanthus* swards dominate swidden fallows (see Lizardo 1955). But with the introduction of cattle in the later Spanish period, *Miscanthus* would have declined while pasture grasses increased. As the fire- and grazing-adapted savannah spread, the montane forest would have retreated to ravines inaccessible to flame. In the more intensively grazed areas of the lower valley, pine would have declined, as yearly burning inhibited its regeneration. In the highest reaches—those above 2,000 meters—perennial saturation would have protected the oak forest, but even here fire could burn a few meters into the woodland each year, allowing a progressive march of grassland vegetation (Jacobs 1972). But for the most part, the higher oak forest would have remained little modified by human activity, except for the few areas cut for uma fields and the selected ridgetops annually cleared for the nocturnal hunting of migratory birds.

The anthropogenic savannah was vital for prewar Buguias subsistence; it afforded graze for the herds and pine wood for fuel, construction, and illumination. But pine regeneration may have been inadequate to sustain this regime in the long run. Pine seedlings require some five to ten fire-free years to become established, and many pastures were burned annually. Most lower-elevation Ibaloi districts had already been deforested well before the turn of the century (Semper 1862 [1975]), owing perhaps to lowered pine vitality in warmer climes (Lizardo 1955) but probably also to the longer history of Ibaloi pastoralism. Certain Kankana-ey areas, especially those, like Mankayan, that supported an indigenous mining and smelting industry, were also deforested long ago (Marche 1887 [1970]). Whether prewar subsistence patterns would have truly allowed a sustainable pine harvest is an open question.

The people of prewar Buguias derived their sustenance from a landscape that was in part their own creation. All peoples transform nature, but here the alterations were especially marked. The vegetation, geomorphology, and even the hydrology of Buguias reflected a history of human activity. Slopes were flattened and streams diverted for pond fields, and even dry fields were sometimes terraced. The original woodland was largely replaced by a savannah grassland, which was then populated by exogenous animals. Of course, the Buguias people did not make their landscape any way they pleased, but rather grappled with their given environment, pushing its vegetation into latent successional pathways and molding its contours with materials at hand.

Deforestation, however, was not the only threat to prewar subsistence. Population began to grow rapidly in the American period, forcing the Buguias people to intensify production and to reorient their management of uncultivated lands.

AGRICULTURAL INTENSIFICATION

Uma cultivation in prewar Buguias deviated most markedly from "classical swidden" in its short fallow and in its labor intensiveness.[6] Following Ester Boserup's (1965) powerful theory of agricultural intensification, one would expect precisely such developments if Buguias agriculture were responding to population pressure. With more persons deriving sustenance from the same area, fallow periods would have been progressively shortened as labor inputs were progressively increased. Demographic history, however, is difficult to establish; during the pre-American period the population of Buguias no doubt fluctuated wildly in response to epidemics, military incursions, and migrations. But during the years of American power, population did mount steadily. American and Philippine census data, although of dubious quality, reflect such growth, the recorded population of the Buguias municipal district rising from 1,612 in 1901, to 5,894 in 1948—the latter figure tabulated after the wartime devastation.[7]

But in many respects, the degree of intensivity exhibited in prewar Buguias agriculture is better explained by ecological than by demographic factors. Since rice would not mature if grown during the wet season, irrigated terraces were necessary for this crop. Once constructed, pond fields do not require a rejuvenating fallow. The motivation for building them, however, rested as much in the ideational as in the material sphere; rice was grown more for the prestigious intoxicant that it provided than for the calories it might afford. Dry fields, however, were allowed only a short fallow, not for lack of land but rather because of the environmental requirements of the staple crop.[8] Sweet-potato vines would produce the whole year only on sites endowed with deep moisture-retentive soils. True, the Buguias people *could* have grown all of their tubers in the wet season, storing enough to last the year. But storage would have demanded its own heavy labor burdens, just as it would have resulted in a less appetizing diet. Moreover, the existence of a separate pastoral sector militated against frequent field relocation; for pastureland to be recultivated, the sod had to be manually turned, an extremely laborious undertaking.

Continued population expansion under the prewar regime would have brought systematic agricultural changes. More careful management could have increased the rice yield, and the pond fields themselves could have been drained and planted to sweet potatoes in the off-season. Dry fields could have been intensified by eliminating their vestigial fallow. But increasing the sweet-potato harvest significantly would have required manuring, a labor-demanding task that also would have stinted the fertile and easily managed door-yard gardens.

A less revolutionary method of increasing production would have been simply to expand the more productive sectors. Additional pastureland could have been converted to dry fields and terraces, while distant woodlands and brushlands could have been cleared for cattle grazing. But since land was finite, constrained ultimately by intervillage boundaries, increased production in this manner would have brought intersectoral spatial competition. Prime dry fields might have been transformed to pond fields, thus forcing new uma construction in previously marginal sites. Pasturelands, cane breaks, brushlands, and forests, however, would have gradually but steadily diminished. Indeed, much evidence suggests that these were precisely the kinds of changes that were occurring in the American period.

If the diet of the Buguias people had continued to be based largely on local subsistence, and had the population continued to grow, labor burdens would have increased, while dietary quality would have diminished. A shrinking pastoral sector would have supported fewer cattle, which would have been divided among more persons. Meanwhile, ever-increasing applications of labor would have been required to convert ever more marginal areas into arable fields or to intensify the output of existing plots.

Beyond this, the potential evolutionary pathways of the intensifying subsistence system are unknowable. As elsewhere, in prewar Buguias a range of potential choices existed, and any developments would have depended on human decisions and innovations. We need only to look at two neighboring peoples, the central Ifugao and the Bontoc, both of whom had much higher population densities in the prewar period than did the Buguias people. The Bontocs had integrated their expansive pond-field system with their dry fields; off-season terraces were drained, ridged, and planted to sweet potatoes (Jenks 1905). Much work was expended, especially since terraces were also manured, but the resulting fields were productive: in 1948, 1,000 hectares of cultivated land in the Buguias regions (reportedly) supported some 9,267 persons, while in Bontoc the figure was 20,966 (Republic of the Philippines 1954, Part I: 53—such figures are, of course, of suspect reliability). In Ifugao, the even more expansive pond fields were seasonally fallowed as in

Buguias, while nonterraced areas were either devoted to brush-fallow swidden or to intensively managed woodlot orchards (see Conklin 1980). Both of these intensified systems were probably sustainable, but neither allowed the meat consumption that was possible in Buguias.

The argument presented above is not merely an exercise in hypothetical reasoning; its purpose is rather cautionary. The latter part of this work will turn to the *commercial* agriculture that replaced the dry-field/pond-field/pastureland complex following World War II. I will argue that the new agricultural system represents an ecological debacle, marked by eroded hillslopes, denuded canyons, poisoned watersheds, and exterminated wildlife. But we should not allow the desolation of the modern regime to lead us into regarding the prewar period as an ecological idyll. Certainly subsistence agriculture was *relatively* sustainable, but with increasing population density, environmental degradation would have resulted nonetheless. Cultural ecologists have shown in many instances the utility of viewing "pre-modern" societies as adapted to their environments, but prewar Buguias shows powerfully that they should also be seen, in the tradition of cultural geography, as remaking their very landscapes—and not necessarily in a positive manner (see the essays in Thomas [1956], and, more recently, Blaikie and Brookfield [1987]).

In continually refashioning their landscape, the people of Buguias were both constrained and enabled by their natural environment. But their environmental-management decisions were also made within a limiting social milieu—within a preexisting (although constantly changing) system of power relations and social ideology. As human society changed, so too changed the relationship between people and nature.

3

Social Relations:
Power and Labor

The Buguias people remade their landscape only through great effort. Their labors were of necessity socially organized; each person's work was determined, in large part, by his or her place within the community. As in most human groups, individuals had widely varying abilities to select their own tasks and to command the labor of others. Such power was generally determined by age, gender, and family position (with permutations for individual ability and personality), but more importantly, by the control of productive resources.

Although some scholars would equate class division with state formation (for example, White 1959:299), most prewar Cordilleran societies were at once village-based and highly stratified. Three social "classes"—taking the term in its most general definition—constituted the population of prewar Buguias. The "commoners" (henceforth, without quotation marks) cultivated their own dry fields and often labored together in cooperative projects. While overtly independent, most remained in chronic debt to their wealthier relatives and neighbors. Commoner men cared for, but rarely owned, livestock. Commoner women, for their part, labored long hours in their uma fields. As was true in all classes, tasks were gender-segregated, and commoner men and women inhabited discrete economic spheres. Members of the elite *baknang* class, however, commanded others to work on their own sometimes grandiose agricultural projects. Servants and slaves, composing the third social class, remained ever at the beck of the rich, who could also entice commoners to work for them with wages. The elite could also tap the labor of still another group, the itinerants from less prosperous Cordilleran communities.

Power relations reflected back on the landscape of prewar Buguias. The territory of any class-based society is characteristically divided into distinct segments over which different individuals hold certain powers. Through the prewar period, Buguias was increasingly subdivided into private and semiprivate plots. This was no smooth progression, however, as three conflicting tenure systems—one indigenous, one American-imposed, and the third of mixed provenance—formed separate arenas of contention. Yet all three systems evinced some movement toward individualized tenure, both reflecting and furthering elite power. Nonetheless, the elite class by no means enjoyed uncontested authority in territorial control or in any other dimension of life.

Prewar Buguias was a society of fluid classes, not lithified estates. A common-born person could rise to wealth, while highborn scions frequently fell. Moreover, class divisions were tempered by interclass genealogical and marital links. Cross-class family ties formed a potential vehicle for upward movement. Each class was marked by its own mobility patterns, closely tied to inheritance customs and redistributive obligations.

Labor and capital, land tenure, and social mobility thus form the substance of this chapter; yet class dynamics also include much more. The exercise of power in local politics, the legitimation of class through ritual, and the creation of wealth in trade all contributed in essential ways to the Buguias social formation. These sundry elements will be taken up in their turn in later chapters.

THE COMMONERS

ANIMAL SHARING

Few persons in prewar Buguias owned the large animals they tended. Commoners typically received their animals on loan, as infants or yearlings, from the village elite, with the understanding that any offspring would be shared. The actual apportioning varied according to the animal lent and the relationship between the borrower and lender.

Hog-lending arrangements varied greatly. When a female piglet was transferred, the caretaker would usually keep the entire first brood, and two of every three in subsequent litters; if the loan were a mature sow, the owner could usually take the choice one of every three piglets. Few commoner women could tend more than two or three brood sows; occasionally they owned one outright, but more commonly they "leased" all. Caretakers could not easily acquire breeding stock, for their own shares were typically devoted to rituals or sold for cash. Most commoners were eager to raise swine for the rich, but a few resisted the entailed subordination. Yet even reluctant individualists could often be pressured by wealthy patrons into building a pigpen and borrowing stock.

Cattle and water-buffalo lending (*pastol*, a Spanish-derived term also referring to the caretakers themselves) was more prestigious though not as ubiquitous as hog lending. Few men could care for more than a few water buffalo, but the ambitious could raise twenty or more cows, steers, and bulls. Enterprising caretakers commonly borrowed stock from several sponsors. Commoners would usually sell their own shares for cash, sometimes to their own patrons— who might immediately "lend" them back again. Pastol agreements typically favored the lender, since he could claim the first offspring, the third, the fifth, and so on; under such terms, the vagaries of reproduction ensured the animal owner a greater share.[1]

The basic pastol contract included provisions for a number of contingencies. Castrated male calves, for instance, might be sold at maturity with the profit divided equally. Yet conflicts sometimes flared, as when cattle fell from precipitous slopes. After such an occurrence the caretaker had to show evidence that the death was indeed accidental. Dead and seriously maimed cattle were usually butchered and sold by weight to interested neighbors, with most of the profit accruing to the animal's owner. A magnanimous baknang, however, would be expected to give a feast and freely distribute his windfall meat.

The customary apportioning of calves and piglets might not be realized if the commoner caretaker were deeply in debt to his or her patron. In this instance, the baknang could claim all offspring, although many often simply let their credits accumulate through subsequent breeding rounds. For the common people, the indebtedness that usually began at marriage was exacerbated by the terms of animal sharing.

LABOR ORGANIZATION AND GENDER

The daily travails of the commoners varied fundamentally with gender. Women toiled primarily in the dry fields. They often would return home, heavily laden with sweet potatoes, only when dark fell. Work in the kitchens and piggeries also fell to female hands. Although women usually labored in their fields alone, some of their arduous tasks could be lightened through cooperative labor exchange (*ogbo*). Overall, women's work was spatially concentrated and temporally demanding.

Male labor, however, was spatially dispersed and much less consuming. The male commoner's only routine job was cattle oversight; the conscientious pastol would once or twice daily determine the whereabouts of his stock. This entailed long hikes, but required only several hours a day unless the animals strayed. Because their daily chores were light, men often tended small children (feeding their babies premasticated sweet potatoes). Men generally cultivated the family dry field only if their wives were ill or recovering from childbirth. Women might complain that their husbands harvested tubers with the care and skill of wild hogs, but those without help were hard pressed. And men's work in childcare was important; one woman, abandoned by her wastrel spouse, had to place her mischievous children in a deep hole so she could attend to her crops. The few men who mastered female farming skills were teased but grudgingly admired, as were those women who reached proficiency in such male tasks as blade sharpening.

The daily schedules of both men and women were punctuated by seasonal and single-occurrence tasks. Here men usually handled the heavier burdens: clearing new umas, weeding pastures, mending and building fences and trails, cleaning canals, constructing and rebuilding terrace walls, cutting and carrying firewood, and preparing rice fields. Other seasonal tasks, such as rice transplanting, fell strictly to women, and still others, such as rice harvesting, were shared by members of both sexes. Women often joined their husbands in digging puwals, usually accomplished in labor-exchange ogbo groups. Ogbo labor debts were strictly accounted, and a woman's contribution was valued the same as a man's.

The people of Buguias usually accomplished their non-routine jobs cooperatively, either through ogbo or through a more commercial arrangement called *dangas*. The individual organizer of a dangas project would acquire labor in exchange for food and drink, with no further obligations incurred. The emoluments provided had to be of high quality; goats or dogs were usually butchered and rice beer provided. Such activities were, not surprisingly, usually initiated by the wealthy.

Day to day, commoner men worked far fewer hours than did women; at the same time, adult males undertook those tasks requiring travel outside the community. Only men served the ten days annually on road corvée duty as required by the colonial government; more importantly, most trade with neighboring peoples was their prerogative. These activities were consistent with the relative lightness of men's quotidian obligations; women simply could not abandon their fields for more than a few days at a time. In the final tabulation, women shouldered the greater burdens in prewar Buguias—as in most societies the earth has known. Buguias women had considerable social standing and authority compared to women in many parts of the world, but men nevertheless held greater political and religious power, and it was they who ultimately ruled prewar Buguias.

Even after accounting for gender differences, the chores of the commoners were not all identical. Some variation could be ascribed to temperament; certain men, for example, avoided the burden of raising cattle, while others maximized their pastol commitments. Certain specialized jobs were limited by their long apprenticeships. Buguias's few blacksmiths did little but work metal, and even expert basket weavers might easily ignore animal husbandry. Both occupations passed from fathers to sons or nephews. Other specialties, such as terrace building (mastered by few) and roof thatching, entailed only occasional, supplementary employment. A few select older men, however, found full employment as ritual specialists.

THE ELITE AND THEIR SERVANTS

THE BAKNANGS

The animal-owning baknang class was internally stratified; the smallest "baknang of pigs" might have a dozen animals let out to neighbors and relatives, while the richest could own hundreds of cattle, hogs, water buffalo, and horses—as many as a thousand animals in all. These very wealthy baknang were few; in the early American period only one, Danggol, lived in what is today Buguias

Central, although by the later colonial period this number had doubled to include Berto Cubangay (Danggol's son), and Paran, an immigrant from a village to the east. The following discussion concentrates on the wealthier individuals.

Most baknang women were little removed from the economic milièu of their poorer relatives; few indeed escaped the drudgery of the uma. The wealthiest were also required to manage female servants and tend to a constant stream of visitors. The topmost men, however, occupied themselves strictly with managerial and financial work: overseeing livestock, supervising rice-field construction and pasture maintenance, and lending money and conducting trade. Unlike their poorer relatives, they seldom directly engaged with the land; rather, they directed others—their servants, assistants, contract workers, and livestock caretakers. Ultimately, the male baknang's role was that of community "leader." These men essentially governed Buguias (both in the indigenous and the American-sponsored systems), organized its religious practices, and headed its traditional courts. These capacities await analysis in later chapters; here we are more interested in the role of labor, as organized by social power, in deriving subsistence from— and thus transforming—nature. We have already seen how the elites acquired commoners' labor through animal lending and dangas "wages"; now we will examine several groups of people over whom they exerted more direct control.

SLAVES, SERVANTS, ITINERANTS, AND CLIENTS

The servile class encompassed a varied group. Some individuals voluntarily tied themselves to wealthy patrons. Elderly widows and never-married women, hard pressed to live alone, could usually enter a baknang household in exchange for hog tending, fire keeping, and dry-field cultivation. In the early years of the century, entire families living to the east of Buguias were often forced by brigands to flee their homes, and many sought the protection of powerful families in Buguias. In return, they would provide labor services for a number of years. A rich man could sometimes protect another accused of a crime, again receiving labor in exchange. In one noted example, after the Kalanguya immigrant Kabading was inconclusively tried, by ordeal, for witchcraft, the baknang Paran protected him from further hazing. Subsequently, Kabading built five rice terraces, four of which became the property of his benefactor.

In the early years of American rule a few individuals were held in slavery. Wealthy traders purchased slaves with animals, blankets, or cash from the Ifugao. Once in Buguias slaves remained bound for life, but they were not traded and their positions differed little from those of the other servants. Their owners sometimes encouraged them to marry local commoners, and their children did not automatically remain in bondage.

The relationships between the elite and their attached clients varied. Servile married couples and elderly women usually lived in small huts near the main residence, while unmarried male retainers (and itinerant workers) more often lodged in crude "bunkhouses." Most dependents, however, were female, since women's work was in more constant demand; the routine tasks of the dry field, house yard, and kitchen could not be accomplished through dangas payments or contract. Some serving women also cared for children, but rarely were couples of child-bearing age so prosperous. Male servants, however, primarily cared for the private herds and pasturelands of a baknang, in addition to providing a host of other minor services. The elite couples always provided patronage for their workers, paying for their funerals and sometimes their weddings, and in general assuring their places within the community. Yet by no means did such relationships approach reciprocity.

The elite could obtain labor for daily, seasonal, and single-occurrence tasks either from commoners (through dangas) or from their dependents. But some projects demanded greater skill and effort than could be locally obtained. Elite men therefore hired, by contract, itinerant workers, usually Northern Kankana-ey or Kalanguya men. These sojourners constructed rice terraces and stone walls, sawed lumber, and occasionally cleared new fields. Remuneration came as cash, animals, or blankets. The Northern Kankana-ey never stayed long, but the Kalanguya, culturally and genealogically tied to the Buguias people (and less secure in their bandit-infested homeland) not uncommonly married and remained.

The wealthiest residents of prewar Buguias commanded yet another set of clients for managerial work, namely their juvenile male relatives. As these younger men (usually sons, sons-in-law, and nephews) acted primarily in trade, their work is discussed in that context in chapter 5. While these underlings could grow wealthy themselves in later life, their careers were anything but secure. Prewar Buguias was a stratified society, but it was also marked by class mobility—particularly striking in the downward direction.

SOCIAL MOBILITY

Class and Family

Social classes in prewar Buguias interdigitated along kinship lines. All baknangs had near relatives of the commoner class, and all commoners were tied not too distantly to elite families. Virtually the entire community traced its ancestry to the Kalanguya hunter Lumiaen, who arrived in Buguias in the early nineteenth century. Most elite families stemmed from Basilio, Lumiaen's wealthy son, while most commoners traced their lineage to Siklungan, his poorer offspring. But since kinship was reckoned cognatically, lines crossed and complex relationships linked most families. The generally poor immigrants were excluded from the Buguias family tree, but they could be grafted to it through marriage. Many individuals married across class lines; since customary law proscribed unions even between second cousins, the pool of potential mates was limited. Powerful families, in attempting to concentrate their wealth, sometimes allowed cousins to marry, or, alternatively, selected for their children elite spouses from other villages. But these were never standard practices, and many elite youngsters married commoners. This did not challenge the village's class structure, however, since local ideology explicitly allowed for individual mobility. Through luck and effort, poor individuals could rise, whereas children of the rich regularly fell.

Inheritance and Downward Mobility

Elite couples periodically diminished their wealth through ritual extravagance, and their fortunes could be entirely consumed at their own funerals. A month-long wake of a true baknang could consume an entire herd. Rice terraces generally devolved as inheritance, but inauspicious funeral auguries might call for their sale to cover additional animal sacrifices. Family heirlooms, especially Chinese vases, also passed to the succeeding generation, but these only displayed *potential* status. Furthermore, since all children of the (usually) large elite families would inherit a share, no one child ever received adequate wealth to maintain class position. Even the sons of the topmost couples had to earn elite status—although they would receive substantial succor all along the way.

Often a single son from a rich family would reoccupy his father's position. Although the successor's personal business fortunes were ultimately paramount, succession could hinge on the parents' funerals. All children had their own funeral-related ceremonies, in addition to being obligated to help finance the main wakes; together these rites might force decapitalization. The wealthier brother (or, occasionally, brother-in-law) could sometimes exploit his siblings' distress and acquire their properties. The eldest sibling, having had a longer period in which to accumulate wealth, was thus advantaged, even though the youngest usually secured the largest share of the family bequest. Not surprisingly, inheritance accords could be contentious; while ailing parents might seek to establish concord before they died, the community's elders often had to negotiate, and enforce, settlements. The elders would weigh many considerations, including the financial assistance the parents had previously given to each child, as well as the help each heir had provided the parents. Education counted as a parental gift, depriving some of the earliest graduates of any property legacies.

Occasionally a baknang line would sink entirely to commoner status. The local sages would interpret this as a sign of ancestral disapproval—in one noted instance, said to have been brought on by incorrectly performed rituals.

UPWARD MOVEMENT

The typical commoner was so burdened with debt (much of it ritually incurred) that upward mobility was all but impossible. But a few managed to rise, usually by working for a wealthy relative. Marrying the daughter of a baknang provided a good business entrée, but the wedding costs, borne by the male party, were restrictive. Still, a young man recognized by his prospective father-in-law as outstandingly clever and industrious might find wedding loans readily forthcoming. Nor was it absolutely impossible for one to prosper through personal efforts in animal husbandry. One man named Calayon, for example, climbed from poverty to mid-level baknang status, although it took him an entire lifetime. Calayon first trafficked in chickens, moved on to hogs, and finally graduated to cattle leasing. He advised others that they too could prosper if they followed his example and if they maintained the proper relations with their ancestors.

Members of the serving class had few hopes for prosperity, although a few skilled immigrants could rise. The accused wizard Kabading, for example, eventually reached a fairly high position. Slaves, however, remained impoverished. Although their children were not necessarily bound, most did remain servile; a good marriage provided their best route to independence. Today, their descendants still constitute the poorest segment of the community.

Class conflict did not rend prewar Buguias society; familial ties and expectations of reciprocity tempered dissonance. Still, certain baknangs were privately censored for self-serving actions, and one was secretly reviled (by some) for abusing his power. Yet no members of the elite could automatically maintain position simply by possessing wealth. Legitimation was a continual and costly burden, albeit one borne (we may presume) reverently. But for this story we must wait for chapter 4; more immediate for the present concern is the land-tenure system that allowed the elite to control key sectors of production within Buguias.

LAND TENURE

Inasmuch as individuals exerted varying degrees of control over different parcels of land, power relations in prewar Buguias were etched on the landscape. Most land remained under what might loosely be termed communal tenure, but elite men were increasingly privatizing individual parcels. Privatization had indigenous roots, but flourished under an American land policy that generated several conflicting tenure systems. The contradictions among them would cause considerable strife, but not until the postwar period.

Indigenous Tenure

Under indigenous tenure, all community members theoretically had unrestricted access to the forests and grasslands surrounding the village, although *de facto* land use even here proved unequal. Open lands used primarily as pastures were divided into semi-discrete sections by natural and artificial barriers. Each caretaker usually grazed his cattle in pastures near his home, although the animals often could wander relatively freely toward the higher slopes. As the baknangs scattered their animals among many commoners and over many pasture segments, most "herds" comprised cattle of diverse ownership lent to sundry caretakers. Still, elite couples usually possessed most of the animals pasturing near their own homes and thus they dominated certain pastures.

Dry fields, in contrast, were semiprivate, since individuals held recognized rights over their own plots while cultivating them. Cultivators gained the privilege of permanent cultivation by investing in permanent improvements, such as stone walls. Since land remained relatively plentiful throughout the prewar period, however, few conflicts erupted here.

By the middle years of American rule, some Buguias cattle lords adopted the techniques of land improvement to lay claim to private pastures. By enclosing and thoroughly cleaning a plot of grassland, a cattle owner could gain the community's consent to his exclusive grazing rights. But few could afford the required fencing, and even the wealthiest maintained private paddocks of no more than a few hectares.

Houselots also formed *de facto* private property since occupation was not easily disputed, but there were exceptions. Door-yard produce, for instance, was considered free to all, and children regularly exercised the privilege. Neither were house sites themselves sacrosanct. As most couples occasionally transferred residence, house sites frequently returned to the village common. In rare cases, poor couples could even be forced out of their homes by individuals with competing ownership claims. Present-day elders tell of one avaricious prewar baknang dispossessing several commoners who had established healthy coffee plantations on land that he was able to claim as his own.

Rice terraces were the most completely privatized element within the indigenous land tenure system; only they could be inherited, bought, sold, and mortgaged.[2] This tenure arrangement may have gradually emerged in Buguias owing to the investments required to establish a pond field, or it may have been adopted from the land codes of other terrace-making Cordilleran peoples. Whichever the case, an individual in prewar Buguias could usurp common land simply by carving out a new rice field. And because of the clear ownership prerogatives, investments in terraces, an option mainly open to the rich, yielded much greater returns than investments in dry fields. The land-tenure system thus reflected and reinforced distinctions of social power.

THE AMERICAN INTERVENTION

The first American surveying team arrived in Buguias in 1903, determined to isolate private land from the "public domain" (owned, in their eyes, by the Insular Government). The surveyors sought out property owners, hoping to award them with genuine titles.[3] But American conceptions of land tenure clashed with the indigenous system, and the officials sent to carry out the work lacked the dedication that would have been necessary for success. They meted only the more accessible sites; Buguias's upper reaches were ignored, and thereby "legally" transferred to the Manila government. Eventually these lands were included within the Central Cordilleran Forest Reserve—reserved for American mill and mine owners elsewhere in Benguet. Although administrators set aside small "communal forests," these were utterly inadequate and largely ignored. Compounding the imbroglio, the surveyors titled large blocks as single properties, blocks encompassing pastures, dry fields, and terraces—and controlled (in varying degrees) by many different parties. The surveyors, it must be said, received little help from the mistrustful residents. Most baknangs, suspicious of the surveyors' intentions, put forward dummy owners; one such newly propertied man was a poor, blind, and completely pliant priest.

American land policy was revised in the 1930s, when two contradictory policies were implemented. A new cadastral survey, less fraudulent than the earlier one, measured only cultivated plots and awarded titles to the actual cultivators. Indeed, the teams preferentially surveyed the fields of individuals requesting the action. But despite this meliorative effort, most land remained either "public" or under titles established earlier. The companion American land program of the period, that of the "municipal tax declaration," formed a strikingly divergent tenure system. Although made possible and encouraged by the Insular Government, the tax declaration arrangement formed, in effect, a quasi-official local tenure system, run by the American-recognized Buguias administration. To confirm limited rights to a parcel, an individual had simply to declare ownership annually and pay a small municipal tax. Such property boundaries were loosely fixed through descriptions of natural features. Any uncultivated plot could legally be declared, so long as the declarant paid the required taxes—regardless of whether it was previously titled to another or officially within the public domain (see Arenal-Sereno and Libarios 1983).

In general, the elite welcomed the tax-declaration system, since it allowed them to aggrandize their own holdings with imperial blessing while retaining control of the tenure system itself. The poor resented it during this period, as they could scarcely afford the requisite taxes. Through the 1930s, considerable pasturage and even some forest stands were made quasi private through tax declarations. Indigenous communal usufruct rights were not thereby cancelled, but the preexisting tendency toward land privatization was strengthened.

Three incompatible land-tenure systems coexisted uneasily at the end of the American period. Many parcels were covered by overlapping claims, each of which could invoke the backing of a different level of authority: the Insular Government in Manila, the American-recognized municipality, or the body of customary law. Individual rights to land and its products varied both within and among each of these disparate systems. The contradictions did not surface until the postwar period, but the inhabitants of Buguias in the later twentieth century are vexed by the land-tenure policies of the American bureaucracy.

LAND TENURE AND CLASS

The elite of Buguias controlled sizable estates and could mobilize the labor necessary to transform them. The baknang household, with its attendant workers, formed a larger production unit than did the commoner's nuclear family, allowing the wealthy couple to cultivate extensive dry fields and door-yard gardens. In addition, elite families held virtually exclusive rights to two further productive sectors: private pastures and pond fields. Wealthy households thus generated a far greater "subsistence income" than did others. Much of this went to in-house consumption, to feed the many guests, family members, and dependents. And of course, the rich led richer lives: they dwelled in substantial houses, wore fine garments, possessed varied tools and utensils, and regularly ate meat and drank rice beer. A true baknang couple would always serve their guests dried meat and alcohol. Yet all told, the truly wealthy still expended fewer resources on their daily lives than their incomes would have allowed; redistributive rituals consumed the greater share. While the elite monopolized the best pastures and converted the prime agricultural sites into private rice fields, a substantial portion of the fruits of these lands flowed back to the people of Buguias at community feasts.

4

Religion:
The Role of the Ancestors

INTRODUCTION

The people of prewar Buguias believed that their lives were continually touched by a host of gods and spirits, both benign and malevolent. The most influential of such beings were the souls of their ancestors. These *amed* involved themselves in virtually all Buguias activities, dispensing luck on their descendants according to the care they received from the living. And they were demanding; lonely for human companionship and hungry for the spiritual essences of earthly things, the amed called for repeated celebration. To placate them, the living were obligated periodically to invite the dead back to earth where they could be honored through feast and dance. The rituals in which this took place formed the focus of communal life, and the climax of most economic endeavors.

Human power relations were inseparable from religious activities. The more wealth a couple possessed, the more they had to dispense in ritual. Yet by adhering to these expectations, the elite found twofold advantage within the system: their earthly prestige was legitimated and enhanced, and their spiritual futures were blessed. True, their wealth was diminished by such expenditures in the short run, but the commoners too had exacting ancestors. With commoners borrowing heavily from the wealthy to carry out their own smaller sacrifices, the baknang class was able to gather in with one hand what it had distributed with the other.

Even outside of ritual context, the supernatural pervaded day-to-day life. Omens called for careful readings, while nonancestral spirits demanded watchfulness, for they could wreak great mischief if not properly propitiated. Accidents, illnesses, and mental disturbances could all originate with supernatural agents, and thus call for sacrifice.

GODS AND SPIRITS

The Buguias Pantheon

Religious ideology was open to personal exegesis. While the Buguias people generally shared the complex Cordilleran hierarchies and genealogies of heavenly, earthbound, and underworld deities and spirits, their interpretations seem to have been heterodox. At least in the modern period, even the relationship between the two chief gods, Kabigat and his brother Balitok, and the secondary members of the pantheon, such as Wigan and Bangan, are uncertain. To some, Bangan and Kabigat are siblings, to others, husband and wife.[1] Above all reigns Kabunian, but again the nature of this ultimate godhead, as well as his connections with the more active heavenly beings, was fluid (see W. H. Scott 1960 [1969]). In one perhaps idiosyncratic conception, all deities are said to occupy dual incarnations: a primary being that remains in the sky-world, and a secondary shadow—intermediary to humankind—dwelling underground.

Gods were considered generally benevolent, and they received numerous petitions for succor. Each deity had his or her specialty. Balitok, for example, offered help in the curing of wounds. To invoke a god's intervention, a priest, or *manbunung*, had to recite the correct prayers and direct the proper offerings. Chickens were commonly sacrificed; after the gods had feasted on the spiritual essences, the participants consumed the flesh.

Spirits: Dangerous, Neutral, and Helpful

Buguias residents had to be wary of a variety of dangerous spirits. Imbag Bagisan, the underworld god of the hunt, provoked great fear. Accompanied by gruesome dogs, he prowled the earth, sating his hunger with human souls. Except on those occasions when his wife intervened on the victim's behalf, he could only be appeased with two chickens, a pig, or a dog. A variety of usually malicious spirits, generally called *anitos*, were capable of causing similar harm. The *mante-es-bilig*, denizens of thickets, caused lingering sickness, curable only through the sacrifice of a female chicken.

The sky-dwelling *mante-ed-tongdo* wielded potent curses that might require the offer of a water buffalo. The *bet-tattew*, visible as flickering evening lights, could carry away unwary human souls. More dangerous still were the *te-tets*, ghostly vampires that sucked life directly from the heart; little could be done to save their victims.

More commonly encountered were *timungao*, beings who could be either benign or vicious, depending on their individual temperaments. Timungao generally dwelled near boulders in clear-running streams, and as a rule they distanced themselves from raucous human activities. Their society closely paralleled that of humans; they were born, grew up, married, bore children, aged, and accumulated property. Usually invisible to human beings, they commonly appeared only in dreams. Occasionally a female timungao would deign to wed a man during such an encounter. The bewitched groom might then abandon the human world, unless he were divorced, at some expense, from his nocturnal companion.

But for the most part, timungao were disgusted by human dirt, noise, and dietary habits. People disturbed them by trespassing in their clear streams, by fighting among themselves, and particularly by killing and eating their pet frogs (distinguishable by their unusual number of toes). As the timungao's revenge could be deadly, one had to be careful to eat only frogs with the normal configuration of digits. Timungao were also known to harm disrespectful trespassers, although most would tolerate a person who called out and apologized beforehand. Sometimes a timungao would intervene in strictly human affairs, dispensing swift punishment on those guilty of deceiving others. Illness usually befell the delinquent party, although a mischievous timungao might be satisfied simply by urinating on the miserable offender. A good-natured sprite could even bring fortune to a deserving human, but in general these ubiquitous beings required continual appeasing since humans could not help but disturb them.

More influential than either gods or nature spirits were the souls of the dead. They usually helped the living, but they too required continual homage. By the late American period, ancestor worship formed the core of local religion, although it is not at all clear whether this was true in earlier times.

The souls of individuals who died horrible or premature deaths could become malicious in their unhappiness. The spirits of the drowned (*nagalnad*) tried to assuage their loneliness by drowning others. More dangerous were the *awil*, souls of those who had died particularly violent deaths. The awil of nineteenth-century Spanish soldiers killed in the vicinity caused untold harm in their never-ending quest for revenge.

To avert trouble, a person had to be on constant watch for signs from the spirits. Negative travel omens, such as the crossing of one's path by an unliked or rare animal, delayed many journeys. Even an impropitiously timed sneeze or an oddly behaving dog could ruin a business transaction. Neither did nightmares bode well, as all dreams were considered serious messages from the other realm. On waking, one would hope that by cleansing in clear water the vision could be washed away. If truly impressed, however, the dreamer would seek expert counsel, hoping that what seemed a fright was actually an encoded charm.

SPIRITUAL CURING, PREVENTION OF HARM, AND BLESSINGS

The person most often consulted in such cases was a female spirit medium (*mansib-ok*). Mediums differed in their diagnostic methods, but most would dangle a bit of iron near the afflicted person's face, and by observing the metal's movement discern the supernatural agent and then recommend the appropriate ceremony (see Sacla 1987). The few male practitioners usually divined by scrutinizing patterns in the dregs of a cup of rice beer.

Having diagnosed her client, the medium would usually refer the individual to a priest (manbunung). Only a priest could perform the requisite sacrifice and chant the correct prayer to the responsible entity. Every supernaturally induced affliction required a different ceremony; one current-day manbunung has recorded the procedures of fifty-nine separate rituals.

Other rituals functioned to secure general blessings from benevolent nonhuman agents. Laymen chanted many simple prayers in the course of daily activities. Drinking sessions formed the most common occasions; before imbibing any alcohol, a person would toss a small amount to the ground, giving its vapors to the gods and ancestors, who would then be beseeched for general assistance. Rituals to secure good harvests, however, were few. Most were concerned with rice culture; the all-important sweet potato was essentially ignored in ritual life.

Not all supernatural signs were negative. An oddly behaving animal, or especially the presence of a specific animal at a specific place and time (*sangbo*), could presage good fortune. A dream too could bode well, depending, of course, on the medium's reading. The ancestors would also convey requests through specific signals. A deceased grandfather, for example, might appear in a dream requesting blankets. The dutiful grandchild would then accord him honor in a blanket-bestowing ritual. Major ceremonies for the ancestors, however, were not usually initiated through such specific requests. Most occurred at intervals dictated largely by the life-stage and social position of the celebrant. Such prestige feasts (*pedit*) formed the heart of religious belief and practice. Before analyzing them, however, it is necessary to link the religious beliefs discussed above with the environmental patterns outlined in chapter 2.

RELIGION AND THE LANDSCAPE

The relationship between community and environment in prewar Buguias was shaped by religious ideology and practices. Rituals guided economic endeavors and social relations, which in turn structured the subsistence activities that transformed the landscape. The supernatural also touched the land directly, as a number of spiritual beings were believed to inhabit specific places where they could influence human activities.

Ritual requirements molded the very dietary basis of subsistence in prewar Buguias. It was, in part, the ancestors' hunger that motivated their descendants to raise hogs. The living, of course, received quality food as their part of the bargain, and materialist scholars (such as Harris 1979) would regard their religious justification as merely a rationale or cultural epiphenomenon. Certainly most humans do crave meat and fat regardless of their forebears' demands. But in settled agricultural areas, meat production entails effort, and different individuals and cultural groups exhibit varying degrees of enthusiasm about exerting the labor needed to produce extra increments of animal flesh. The people of Buguias could have thrived on less meat; their neighbors, the Bontocs and Ifugaos, did so without much ill effect. But the Buguias villagers, motivated in part by their beliefs, produced a surfeit of meat. As hogs and people ate the same laboriously cultivated sweet potatoes, dry fields had to produce tubers well in excess of minimal subsistence requirements (see Brookfield [1972] for a discussion of "ritual intensification").

Much the same could be argued for pond-field agriculture. Rice, even though usually fermented, did provide quality nutrition, and since rice terraces produced abundantly, their construction might well have been justified without a ritual rationale. But rituals required great quantities of rice beer—the ancestors demanded as much. Beer could be brewed from millet or corn, but the resulting product was considered contemptible. Prestige, wrapped in religion, played an inescapable role; no baknang couple could claim respect unless they were generous with alcohol made from rice.

The spirit realm also reflected directly on the landscape, albeit in relatively minor ways. Buguias religion was focused on a sky-world that touched the earth more at sanctified times than in sacred places. And while consumption in ritual feasts could be a holy experience, production was generally rather mundane. A few meager rituals blessed the rice fields, but other crops were ignored. It was rather through the timungao and other nature spirits that the supernatural directly impinged upon the landscape.

Each of the many timungao dwelled in its own specific abode. Such places were separated from human life not because they were sacred but rather because they were dangerous. If a man tried to cut a sprite's tree, his hand could be severely and immediately "deformed." Buguias residents usually left untouched the large trees and brushy thickets known to harbor timungao. Several potential irrigation sources remained untapped, as timungao were especially vexed when their waters were muddied. But ultimately, even the timungaos' favored havens were vulnerable if any one individual was willing, and able, to offer the necessary propitiation. Here too, class had its way.

The distribution of timungao may also have shaped conceptions of the community's territory. In one specific prayer, a manbunung had to ask forbearance of every timungao inhabiting Buguias and surrounding locales. These beings were not known by personal names, but rather by their locations of residence, and if any dwelling sites were ignored in this petition, bad luck could ensue. This perhaps helped create and sustain Buguias's extremely intricate system of toponyms, in which even inconsequential sections of uninhabited slope are individually named.[2]

PRESTIGE FEASTS IN PREWAR BUGUIAS

The Wedding Ceremony

A couple's ritual career would begin with their wedding ceremony. A respectable groom had to furnish at least one buffalo and several pigs. In an arranged marriage, butcherings could begin with the betrothal of infants, but this practice was uncommon even among the elite. Most engagements proceeded slowly, through the office of a go-between (usually a male elder), and each step of the deliberations required its own rituals.

Marriage conferred ritual independence, although some couples continued to reside for a time in a parental home (usually the wife's). Children were expected to follow soon, but not before the newlyweds had given a second offering to the ancestors. This ceremony (*sabang*) formed the first step in a graded series of prestige feasts called pedit (referred to earlier), but it was the only one incumbent on all couples. As in other prestige feasts, its ostensive purpose was to invite the ancestors to dance and eat with their living descendants. Specific to this rite, however, was the asking of favor for the young couple's progeny.

Graded Prestige Feasts: The Pedit

While all households performed many minor curative or preventive rituals, roughly one-fourth of prewar Buguias couples did not progress beyond sabang in the prestige-feast ladder. The rest moved on to *tol-tolo*, the first real step of the pedit series, and all respected members eventually progressed to *lim-lima* (*lima*, or five, refers to the number of pigs sacrificed on the second day). The following several pages describe a typical pedit ceremony, using the lim-lima as an example.

As with other stages, butchering would begin during an organizational meeting held several days before the actual observance.

Here the celebrants, ritual experts, and elders would immolate a single pig while they planned the celebration's logistics. On the first day of the ceremony proper the ancestors and some of the living guests arrived to be feted with two pigs of either sex.

The following day marked the essential sacrifices of *otik* ("swine with tusks"). The guests, representing several villages, assembled at dawn, when five ritual hogs, four males and one female, were released in a sanctified enclosure. Young men then scrambled to catch and tie down the boars, avoiding the sow for the time being. They then lashed the boars together in a line; the connecting rope allowed the ancestors to lead the spirits of the animals to the afterworld. After prayer and ritual, four high-status men drove sharpened stakes into the pigs' hearts. The screams of the dying beasts pleased the ancestors, while their blood gushing to the ground foretold fertility.

After the hogs expired, the manbunung would burn blood-soaked taro slices and rice stalks on their backs, bringing prosperity to the celebrants' household. The animals were then butchered, with their livers and gall bladders carefully exposed so that the manbunung and other experts could read them as oracles. The carcasses were then singed, scraped, dismembered, and boiled. After this, members of the "meat committee" would distribute the flesh, making sure that elite (and the ancestors) were first honored with the best portions. All guests were also given raw meat to carry home. To fill the enormous appetite of the gathering, the celebrants might have to slaughter water buffalo and sometimes even cattle in a purely secular context off to the side of the main proceedings.

Once the sacrifices were completed, attention turned to dance. A man and a woman invariably danced as a pair, while brass gongs, iron bars, and wooden drums maintained the rhythm. The performers would alternate between several different dance styles, each associated with a particular geographic region. The celebrating couple danced first, followed by the village elite, with each dancer performing in the stead of a specific ancestor. All dances were punctuated by the manbunung's blessings. Eventually the roster of the ancestors would be completed, and the dance opened to the wider community. At this point even the young participated, often reveling through the night. The mood was now one of pure festivity, the participants well lubricated with rice beer. One of the first Europeans to visit Buguias, the German traveler Carl Semper, must have arrived at such a time, for he wrote, "When I arrived in Buguias the people had been drinking . . . for five days and nights, and the general drunkenness lasted during my three day stay" (1862 [1975]: 29).

After the second day most guests returned home; only the immediate family, the village elders, the ritualists, and the ancestors remained. On the third day the elders would sacrifice another hog and possibly a water buffalo, and the fourth day marked a simple "party" for the ancestors. On the fifth day, ritual specialists would clean and bind together the heads of the ritual pigs, then slaughter a new pair of swine, male and female. The following day was uneventful, but the seventh day again required a pair of hogs as the remaining guests prepared for the departure of the ancestors. This signified the formal conclusion, even though on the following evening the celebrants' close relatives often performed their own subsidiary rites. The celebrating couple might also observe a last single-hog ritual to "dam up" the good luck bestowed by the ancestors.

The celebrating couple bore the feast's financial brunt, but some of the other participants also contributed. Close relatives had their own secondary rituals, and both relatives and neighbors always prepared rice beer used to entertain guests during the initial gathering. Throughout the festivities, a markedly communal character remained.

During the feast's public events, the ancestors were entertained, provisioned, and beseeched. But within the house, the celebrants and ritual experts strove for more intimate communication, chanting and singing to the ancestors well into the night. Some of their intonations were simple requests; others were ritual utterings meaningless in ordinary speech. During these occasions the spirits could possess certain women; through these media the ancestors prophesied and demanded additional favors, often requesting that another specific couple also celebrate a major feast. Such a woman might remain in a trance, alternating between anger, sorrow, and elation, for hours. Occasionally a man would be entranced, but most participants would regard such an event with skepticism, wondering openly whether he were only drunk.

Few couples progressed beyond the lim-lima pedit, but those with social pretentions were obligated to continue up the prestige ladder. A given pedit ceremony was ranked by the number of hogs chased on the second day; at each successive rung the number increased by two, the scale thus ascending in odd numbers.[3] The essential observations remained the same, but the number of villages invited and the number of animals butchered increased markedly with each step. Cattle especially were slaughtered in large numbers, as the take-home meat requirements escalated faster than did the sacrificial obligations. Swine killings roughly matched those of the lim-lima for the first seven days, but they continued for a longer period of time, determined ultimately by the advice of the ritual experts. Seventeen days was typical for a "number nine," but any untoward occurrence, even the appearance of a rat, could prolong it. Through the entire period the celebrants observed taboos; they could not eat pungent vegetables, nor could they engage in any sexual activities.[4]

"Nine" (*siam*) marked the graduating pedit, confirming a couple's baknang status. After this their prime responsibility shifted to helping their children ascend the prestige ladder. But the wealthiest could still continue their own series, celebrating "eleven," "thirteen," and so on. Upon reaching the stellar level of "twenty-five," the couple had completed one full ritual cycle and was expected to withdraw. In the "retirement ceremony," five hogs would be shared with the other baknangs.

THE BUGUIAS FUNERAL

Funerals, except for those of suicides, replicated the essential structure of the pedit ceremony. Both centered around communion with the dead, and both reflected the status of the honored individual.

On the first day of a wake, the survivors would lash the corpse to a death chair, where it would remain throughout the ceremony. A smokey fire and watchful fly-shooer at its side fought off the worst effects of putrefaction. On the initial day a male and a female pig were butchered, and, if necessary to feed the guests, a cow or steer also. The second day would pass with little ritual, simpler food being prepared for the guests. On the third day, the deceased's children huddled together under a blanket holding a single fiber, signifying the continuity of generations. Now the most sacred rituals began. Sacrifices ensued, always in male and female pairs, until a number commensurate with the deceased's stature—and with the wealth of his or her survivors—was reached. Duality was a constant theme; guests brought paired presents (designated male and female), and were required to attend for an even number of days. Buguias wakes were often rather festive; food and drink were plentiful, and the participants commonly remained awake through the night, drinking, telling stories, and singing to the corpse.

Poorer individuals were buried at the end of the third day, but most were interred on day five. On the fifth day, three pigs, the first odd-numbered offering, usually signified the funeral's conclusion. But such an abbreviated wake would not suffice for a baknang, and the wealthiest remained in the death chair for one month or longer. (One story tells of a funeral beginning on the day a particular dog gave birth, and ending after the pups were as large as the mother.) The higher a person had progressed in the pedit series, the longer his or her corpse was expected to remain unburied. A baknang's entire cattle herd could be consumed in the process, although half of it would usually be saved if there were a surviving spouse.

At the close of the public sacrifices the corpse was placed in a coffin carved from a single unblemished pine log. But the ceremony had not yet ended. On the following night, close relatives and ritualists would retrieve the coffin and again expose the body, offering one last hog and chanting again through the night. Thirty-six hours later came the final burial. The next day, barring bad omens, each married child of the deceased would offer two hogs in their own homes. A final ceremony, also incumbent upon the married children, took place three months to a year later. During this rite the deceased, now a full-fledged amed, or ancestor, returned for the first time to socialize with the living.

But the initial burial site was not necessarily the final resting place. Not uncommonly, an ancestor would visit one of his or her descendants in a dream, pleading that his or her bones be transferred to a new gravesite. This entailed a new round of ceremonies and sacrifices. In the Spanish period, the movement of the coffin had been easily accomplished, as most were put to rest in natural caves and crevices. In that era entire families were sometimes interred in a single carved, zoomorphic casket. In a still earlier period, secondary burials were made in ceramic jars. Evidently, it was only in the American period that coffins were buried under earth; after the war, above-ground concrete-block crypts were adopted, facilitating once again the periodic transfer of bones.

OTHER RITES

Several unusual ceremonies punctuated the lives of a few individuals in the Buguias community. If a couple could not reproduce they would perform fertility rites; if these failed, divorce was the usual recourse. (In the disjoining ritual the couple's hog-feeding trough would be split in two while a single animal was sacrificed.) Individuals sometimes tried to hide from bad luck by changing their names, and this too called for specific rituals and sacrifices.

Overall, ritual practices were not rigidly fixed; requirements were flexible, with specific actions negotiated by celebrants, elders, and ritual experts. Moreover, innovation and borrowings from neighboring peoples brought ever greater complexity. While some rituals remained specific to a single family, change occurred readily in the community at large, for all significant actions took place within a context of shared meanings that was itself open to discussion and debate. But remaining central to the whole was the display of status during all major ritual occasions.

STATUS DISPLAY

Religion was inseparable from social stratification. The magnitude of ceremonial expenditure varied directly with the wealth of the celebrating couple, and individual status reflected a history of ritual performance. Moreover, in community-wide ceremonies the relative social position of many individuals attending was publicly and precisely displayed. The exact standing of any given person was the subject of intermittent negotiation, with the ritual specialists acting as the ultimate arbiters.

High-status persons were accorded honors at all feasts. They dined first, received the choicest meats, and were provided the freshest rice beer. They also received ample shares of take-home meat. Dancing order also depended on status; the elite danced first, representing their (usually) elite ancestors. The truly poor were often too ashamed to participate at all. High-status individuals were also privy to the inner ritual circles; they, for example, along with the religious experts, often chanted through the night in the celebrants' house. At their own ceremonies, the elite advertised their positions clearly, in part by displaying collections of Chinese porcelain vases.

BLANKET RANK

The elite received special treatment at ceremonies as a prerogative of power rather than as a display of status. But ritual dancing pegged status exactly, since performers indicated their ranks with funerary blankets and accessory garments of known prestige value.

The five different blankets, which would ultimately serve as burial shrouds, reflected their owners' status in reinforcing ways. The intricately woven higher-rank blankets were elaborately patterned and very expensive. The topmost blanket, *alladang*, along with its five complementary garments, could only grace the community's highest echelon. The second highest, *pinagpagan*, was also restricted to the elite. The lower *kwabao* could adorn the older and more respected commoners, but most common people were entitled only to the cheaper *dil-li*. The poorest individuals donned only *bandala*, a cheap, essentially secular covering. Combinations of blankets and accessories displayed intermediate ranks; an elderly and respected commoner, for example, might be allowed kwabao complemented with a few secondary items normally associated with pinagpagan.[5]

Four considerations determined an individual's blanket rank. These were, in order of importance: level of achievement in pedit, status of immediate ancestors, wealth of close relatives, and age. A person's position at marriage was largely inherited, but one could subsequently ascend the status ladder, even moving a rung or two during the death ceremony itself if unstinting sacrifices were offered. Such social climbing had its limits, however, as only members of the most exalted lineages could ever hope to wear the alladang.

The ultimate ranking decision, at death, rested with the elders and ritual experts. But arguments from the family of the deceased who usually hoped for higher status regardless of cost could sway opinion. In one noted case, the alleged wizard Kabading rose two full levels during his wake, as his corpse sat in the death chair through an entire month of deliberation. Since Kabading was not notably wealthy and had not progressed far in pedit, his station at death was only dil-li. But his relatives successfully contended that because he was both a priest and a prophet, because he had produced many descendants, and because his wife had rich cousins who had helped defray the funeral costs, he should be inhumed in pinagpagan.

Ritual Experts

Knowledge of ritual matters could also influence status determination. While the office of manbunung, or priest, appealed little to the wealthy, it did provide an avenue by which a common man could gain prestige. Manbunungs led many exclusive activities, and their blanket ranks could be boosted if they had gained renown.

The Buguias priesthood was internally stratified according to depth of knowledge and performance skills. Obscure rites escaped the mediocre, and only the most capable could officiate at the distinctly different and generally more complex rituals of Kalanguya immigrants. The best of the priestly elite solemnized charismatically, gracefully covering forgotten stanzas and evoking heartfelt emotion from the participants. The worst were castigated as lazy if not greedy; one could earn such a reputation, for instance, by refusing to perform any ceremony that required only chickens.

Although manbunungs occupied an essential ritual office, they were not the most important religious figures. Real ideological power resided rather with the *mankotoms*, the ritual advisers and prophets of Buguias. Although a manbunung performed ceremonies, he could not determine what they should include; priests could not be so entrusted, it was thought, since they might choose the most expensive ritual in order to increase their own remuneration. A spirit medium would recommend minor curative rites, but a mankotom would specify the procedures of the major ceremonies honoring the ancestors. These several men determined the sequence of pedit and the magnitude of funeral rites; they also served as the ultimate arbiters of social standing. This was not a position for the poor, although a few men of intermediate standing did reach it, and while it was coveted by the rich, few from that class ever achieved it. The mankotom's position was always tenuous, for his authority finally rested on his ability not only to remember the past but also on his ability to predict the future.

THE IDEOLOGY OF
RITUAL PERFORMANCE

Wealth in prewar Buguias permitted lavish ritual performance, which in turn conferred social status. But underlying the feast system was a more recondite economic calculus; couples performed ceremonies primarily in hope of enlarging their own stores of material wealth, which would allow even more grandiose future celebrations, hence even more prestige, and so on. The seeming paradox posed in the proposition that consumption was the route to accumulation was resolved in beliefs concerning the rapport between the living and the dead. In all likelihood, such ideas evolved slowly in the Spanish and American periods, as they have continued to do during the postwar era; as a result, it should be kept in mind that later innovations may have inadvertently been introduced into the oral accounts upon which this analysis is based. The basic workings of the system, however, have clearly been in place for the entire reach of present-day lore.

THE LUCK OF THE ANCESTORS

According to the local economic-cosmological model, luck—vital in every endeavor—was controlled by the ancestors. Certainly the Buguias people considered hard work essential for realizing potential good fortune, just as sloth was considered capable of bringing its own destitution. But fortuity was primary. The nature of a couple's luck hinged on their concourse with their deceased parents, grandparents, and more distant ancestors. To ensure blessings from above, they had to please these amed, and since the dead yearned to return periodically to feast with their descendants, pedit was mandatory. If the offerings were inadequate, the amed would readily indicate their displeasure.

The ancestors relished dance, but they were also greedy for the spiritual essences of hog flesh and rice beer. They also rejoiced in blankets and even money; a cache of silver peso coins, placed upon a stack of funeral blankets, adorned every pedit ceremony. The dead needed such (non)material things because they too existed within a wealth-based, and mutable, social hierarchy. A soul entered the afterworld with a blanket-signified rank, but could subsequently rise or possibly even fall according to the oblations offered by living descendants. To cinch the matter, an ancestor's power to bestow bounty on the living depended, in turn, on his or her afterlife position. The welfare of the living was thus partly contingent on the gifts that each couple managed to send skyward. The newly rich encountered a special burden here, since to ensure continued success they had not only to placate but also to empower their low-status spiritual allies.

Normal communications between earth and heaven were indirect, vague, and subject to misinterpretation. A clear channel, however, opened with every death. While in the death chair, an individual remained in limbo, shuttling back and forth between the two realms until the final burial on earth, corresponding to acceptance in the afterworld. Hence the extravagant attention lavished on the corpse; revelers at the wake sang and chanted unceasingly to the body, asking it to convey special requests to the ancestors. Here also lay the significance of the double burial; with the first interment the soul sojourned in the afterworld, gathering a store of luck that it could redistribute if brought back to earth for a brief period. Since the cooperation of the recently released spirit was vital to the success of this endeavor, the living hoped that through flattery they might secure an enthusiastic messenger. A funeral of an elder was thus not an entirely unhappy occasion. Story telling, joking, and drinking lightened the somber ceremonies at the house of the dead.

Even if well-feted, the ancestors still constituted a threat, thus requiring additional ritual precautions. Two parallel dangers lurked here: an amed might pine for a specific living person's companionship; or, a certain living soul might opt for more constant spiritual communion. In either instance, death could come prematurely. Here lay the peril in visiting a wake on an odd number of occasions; if the pair (essentially a sexual metaphor) were not completed, one's now unbalanced soul could more easily be lost. Special ceremonies were also needed to resegregate the quick from the dead. In nonritual settings, however, the afterworld was not so beckoning; in fact, languishing elders would occasionally bundle themselves within their own death shrouds, hoping to frighten their souls into remaining earthbound a while longer.

RITUAL AND POWER IN HUMAN SOCIETY

During rituals the Buguias people generally feasted together in communal harmony. Disputes were put to rest for the nonce, and the few rivalries exhibited were playful. For example, if someone were to fall asleep during a wake, another might regale the corpse by saying: "Look here, this fellow is ignoring you, so why don't you give to me the favors he requested?" But good will did not always infuse human relations, and mundane disputes were sometimes referred to the afterworld. In trial by ordeal, for example, the ancestors and gods were asked to judge, and were expected to give immediate evidence of guilt or innocence. Moreover, the threat of supernatural sanction always made perjury a dangerous litigation strategy. A curse befalling a liar might persist for years, fomenting perennial ill feelings between contesting families.

On the whole, the Buguias people prized amicable settlements and were proud to note that the blood feuds endemic to many other Cordilleran regions did not plague their society. Yet violent disputes did occasionally erupt, and the opposing parties could try to curry favor from the more powerful ancestors. Since both parties could do the same, human quarrels could escalate into contests between different afterworld factions. A few individuals, usually Kalanguya immigrants, were judged guilty of manipulating malignant spirits for their own benefit; these *mantala* were greatly feared and occasionally killed, secretly or in public.

THE TONG TONGAN JURAL SYSTEM

Regardless of ancestral advocacy, most disputes were ultimately settled in the *tong tongan,* or indigenous court system, the focal point of political power in prewar Buguias. Here the male elders arbitrated suits and sentenced criminals; the issues they faced

ranged from murder to divorce to animal damage in an uma. Not
surprisingly, power and to some extent, even membership, in this
jural body were not merely functions of age, but also of pedit performance. While an elder of the lowest respectable rank would rate
the status of elder, the dominating voices were those of the more
elderly elite. But even the richest could not rely merely on their
ceremonial renown or economic muscle; a powerful voice had to
be eloquent, reasonable, trustworthy, and ultimately convincing to
the other jurors. Lower-status elders, however, were usually reluctant to contest their higher fellows. Thus a strong bias pervaded
cross-class tong tongan proceedings; poor parties often prosecuted
their cases with reluctance, relying instead on the high-class jurors'
sense of justice.

Religious significance imbued the tong tongan. Contestants
would always purchase a pig for joint sacrifice, while both winner
and loser offered additional animals (*batbat*) after the settlement—
the losing party paying for both. The Buguias people trusted these
rituals to quell the ill will and bad luck engendered in litigation.
Here too status nudged the scales. A batbat, for example, required
only a chicken, but a victorious baknang, if callous, could demand
of the loser a pig, the theory being that a man of stature should
always perform a lavish rite.

Grounds for Belief

The purported economic linkages between the sky-world and earth
rested as much on quasi-empirical demonstration as on faith. The
efficacy of prestige feasting was superficially palpable; those couples who held the grandest feasts possessed the greatest wealth,
which implied ancestral favor—itself derived from gifts offered in
ritual. But this tautology did not suffice. Rather, the Buguias people
called for direct evidence tying past performances with present conditions. This was the province of the mankotom. It was his duty to
keep track of many individuals' supernatural messages (dreams,
sangbos), their subsequent ritual actions or omissions, and their resulting economic successes and failures. It was on the basis of this
body of narrative evidence that the mankotom gave advice and
offered prophesies.

If an advisee followed the recommended course but garnered no luck, he could always question the skill of the mankotom rather than the verity of his own beliefs. Those mankotoms with poor records found their careers abbreviated, but successful forecasters enjoyed ever increasing renown. Of course, even an ascendant prophet occasionally blundered, but then he could always accuse the celebrant of neglecting some minor but essential duty. As a person of considerable ritual power, the mankotom could be tempted to serve himself. One adviser was suspected of having intentionally staged an inappropriate and incomplete ritual so as to offend the ancestors and bring down a disliked advisee. But such a ploy was perilous, since it could destroy a mankotom's reputation, the very stuff of his power.

The Economics of Ritual Expenditure

All rituals entailed expense. An angry nature spirit could usually be appeased with nothing more than a chicken, although an irritated timungao might exact an expensive white pig. But the ancestors, and the living persons honoring them, demanded real livestock slaughter. In any given ceremony this could escalate beyond original expectations, as bile omens might require additional sacrifices. With this eventuality in mind, celebrants sometimes stockpiled small, cheap pigs. In funerals, the paired offerings increased the risk, since a single malformed gallbladder might call for two new animals.

Nor was livestock the only expense. The guests also required carbohydrates and plenty of expensive rice beer. Furthermore, the ritualists demanded pay: the manbunung received the hind leg of a pig or the foreleg of a water buffalo, and the mankotom was given a large portion of the finest meat. As major ceremonies called for several manbunungs, the outlay here could be significant.

A funeral burdened both the estate of the deceased and the personal fortunes of the surviving children. Guests brought alms (used spiritually by the departing soul and materially by responsible family), but these could never cover the entire cost of the funeral. Many believed that if the personal property of the dead (animals and rice terraces) were spared, his or her spirit would be prone to haunt. Further, the alms givers received raw and cooked meat to take home in proportion to their contributions. And finally, the married children of the deceased were further burdened with private postfuneral observances for which no assistance was forthcoming.

Social Stratification and Religious Expense

On the surface, ritual expenditures disproportionally taxed the rich. This was especially marked in funerals and above all in pedit, where each step entailed geometrically inflated expenses. But on all occasions, elite couples demonstrated their stature by redistributing lavishly. This also extended to the nonritual feasts (*saliw*) that accompanied such occurrences as the completion of a house or the engagement of one's child.

The Buguias ideology demanded the redistribution of wealth. The elite could accumulate only so much; eventually public pressure, or the desire for supernatural favor, would force them to some extent to decapitalize.[6] No one could live on the fruits of wealth alone, and even the richest had to pursue income actively. But, in the great irony of Buguias religion, a favored method of reacquiring wealth was to exploit the religious observations of the commoners. Here was a fine opportunity for usury.

Every self-respecting commoner had to begin adult life with a series of expensive rituals, beginning with the wedding ceremony. Social pressure motivated laggards; villagers denigrated any woman who married a man too poor or frugal to supply a buffalo ("Are you so cheap that he could take you with just a chicken?"). Couples who failed to perform the postwedding ceremony of sabang humiliated their parents, who feared for their own status—both on earth and in the afterlife. If a couple did not at least initiate the pedit series they suffered continual shame. Everyone was obligated to entertain the ancestors and to feast the living; the well-being of the entire village rested here. Further costs were encountered with sickness, and, more importantly, with funerals. Only members of the servile class could ignore the demands of the spirits and the corresponding responsibilities of community life.

One may well wonder how people of little property were able to afford such celebrations. The only answer was long-term debt. Few managed easily to return the principal, and interest charges—often hidden—exacerbated their plight. Most commoners remained constantly in debt, often owing their labor as well as their livestock to the village financiers. This put them at a psychological and monetary disadvantage in communal affairs. Debtors were often cowed, and wealthy creditors could argue with little opposition the right to dictate a poor couple's ritual schedule, saying, "You couldn't do anything if we didn't lend you money, therefore you should do as we say."

Interest arrangements for ritual expenses varied. Loans were often "on the hoof," in which case the lender immediately received a large chunk of flesh as partial compensation. On other occasions the baknang would lend money for the purchase of a specific animal. In this instance, several parties might claim "interest meat," including the creditor, the animal's caretaker, and its owner. Interest on simple cash loans also varied; usually a year's grace period was allowed, after which rates ranged between zero and 30 percent annually, depending on the generosity of the lender and on the familial ties of the two parties.

A few debtors escaped altogether by moving away, either to Baguio City or to a more remote district within Benguet. But most commoners continued to pay off their old debts—although they usually accumulated new ones in the interim. If a borrower owned rice terraces, the lender could take possession after several years of nonpayment and eventually claim them outright. One baknang in particular was alleged to have amassed extensive terrace holdings in this manner.

One could not claim baknang standing if one did not lend animals for prestige feasts. This was a responsibility of rank, albeit one that *could* be used to advantage. But by exploiting the poverty of neighbors and relatives the unscrupulous baknang would arouse community censure. In characteristic circularity, however, communal approbation could readily be reacquired through further ritual expenditures. Both despite and because of their considerable outlays, a few powerful individuals retained control of the community's underlying financial structure.

POWER AND RELIGION RECONSIDERED

Political power in prewar Buguias rested largely on wealth legitimated by ritual performance. If any baknang couple had tried to shirk their ritual responsibility (an unthinkable occurrence), their position would have faltered, for it depended critically on popular support. The elite had few real means of coercion in the indigenous system; even in exercising political power they worked with, not against, the public. The commoners accepted elite domination in part because the wealthy, by feasting the entire village, proved themselves worthy of respect, and, by honoring the ancestors, helped ensure the prosperity of all Buguias people.

Most Buguias residents considered the differentiation of human society into rich and poor, powerful and weak, to be the natural order of things. Social stratification pervaded their universe, being marked just as strongly in heaven as on earth. The gods of Benguet were noted above all else for their wealth, as is evident in Sacla's (1987:53–56) masterful translations of ritual chants:

> It is said, Pati came down;
> The progenitor of the wealth and mighty;
> He came down with pigs, your pigs . . .
>
> It is said, Balitoc came down
> Whose gold scales balance perfectly;
> A precious scale used in Suyoc;
> Yes, because he is wealthy and mighty;
> He came with pigs, your pigs . . .
>
> It is said Kabigat came down;
> With precious coins in the amount of twelve and a half;
> He used to purchase pigs for *pedit*;
> Yes, because he is wealthy and mighty;
> He came down with pigs, your pigs . . .
>
> It is said Lumawig came down;
> He has power to cast out evil;
> Yes, because he is wealthy and mighty;
> He came down with pigs, your pigs . . .
>
> It is said, Bangan came down,
> Bangan from Langilangan;
> Wearing an *alad-dang* blanket;
> She wore such garment because
> she is rich and mighty . . .

Even nature spirits in Buguias were class-divided. The wealthy timungao, of course, could cause much greater harm or bestow much better fortune than their more modest colleagues. If a human were to break an (invisible) porcelain jar of a *baknang ni timungao,* serious consequences could be avoided only through a very expensive ritual.

But individual class positions, whether in human or ancestral society, were never regarded as ordained; it was rather the economic interactions between these two spheres that allowed mobility in both. As everyone hoped to prosper, the luck-bestowing ancestors lay at the focus of religious life. Although individuals competed for material gain, their relations with their forebears ultimately hinged on communal engagements. The centrifugal tendencies of a commercial and competitive society were partly balanced by the centripetal forces inherent in common worship and food sharing.

In more immediate material terms, however, the resources necessary both for upward mobility and for the wealthy to maintain their positions were derived largely from interregional trade. It is this mercantile sphere, which also formed the essential preconditions for Buguias's later commercial transformation, that we shall now examine.

5

Commercial and Political Relations

INTRODUCTION

Prewar Buguias was by no means a wholly self-sufficient community. The inhabitants of the upper Agno Valley were widely noted as long-distance merchants. Through trade the Buguias people procured part of their subsistence needs; more importantly, through incessant buying and selling they developed a mercantile orientation. In Buguias it was commercial endeavors, not agrarian practices, that formed the pivot between the economic and the ideological realms, the mundane and the spiritual. And it was the legacy of prewar trade that nurtured the postwar vegetable industry.

Paralleling the community's economic linkages were political ties. For just as prewar Buguias was not self-sufficient, neither was it wholly autonomous. From the beginning of the twentieth century, the village lay within an international structure of power relations centering on the American colonial government in Manila. Compared to many other peripheral regions of the world economy, imperial power was relatively light here, but in many respects American policies, intentionally and accidentally, molded the development of Buguias society.

TRADE RELATIONS

HISTORICAL BACKGROUND

Well before the Spanish era, southern Cordilleran miners exchanged gold in coastal villages for Chinese porcelains, raw iron, cloth, livestock, and other goods (Scott 1974; Keesing 1962). Highland-lowland commerce in all probability expanded through the Spanish period as the population erratically grew and as the mountain people responded to new trade opportunities. After the state mandated a tobacco monopoly in the 1780s, for example, highlanders soon began exporting large quantities of contraband tobacco to the lowlands (Scott 1974: 232).

In the late 1700s, Francisco Antolin, a Spanish friar stationed in a remote mission in the Magat Valley to the southeast of Buguias, documented an extensive and closely knit exchange system in the southern Cordillera. At that time, gold-mining communities typically procured food from nearby agricultural villages and even from the lowlands; the more prosperous mining districts regularly imported slaves from peripheral communities as well. Other villages specialized in manufacturing ironware and copperware, which, along with other handicrafts, were exchanged over long distances. Villages located athwart trade routes profited by charging tariffs on goods passing through their territories (Antolin 1789 [1970]).

At the time of Antolin's writings in the late eighteenth century, the southern Cordilleran trade network centered on two villages in the eastern cloud forest: Tucucan, located eleven kilometers east of Buguias, and its neighbor Tinoc, some twelve kilometers east-southeast of Buguias (Antolin 1789 [1970]). In this period, Buguias itself was noted for its production of copper vessels and iron tools and weapons, rather than for long-distance exchange (Scott 1974; Meyer 1890 [1975]; Semper 1862 [1975]). Sometime in the middle or late nineteenth century, however, Buguias gained ascendancy in transmontane trade—an abrupt shift evidently owing to the migration of Tinoc and Tucucan traders to the Buguias region, perhaps in response to Spanish incursions from the east. Virtually all present-day Buguias genealogies trace back to one wealthy Tucucan trader, Lumiaen, who migrated to Buguias during this period, and the Buguias people remember Lumiaen's son Basilio and his grandson Danggol as powerful merchants.

Buguias Trade in the American Period

Buguias trade patterns in the American period owed much to environmental and cultural variation within the southern Cordillera. Complex topography, vertically banded production zones, monsoonal seasonality, a patchy distribution of mineral resources, and a diversity of cultural groups all contributed to pronounced differences in local production over short distances. Trade linkages cen-

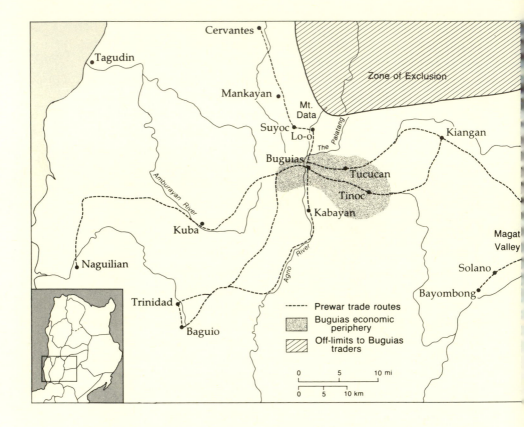

Map 6.   *The Buguias Trade Sphere*. Only the most important trade routes are indicated on the map.

tered on Buguias integrated multiple environmental zones and several different peoples (see map 6).

The Buguias mercantile system was predicated on a consistent pattern of exchanges carried out between specific centers of production. In the immediate neighborhood each substantial village occupied a unique position in the network. Beyond this local zone, trade involved exchanges across broad cultural and ecological zones; these included both the cloud forest (or kalasan) and the Ifugao culture region to the east, the lower elevation areas of Benguet to the south and west, and the Ilocos Coast along the South China Sea.

Kabayan, 10 kilometers to the south, was a major local partner.

At 1,200 meters, this Ibaloi village is 200 meters lower than Buguias, hence distinctly warmer and drier during the low-sun season. Its steep hillsides, however, offered fewer suitable sites for dry fields. Whereas Buguias umas yielded sweet potatoes abundantly throughout the year, those in Kabayan were barren in the dry months. Rice, by contrast, flourished here and was produced in great abundance. Kabayan's terraces were not only much more extensive than those of Buguias, but they also gave larger and more assured harvests. The residents of the two villages thus found each other natural trade partners, and many Buguias households bartering dried sweet potatoes here for rice. In addition, some Buguias residents purchased Kabayan rice with cash, clothing, or other trade goods, and not a few poorer individuals labored in Kabayan's fields in exchange for harvest shares.

Buguias residents also exchanged foodstuffs with the Kankanaey villages of the upper Agno Valley. Occasional frosts in Lo-o, 8 kilometers north, precluded the cultivation of ginger and other crops. Furthermore, the Lo-o people grew no rice until cold-tolerant strains appeared in the 1920s; earlier they had purchased necessary stores in Kabayan and occasionally in Buguias. In exchange, Lo-o exported, among other goods, meat-horses raised on its extensive bottomland pastures. Residents of the smaller settlements on the slopes above the Agno River also procured rice in both Buguias and Kabayan, usually in exchange for hogs or chickens. Hogs and cattle also flowed from these marginal communities to Buguias as interest payments, as the local system of animal lending bound these small villages tightly to Buguias financiers.

East of Buguias, along the main ridge of the Cordillera and into Ifugao province, lay the extensive cloud forest, dominated by oak and other hardwoods. The Kalanguya-speaking inhabitants of this mossy oak woodland were closely connected, genealogically and commercially, to the Buguias people, and during the American period a good part of the region was an economic hinterland of Buguias. Unlike the Agno Valley, this area was the province of professional traders, men who had learned the art of "buy and sell" and who could profit by their knowledge of the geographic variation of commodity prices.

The cloud forest produced hogs in great abundance. Its thick forests yielded ample mast, fungus, and earthworms, and its perennial humidity allowed year-round sweet-potato harvests while militating against porcine skin disease. Here Buguias traders could also obtain forest products, such as rattan and various species of bamboo, unavailable at home. Minor cloud-forest specialties included chickens, eggs, mushrooms, honey, and migratory birds (attracted by torchlight and captured with nets on foggy autumn nights along the main ridge).

The Buguias traders brought copper pots, ironware, and textiles (especially funeral blankets) to exchange for these coveted products of the cloud forest. In addition, the local residents were eager to obtain silver pesos and copper coins—scarce items in this remote area but readily obtained by the Buguias people elsewhere in their trading sphere.[1] Buguias merchants would also extend credit, both in cash and in livestock, to cloud-forest dwellers. In fact, the wealthiest Buguias residents managed to accumulate hundreds, and at times thousands, of hogs and cattle throughout this region, and many kalasan dwellers remained perpetually in their debt.

One thread of the Buguias trade network continued east across the cloud forest to the Ifugao district of Kiangan. An expedition to this region required some ten days, but Kiangan supplied high-value goods, particularly water buffalo. The Buguias people valued buffalo for rituals and sometimes as work animals, but they resold most of them for profit in other Benguet communities. The Kiangan people did not raise these animals themselves, but rather imported them from the adjacent Magat Valley. Only occasionally would Buguias merchants travel so far to purchase directly from the stock breeders. Human chattel formed another element of the Kiangan trade in the early American period. Kiangan slavers typically trafficked in debtors, convicted thieves, and captives from other Ifugao regions. Buguias residents recall the average Kiangan slave as selling for roughly the same price as a large cow or water buffalo, a value similar to that found by Worcester (1903) for the lowland areas of northern Luzon.[2]

Buguias traders traveled extensively through the northern two-thirds of Benguet, primarily to purchase swine. Benguet hogs, especially ones from the lower, warmer areas, were different animals from those of the cool, moist cloud forest. Never as fat, they were however more easily fattened. According to local theory, Benguet hogs were accustomed to such an impoverished diet (of sweet-potato leaves, rice hulls, garbage, and human waste) that they would readily eat—and even batten on—the *raw* sweet potatoes that their spoiled cloud-forest cousins found indigestible. Buguias traders therefore keenly purchased such animals for fattening at home. Cash-hungry Benguet villagers would also sell their aged hogs, prized throughout the Cordillera for their long tusks. Buguias traders sometimes sacrificed tuskers in their own rituals, but more often they sold them to Ifugao and Northern Kankana-ey itinerants who were willing to pay well for this particular form of ostentatious display.

Through their extensive trade network and local production, the Buguias elite had access to a larger supply of hogs than could be consumed at home. Their outlet for this meat supply lay in the gold-mining village of Suyoc (see Lednicky 1916; Marche 1887 [1970]), 12 kilometers to the northwest. Suyoc supplied cash for the entire Buguias trade network and formed its most concentrated consumption point: its miners had both abundant coins (obtained from local traders who sold their gold in the lowlands) and a prodigious appetite for pork. Above all else, the Buguias merchants' profits came from provisioning this mining community.

The steady, high level of demand for pork in Suyoc stemmed from the exclusive concentration of the community on the mines. The miners spared no time for agriculture. Instead they imported their food: rice from the Northern Kankana-ey, sweet potatoes and vegetables from Lo-o, and hogs primarily from Buguias and Lo-o. Although the wealthy among them sometimes owned substantial cattle herds (raised in other communities), the miners could not consume beef in the rainy excavation season: the spirits guarding the ore were believed to find its odor offensive. Pork, however, was a ritual necessity as well as a staple food. Every strike called for a thanksgiving feast, and the miners performed other elaborate rituals as well. One funeral in the late Spanish period reportedly lasted three months, during which time sacrifices continued and the entire community abstained from labor (Scott 1974:286). And pork formed a staple as well, since the miners believed that only a diet of meat would provide them sufficient strength for their arduous work.

Along the coast, the Buguias merchants' main destination was the old commercial center of Naguilian (see Keesing 1962:107). Here the Buguias traders brought coffee, dried legumes, and cash. In return, they primarily purchased cloth, a good generally not produced in Benguet. Lowland Ilocano weavers furnished several varieties of funeral blankets, loincloths for men, skirts and jackets for women, and plain white fabric. The intricate designs in funerary blankets may have followed patterns designed by the highlanders and originally used in decorating the local bark fabric, and the lowland weavers had to meet the exacting standards of their highland customers. Other notable products of Naguilian included dogs, tobacco, salt, and sugar, all of which could be obtained in Buguias but were cheaper and often of better quality in the lowlands.

Buguias merchants also conducted business in other lowland Ilocano towns. Cervantes, probably the second most important lowland destination, furnished pig iron (used in the Buguias foundries), cotton cloth, cattle, and horses. Buguias merchants occasionally visited the coastal town of Tagudin to buy Chinese porcelains. But most of these lowland trade partners began to be replaced after the first decade of American rule by the new highland city of Baguio, which grew to rival even Naguilian as a commercial center once the American colonialists established their summer capital and hill station there (see Reed 1976). Although well within the mountains, Baguio functioned as an imperial and lowland-Filipino outpost, and it eventually emerged as the preferred source for many lowland products.

As for economic relations with the far north, animosity with the Bontoc people of the central Cordillera prevented Buguias traders from venturing north of Mount Data. Since the Northern Kankana-ey (living north of Data but south of the Bontoc) produced goods desired in Buguias and were themselves in need of cash, commerce did occur, but it could only be carried out by the northerners. Northern Kankana-ey men, who visited Buguias primarily for contract work, sometimes traded; northern women came specifically to sell their handicrafts, especially ceramic vessels (neither Buguias nor its neighbors produced pottery). The Northern Kankana-ey also wove and sold funeral blankets and other fabrics, in increasing competition with the Ilocano weavers.

THE ORGANIZATION OF TRADE

FINANCIAL AND SOCIAL STRUCTURES

The southern Cordilleran economy was partly commercialized well before the American era. In the 1700s, traders usually carried scales "with which they measured out gold dust like cash" (Scott 1974: 181), and by the late 1800s, while other subjugated Cordilleran areas still paid in kind, most Benguet villages yielded their tribute in coin (Scott 1974:285). Copper-working villages even minted their own copper coins modeled on Spanish currency. Indeed, the American government considered it necessary to purchase and remove these coins before issuing its own coinage.[3]

If cash-based economies were unevenly distributed even in the southern mountains, Buguias traders turned this differentiation to their own advantage. Virtually all villagers desired cash, but few could obtain it locally. Yet Buguias merchants could acquire an abundance of coin through their foothold in the far periphery of a global economic network.

As Suyoc suffered the chronically inflated prices typical of gold-mining camps, a good profit could always be made by buying low in the interior and selling high in Suyoc. Buguias elders remember well the price gaps they exploited in the prewar period. In the 1930s, one could often purchase a sizable hog in Kabayan for 25 pesos and sell it the same day in Suyoc for 35. A chicken bought in Tinoc could fetch twice as much money in Buguias, and even more in Suyoc.

A successful trader needed a good economic understanding and a facility with numbers, unaided (in the early period) by formal mathematics. One Spanish observer noted in 1877 that the mountain people "are familiar with coins, recognizing and evaluating them exactly . . . [and] they count with precision from one to the hundreds of thousands" (quoted in Scott 1974:239). The Buguias traders also recognized the utility of keeping their cash circulating. Residents of certain other Benguet villages guarded their money more warily; many of the Ibaloi elite buried substantial hoards under their dwellings (Scheerer 1932 [1975]: 199). But Buguias traders even found ways to profit from this: when the value of old coinage suddenly jumped in the early postwar years, several returned to their old Ibaloi trading partners to repurchase coins they had previously spent.

Buguias merchants customarily traveled in groups of four to eight, seeking companionship and mutual protection. Most men began trading as teenagers, usually working under a wealthy sponsor for cash wages (in the 1930s, often one peso per day, respectable pay at the time). When the party reached its destination, the

senior members would seek lodging with relatives, business partners, or local leaders. The actual transactions, however, usually required canvassing, as each trader had to seek individuals willing to
sell (or buy) and ready to settle at a good price. In a few regions,
however, exchange sometimes took place at customary sites, such
as Abatan ("meeting place") between Lo-o and Suyoc.

To prosper, traders had to know how to handle animals as well
as to make deals. Simply staying upright on the slippery cloud-
forest trails during the rainy season was arduous for the uniniti-
ated; leading recalcitrant hogs and water buffalo along these trails
was an enormously exacting job. The young merchant had to master the art of *man-dodo,* or "hog-following." In this technique, ropes
were affixed to a hog's hind feet; by expertly alternating jerks on
each rope, the trader could urge the animal in the desired direction. The most skillful men could manage as many as four hogs
and two water buffalo at a time, but two hogs was the usual quota.

Successful merchants also had to cultivate friendships with their
trading partners. Many did so through gift giving. In the Ibaloi village of Nagey, one Buguias trader is still fondly recalled for his presents of delectable dried locust. Kinship also softened commercial
relations, just as it partially molded trade patterns; many traders
worked primarily in areas where they could be aided by relatives.

A young trader needed an apprenticeship, but after acquiring a
small store of capital and the necessary skills and connections, he
faced no barriers to independence. Although many did manage
their own ventures, few developed large businesses. To do so required fortitude, skill, luck, and continued patronage, for as one
began to accumulate, one's social obligations increased apace. Redistributive rituals were never-ending, and even secular feasts burdened the rising merchant. A profitable trip had to be commemo-
rated; a trader who had earned 10 pesos selling a Kabayan hog in
Suyoc, for example, was expected to devote at least half to feasting
his neighbors.

Several traders prospered by reaching into new territories. The
Buguias trade network ramified so intricately that no individual
could master its entire extent, leading ambitious men to explore
unknown districts in search of inexpensive swine. Others sought
out new commercial niches. The second wealthiest person in prewar Buguias, Paran, initiated his career by purchasing coffee in

Tinoc and reselling it in Naguilian. In doing so he contravened the wishes of his father, who had advised a traditional business entree in the animal trade. Paran was disinherited for his disrespect, but he prospered nevertheless.

The supreme traders, who functioned equally as financiers, comprised the elite class of prewar Buguias. These men conducted most of their deals through intermediaries, usually sons, sons-in-law, and nephews. Their business partners also traveled to Buguias to work out new agreements and to renegotiate old ones. The varied enterprises of the master traders also demanded specialized labor. Information had to move rapidly, and the swiftest runners found periodic employment as messengers. Immigrants often served as couriers to, and mediators with, their natal villages. Business accounts—complex ledgers of debts and credits (in cash and animals)—also required unerring attention. Although arrangements of knots in loincloth threads registered appointments, such mnemonic devices were not used to record finances. Rather, memory alone sufficed until literacy became widespread later in the American period. But the wealthiest merchant in the early twentieth century, Danggol, could rely on a famed "verbal mathematician," Palbusa, to keep track of his many accounts.

GEOGRAPHICAL PATTERNS

Although Buguias may well have supported the largest trade network in the southern Cordillera, every important village nested in its own web of exchange. The larger Ibaloi settlements trafficked mainly with the lowland towns of Pangansinan and La Union. Their ties to the east and north were tenuous; compared to Buguias, they were not trade oriented (see Moss 1920a:214). But the other sizable villages of the upper Agno, Amlimay and Lo-o, exhibited a similar mercantile bent. Villages specializing in mineral extraction (Suyoc) or metal-goods manufacture (such as Ubanga, a small copper-working village) maintained different kinds of exchange systems, as they attracted many traders from other areas into their territories. Suyoc merchants themselves were concerned with little other than the gold trade. Adding another layer of complexity, the trade routes of many central Cordilleran villages also extended well into the southern mountains (Conklin 1980:98).

Ifugao miners and traders returning from the Baguio area, for example, often lodged in Buguias where they commonly purchased cattle to lead home. One Buguias family actually specialized in this narrow trade.

In short, prewar Buguias lay at the center of two very different spatial economic structures. One, an extensive trade network, was perpetuated through the efforts of numerous individual traders, its many strands enmeshing with webs centered on other commercial villages. Buguias formed this reticulum's organizational hub, despite the fact that the village proper was not, strictly speaking, a market center. Buguias traders rather established a *price-setting market* wherever they went, bridging the area of supply (western Ifugao and most of central and northern Benguet) with the seat of demand (Suyoc). This was certainly not a "perfect" market, for the backwoods people had limited access to price information. But it was a market nonetheless; prices varied according to supply and demand, and deals were haggled, not instituted (on the theoretical implications of the Buguias trade system, see Lewis 1989).

Buguias's second economic region was more exclusive, more cohesive, and smaller than this long-distance trade network. At the local level, the village integrated the economies of several neighboring settlements, largely through its financial role. As purveyors of capital, the Buguias elite influenced, and to some extent dominated, the indebted economies of the village's immediate periphery. Their effective hinterland extended along the Agno River north toward Lo-o, south toward Kabayan, and eastward well into the cloud forest of Ifugao province. In so doing, it sliced across several cultural boundaries, encompassing peoples of all the major southern Cordilleran language groups.

LOCAL SPECIALIZATION OF PRODUCTION

The Buguias region had long provided the southern Cordillera with quality ironware and copperware. During the American period, few smiths lived in Buguias proper, but nearby villages continued to supply cooking pots and cutting tools for a wide area. This geographically segregated production system both depended on and helped to support the local trade networks. Within Buguias itself, diverse artisans also provided goods to help fill the backpacks of local traders. While craft specialization was at best a secondary impetus for exchange, it nevertheless contributed to the integration of the southern Cordilleran economy.

IRONWORK

Most larger Cordilleran villages possessed an iron smithy. The smiths of the Buguias region, however, had long been noted for their expert work; others simply could not match the temper they imparted to their implements. Accordingly, they worked in secrecy. The German naturalist Carl Semper (1862 [1975]: 29) could not even learn the locations of the local workshops. Buguias wares—and the smiths themselves—were thus in demand through much of Benguet. Local traders often carried iron goods on their rounds, while outsiders traveled to Buguias to purchase them directly.

In the late American period, iron forging was centered in the small village of Lingadan just north of Buguias proper. The smiths had to live and work in remote, wooded areas, so great was their demand for charcoal. Although legends tell of iron ore once being gathered in the river bed, it is more likely that raw iron was always obtained through coastal trade, its ultimate source being eastern China (see Scott's note in Meyer 1890 [1975]: 63). Buguias smiths fashioned sundry iron tools, most notably bolo knives, culinary knives, digging trowels, iron or iron-tipped bars, and axes. Different grades of iron served for different kinds of bolos: soft but cohesive metal for rough tasks, such as smashing bones, and harder but brittler steel for finer work.

COPPER

Copper work was the true specialty of the greater Buguias region, and by the American period the area's forges supplied the entire southern Cordillera. But rather than Buguias proper, it was the small, peripheral village of Ubanga that formed the preeminent copper-working center.

Copper ore originally was extracted in the mineral district extending from Suyoc to Mankayan (see Wilson 1947). A dwindling fuel supply here probably forced the wide separation between the workshops and the mines that was later evident; Mankayan in particular was deforested early (Marche 1887 [1970]: 125). Ubanga, sitting on the edge of the heavily forested Palatang region, offered a prime site for copper works. In any case, by the later American period, imported copper wire purchased in Baguio substituted for local ore in the Ubanga forges.

In Spanish and early American times, the local artisans fashioned a variety of copper and bronze items. Fine ornamental works included bracelets, arm and leg bands, and earrings, the latter finding their main market among the Northern Kankana-ey. Copper smoking pipes moved rapidly throughout the southern Cordillera. Elders still tell of local manufacture of ritual gongs, but these vital items may have always been imported. Certainly in the later American period, richly resonating Chinese bronze gongs were everywhere in use (Goodway and Conklin 1987). Completely discontinued was the making of copper coins, as the imperial government could not abide their circulation.

The large cooking vessels called *gambang* ("copper"), used for preparing the food of both hogs and humans, overshadowed all other copper goods. Any person raising swine needed at least one large copper pot for boiling sweet potatoes. The Ubanga smiths fabricated gambang in several sizes and shapes for the extensive market; the largest allegedly could shelter a traveling merchant from a downpour. In earlier times, more decorative urn-shaped vessels were also made, the German traveler Schadenburg having purchased one in the late 1800s for the princely sum of four water buffalo (Scott 1974:312).

Copper working required a team of at least seven, with each individual specializing in one or two tasks. In general, it required more skill and was more arduous than ironwork, which could be done in groups of only two or three. Virtually the entire male population of Ubanga labored in this industry. Boys too young for the workshops made charcoal and gathered the pine bark and half-rotted wood well suited for the slow-burning fires necessary at certain stages of the manifold manufacturing process. The copperware industry also created linkages with nearby villages; forges were made in the neighboring hamlet of Sebang, while clay molds (used for casting) came from the Northern Kankana-ey.

Copper vessels were marketed through a complex network of intermediaries. Buguias and Lo-o merchants carried copper pots deep into the cloud forest, while Northern Kankana-ey and Kalanguya traders traveled to Ubanga to buy directly. Individuals also brought in broken pots and gongs for repair, and one Ubanga man made a special trade of searching out and fixing broken copper-ware throughout the Agno Valley. As a by-product of such business dealings, the smiths had a much better geographical knowledge of the central Cordillera (north of Mount Data) than did most other residents of the Buguias region.

OTHER LOCAL SPECIALTIES

The Buguias people of today do not recall other significant local products, but the American administrator David Barrows, who visited Buguias twice (in 1902 and 1908), was so impressed with their crafting of smoking pipes, wooden spoons, and effigy figures that he devoted a three-page journal entry to them (1908:91–93). Evidently, several Buguias artisans made four different kinds of pipes from three different materials (copper, wood, and clay). Pipe making must have disappeared soon after his visit; in the later American period Buguias traders were purchasing old pipes from the Kalanguya. Barrow's attention to wooden spoons indicates a subsequent decline in workmanship; the later examples of this art are simple utilitarian objects. The carving of representations of deities and spirits disappeared completely; evidently, as trade opportunities grew, the Buguias people abandoned several of their customary arts. A number of smaller neighboring villages, however, retained notable craft specialties, including basketry and wood-platter carving.

THE PREWAR VEGETABLE INDUSTRY

VEGETABLES IN BENGUET

The Spanish introduced cabbages and potatoes to the Cordillera well before they had established political control. Potts (1983) argues for two separate potato disseminations, the first in the late 1600s or early 1700s, and the second, linked to Benguet's first Spanish governor, Blas de Baños, in the nineteenth century. The southern Cordillerans readily adopted both cabbages and potatoes for their door-yard gardens. Both crops were casually traded among Igorot communities and some produce was sold in nearby lowland market towns (Perez 1902:118); as early as the 1860s, Benguet potatoes appeared in the Manila market (Scott 1974:239).

AMERICAN ENCOURAGEMENT

When the Americans occupied the Philippines, the demand for temperate vegetables grew. Chinese and Japanese laborers, brought to southern Benguet to build Baguio City and its connecting roads, soon began cultivating a variety of market-garden crops. Trinidad Valley, near Baguio and endowed with fertile and easily irrigated soils, formed the center of the emergent vegetable industry. Japanese capital dominated until independence, and local Ibaloi villagers eventually supplied most of the labor. A second cradle of vegetable culture emerged on the high plateau of Paoay (in Atok Municipality, north of Bagio), where an American soldier, Guy Haight, established a residence and rest house while recovering from tuberculosis (Davis 1973:58). Despite his distance from Baguio, Haight managed to deliver vegetables to the city, and he also supplied the travelers who lodged at his place. Through their association with Haight, many of Atok's residents learned the techniques of market gardening.

American officials encouraged vegetable culture among the Benguet people. As early as 1901, they distributed seeds from an agricultural office (Fry 1983:216), and not long afterward they established an experimental station largely devoted to temperate vegetables in La Trinidad. The Catholic Church also fostered vegetable growing in the districts it missionized (Russell 1983:192).

With such encouragement, the market-garden frontier began to advance. In Baguio and environs, vegetable growing spread among the local Ibaloi; by 1907 they were reported to be abandoning their mining works in favor of the more profitable truck gardens (Philippine Commission 1907, v. 1:282). By 1908, nearly 4,000 baskets of potatoes were sold annually in the Baguio market—but demand was still not satisfied (Philippine Commission 1908, v. 1:245).

VEGETABLES IN BUGUIAS

This commercial frontier reached Buguias in the last decade of American rule. In earlier times, transport to Baguio had been too costly to justify the enterprise on any scale. Only a handful of individuals had grown unimproved cabbages and potatoes for sale to the Japanese workers and American managers employed in the large sawmills to the north and west of Buguias. Local vegetable growing first took hold when the Mountain Trail, snaking along the ridgetop west of Buguias, was made passable to vehicular traffic in the 1930s. Bus service, organized by the Kankana-ey entrepreneur Bado Dangwa, soon provided ready market access. By 1940, the Dangwa Company ran some 173 vehicles, traversing much of the Cordillera (Fry 1983 : 130). Even so, Buguias vegetables first had to be ported up to the ridge, a grueling 800-meter climb.

The residents of the small village of Nabalicong, located a few miles southwest of Buguias, soon discovered that dry fields cleared in the oak scrub along the new road produced prime tight-headed cabbages while enjoying easy road access. An American road-construction foreman, one "Mr. Clark," also experimented with vegetables in the same area. The Buguias baknang Paran envisaged profit here, and he soon engaged several of his clients to clear new plots in the area. At roughly the same time, two of Paran's sons returned from the agricultural school in Trinidad, seeds in hand, and set about growing cabbage in Buguias proper, first in fallowed rice fields and later in dry fields.

These early vegetable gardens demanded more labor than did subsistence crops. To supply the necessary nutrients, gardeners had to haul ashes and sometimes even composted manure to their garden plots. The Buguias people had long known that such materials would enhance soil fertility, but they judged the effort worthwhile only for the remunerative vegetables. Insects also plagued the new crops much more than the old. Growers dispatched caterpillars and other large insects by hand; fortunately, thrips and other pests too small for manual removal had not yet emerged as serious problems.

While temperate vegetables presented a lucrative trade opportunity, production in the prewar was dominated by the Paran family. Paran's wife, Albina, developed her own specialty in trading peas. A garden pea with a nonedible pod had long been grown in the higher elevation zone immediately east of Buguias. Albina purchased peas from the growers and arranged to have them trucked to Baguio. Pokol, son-in-law of the baknang couple, organized the

Baguio trade. As operator of the village's only store, Pokol frequently traveled to Baguio to purchase supplies; on these trips he began dealing in vegetables as well, acquiring produce both from his family in Buguias and from a few gardeners along the Mountain Trail and selling it in Baguio to Chinese agents.

The vegetable trade was in its infancy when war broke out. The movement to the Mountain Trail, which would become a torrent after the war, was still a trickle. In Buguias, only one family engaged substantially in vegetable growing and trading. Yet only a few years after the return of peace virtually the entire village would be occupied in the vegetable enterprise.

IMPERIAL POWER

Throughout the prewar period, Buguias was subjugated territory. Not since the mid-1800s had it been a truly autonomous community. Colonial designs and exactions impinged on the village in several important areas. We have already examined the effects of American land-tenure policy and have noted the role of the colonialists in fostering the vegetable industry. Imperial administrators also influenced—or at least attempted to influence—other aspects of local life, most importantly by funneling highland resources toward the nascent enterprises of American residents.

Even though well-meaning colonial authorities devised plans that were potentially destructive, few of their designs came to fruition. Colonial policy often proved feckless, and in comparison with many other colonized places, the imperial tread fell lightly here. What the Americans did accomplish, to some extent inadvertently, was to enhance the position of the indigenous elite.

THE SPANIARDS

All Spanish attempts to gain control of Benguet ended in failure until the middle of the nineteenth century, when a series of well-equipped military expeditions subdued virtually every village. Although the inhabitants of the Amburayan Valley continued to resist until the 1880s, Buguias and its neighbors resigned themselves to paying tribute shortly after mid-century (Scott 1974:306).

Evidently, the Spaniards maintained their position in Benguet partly by scaling down their usual tribute demands: highlanders paid only one-seventh the dues exacted from lowlanders (Scott 1974:238). Yet even these relatively light demands heavily burdened the majority of Benguet's people. Commoners could not easily afford these "tokens of non-Christian vassalage," while the additional labor duties, purportedly for public works, were much abused and universally despised. It was mainly the elite who found advantages in Spanish hegemony, gaining further leverage over their subordinates as their political power was formalized, and encountering safer conditions for their trading endeavors (Scott 1974: 239; Wiber 1986:17).

THE AMERICAN REGIME

When American imperialists replaced the Spanish at the turn of the twentieth century, the Ibaloi of southern Benguet put up some resistance, and several local baknangs even sent cash to the independent Philippine government (Scott 1986:82). Benguet as a whole, however, was quickly brought under American rule.

The early American administrators, availing themselves of the stable political structure they had inherited, undertook a self-conscious "experiment with civil government" in Benguet as early as 1900 (see Philippine Commission 1901, v. 1:33,34). Although Dean Worcester (n.d.:4) assumed credit for "[establishing] a provincial government in Benguet and . . . small autonomous township governments," in actuality his office had simply recognized the existing local governments. Since official correspondents found the local *presidentes* able administrators (Philippine Commission 1901, v. 1:34), this was simply the most effective and least troublesome mode of administration.

American tax policy, in contrast to that of the Spaniards, was intended less to demonstrate vassalage than to finance local government and public projects. Yet the Benguet region continued to run chronic deficits—a situation tersely justified by Governor Pack's relegating of the Igorots to the status of "governmental wards" (Philippine Commission 1906, v. 1:199). The colonial government's overall fiscal design in Benguet was to facilitate resource exploitation by Americans and to foster economic "modernization." Local public works, such as bridges and trails, were financed by poll taxes and through corvée requirements (two pesos or ten days annually [Worcester 1930:44]). Governor Pack insisted that labor dues, the earlier regime's greatest curse, were instituted by the Igorots themselves (Philippine Commission 1904, v. 1:410); one can only wonder what coercive tactics may have been employed to enforce them.

In theory, the municipal governments were autonomous. Local councils passed their own ordinances, subject to the provincial governor's approval. But present-day Cordilleran scholars argue that the municipal governments held no real legislative power, functioning merely to rubber-stamp American orders (Hamada-Pawid and Bagamaspad 1985:192). But aside from the critical areas of land and resource policy, the Americans interfered relatively little.

Such noninterference reflected the limits of colonial power more than a lack of interest. Benguet funeral ceremonies, for example, appalled the hygiene-obsessed American functionaries (Philippine Commission 1903, v. 2:225), yet villagers easily tricked the sanitary inspectors sent to stop them. The Benguet colonial government was similarly frustrated in trying to limit interest rates on local loans (Moss 1920a:225), and in proscribing range fires (Philippine Commission 1906, v. 1:178). Overall, the most concerted police actions were directed against gamblers and "unemployed Americans" (Philippine Commission 1906, v. 1:265; Lehlbach 1907:11). Few civil or criminal cases internal to Benguet society ever reached colonial courts; Governor Pack reported in 1903 that he had served as Justice of the Peace on only eight occasions, as he could rely instead on the tong tongan system (Philippine Commission 1903, v. 1:795).

The American authorities, like the Spaniards before them, did encounter one persistent military challenge in Benguet: the *busols*, or bandits, of the Palatang region northeast of Buguias. The busols ("enemies"), according to Buguias lore, were less a distinct community of people than a gang of thugs who plundered and terrorized their Southern Kankana-ey, Ibaloi, and Kalanguya neighbors. The American bureaucrats totally misunderstood the "busol problem," yet by the second decade of the century the brigands had been dispersed and pacified. Whether this was owing to the steadfast actions and conciliatory negotiations of the American military, as its chroniclers would have it (see Philippine Commission 1906, v. 2:265), or to the unyielding opposition of Benguet citizens, newly fortified with a few shotguns, is another matter. Benguet elders insist that the busols disbanded only after one Carbonel, treasurer of Atok, dispatched their leader, Samiclay, with a well-aimed blast.

EDUCATION, RELIGION, AND ECONOMICS

Hampered as they may have been in other policy areas, American officials directed considerable attention toward public education. The Spaniards had constructed a few schools, but because the graduates—automatically regarded as *nuevo Christianos*—became subject to full taxation (Philippine Commission 1901, FF:545), education had not been popular with the highlanders (see also Russell 1983:271). American secular schools, by contrast, were accepted in almost every Benguet district; the leaders of Buguias even offered to build a schoolhouse without state assistance (Philippine Commission 1901, FF:547–548). Within a decade, local residents educated in village schools began to replace Ilocanos as teachers and municipal secretary-treasurers throughout the Cordillera (Fry 1983:68).

American missionary activity largely bypassed northern Benguet, ensuring religious continuity and concord throughout the prewar period. Buguias Christians today argue that missionaries neglected their region because it was too peaceful; the bellicose central Cordillerans presented a more urgent target. But whatever the motives behind it, this bypassing of Buguias by church agents was to have significant consequences for subsequent cultural change.

American capitalists were a more potent force in the area. They excavated several gold mines in southern Benguet, inherited a Spanish copper mine at Mankayan, and for a period mined gold at Suyoc. They also claimed vast stands of pine to supply supports and headworks for their many mining operations. These actions were to have damaging repercussions on the indigenous peoples in the postwar period, but before the war their effects *in Buguias proper* were relatively benign. Most mine workers were immigrants from the more densely populated central Cordillera, and they presented a good market for Buguias traders during their periodic trips home. American mineral operations in the Suyoc/Mankayan

area simply bolstered the Buguias economy; the indigenous diggings were left to their rightful owners, and the laborers brought in
to work the deeper American mines formed a new set of customers.

The American rulers also sought to "create new wants" among
the Benguet people to spur development, but it is uncertain how
they hoped to accomplish this (Fry 1983:100). If Buguias prospered
during the American period it was because of local initiative rather
than American agency. Overall, the generally well-meaning administrators had poor understandings of the local economy; Governor Pack, for instance, hopefully proclaimed in 1907 that the cattle
industry was "only in its infancy" (Philippine Commission 1907,
v. 1:278), evidently unaware that most suitable pasture areas had
long since been developed.

THE GEOGRAPHY OF IMPERIAL RULE

The remote Kallahan/Kalanguya-speaking areas of the southeast
Cordillera were for the most part ignored by American officials,
and the local residents, largely unsubdued by the Spaniards, had
no desire to submit to the new authorities. Some efforts were made
in the early years to bring the relatively accessible village of Kayapa
into the imperial fold, but the *de facto* American policy was to leave
the entire area alone. In 1934, J. W. Light reported that the Kayapa
people were peaceful and industrious, and although they paid no
taxes and did not want a school, they presented no problem for the
state. The northern Kalanguya (many of whom lived within the Buguias economic sphere) were even less bothered by colonial interference. The American hope was that these "wild" people would be
gradually "civilized" through contact with their Benguet neighbors.

The American policy makers hoped to encourage both economic
development and social integration in the Cordillera by constructing an extensive system of graded trails (Fry 1983:77). (A trail-
building program had been initiated by the Spaniards, but as late
as 1906, S. C. Simms (1906b) found it necessary to take a detour
through Cervantes when traveling from Baguio to Kiangan.) The
rationale behind the transportation program was given dramatic
expression by Governor Early in 1931 (Early 1931:41): "[to coalesce]
the warring mountain tribes into a homogenous society which will
have solidarity of interests in the next generation as it has found
peace and mutual understanding in this."

COLONIAL VISIONS

To appreciate why colonial policy worked as it did one must examine imperial agents' assessments of their own roles and of the highlanders they presumed to rule. Most American administrators saw themselves as protectors and guides, bearers of civilization to a benighted land. As Benguet's Governor Pack saw it, the first Americans in the Cordillera found a group of "poor, timid and oppressed barbarians" (Philippine Commission 1907, v. 1:277). But officials stationed in the Cordillera, especially those in Benguet, quickly developed a deep respect for their hard-working "subjects." This—combined with a strong sense of frugality—contributed to the general policy of minimal interference, just as it led to prognostications of rapid economic development. At the same time, most Western observers thought that an unfortunate but inevitable concomitant of material progress was the destruction of indigenous culture—a forecast that turned out to be less prescient.

Many Spanish observers had regarded the Igorots as lowly beings indeed: filthy, vicious, scheming idolaters was the typical picture (see Scott 1974, especially p. 70). With the occupation of Benguet in the mid-nineteenth century, however—their dismal failure to missionize the area notwithstanding—local administrators began to report highly positive qualities. One Benguet governor praised the highlanders in quite extraordinary terms: "The character of the Benguet person is loyal, honorable, humble, and, above all, very respectful. His intelligence is lively, and his natural talent is superior to that of the lowlander [quoted in Perez 1902:317; translation by the author]."

Most American commentators also considered the highlanders superior in many respects to the lowland Filipinos. This reflected at once a racist disdain for Filipinos, compounded by scorn for Hispanicized culture and a "rough rider" respect for the rugged, disciplined, and sometimes belligerent highlanders (see Jenista 1978). In the early years of their rule, the Americans' tone was set by Dean Worcester, Secretary of the Philippine Interior. All the mountain people needed, Worcester was convinced, was American tutelage and protection from the lowland Filipinos.

The American administrators' admiration of the Benguet peoples is well expressed in an official report of the era: "In their town government the Igorrotes are considerate and just, and on the whole conduct the business of the town intelligently and wisely [Philippine Commission 1904, v. 1:410]."

In part, Americans attributed the virtues of the Benguet people to a perceived meritocracy in their class stratification. Governor Pack reported that "[above the common Igorot there is a] higher, richer, cleaner class—whose individuals think and study and somehow and from somewhere glean valuable information, and to this class all other classes render implicit faith and obedience [Philippine Commission 1904, v. 1:410]." It is thus hardly surprising that American policy bolstered the position of the indigenous elite.

THE FUTURE

Because of their perception of the Benguet Igorots as a hardworking people led by a capable elite and guided by a beneficent metropolitan power, the American officials foresaw a prosperous future.[4] As Pack self-servingly and naively reported:

> Owing to the public works being carried out by the insular government in Benguet Province, the Igorrotes have plenty of money with which to go to the coast and buy stock according to their ambitions, for the Igorrote is never a rich man (or Bocnong) no matter how much money he may have, unless he has animals to show for it. So the ambitious convert their hard-earned cash into hogs or cattle, and possessors of such may take a place among the counselors of their race. This traditionary custom will make these people wealth producers instead of consumers, and as they have a thorough appreciation of the protection of property afforded them by our American Government, they will become valuable allies in pushing our methods of progress still further over the mountains among our natives not yet wholly tamed [Philippine Commission 1904, v. 1:411].

The Keesings (1934:199) also saw a connection between class stratification and economic "progress": "The presence of *baknangs* in these mountain communities gives the people, in this sense, something of an advantage in the modern struggle toward a wider competence over many backward people whose customs are more communal."

Neither were such optimistic forecasts confined to American observers. Perez (1904:206) articulated the same sentiment in most unambiguous terms: ". . . no doubt, that within a few years Benguet will be one of the richest areas of the Philippines [translation by the author]."

The Keesings (1934 : 196,219), at least, did worry that communal feasting might thwart economic growth (and harm the breeding stock), although they also appreciated its role in equalizing wealth. A more common forecast, however, saw Igorot culture as doomed by the forces of modernity. Its imminent demise had, in fact, been announced well before the American conquest: in 1890, Meyer (1890 [1975]: 128) declared that ". . . the Igorots are doomed like every other primitive race which comes into sudden contact with European civilization." Some observers thought that "Ilocanoiza-tion" would demolish local identity; in 1914, Robertson (1914 : 471) warned that with the lowlander influx, "pure culture" was disap-pearing and "real Igorots are becoming hard to study." Others thought their undoing would come at the hands of American sight-seers: "[R]oads are to be built, automobiles, stage relays, etc. are to connect this place. Then come easy travel and tourists and then the prostituted work of the natives . . . [Simms 1906a]."

Regardless of the postulated agent of change, indigenous reli-gion was repeatedly predicted to be the first casualty. Several of the most discerning American Cordilleran scholars thought that they could already see this transformation at work in Benguet, the most advanced highland province. The Keesings (1934:228) found Pa-ganism on the decline in Benguet; and as Barton (1930:123) wrote: "In Benguet foreign influences have been changing the culture and have introduced a laxity of religious observations."

As will be shown, the economic predictions of the early twen-tieth-century observers were remarkable for their accuracy; their corresponding cultural forecasts were remarkably erroneous. For the people of Buguias would accomplish what seemed impossible: to accept and indeed prosper in a Western economic framework while maintaining their indigenous beliefs, practices, and social identity. But before this was to happen, their old economy was to be utterly demolished in the flames of World War II.

Interregnum
The War

The Japanese occupied the southern Cordillera with relative ease. On December 24, 1941, the Americans evacuated their military facility at Camp John Hay, and retreated east to the sawmill at Bobok, Bokod municipality. When they found their planned escape route a dead end, the soldiers scuttled much of their war matériel, lest it fall into Japanese hands (see Harkins 1955:22–24). When the Japanese threatened to bomb Baguio City, American officials entered negotiations; within weeks Japanese troops marched in unopposed. A few American civilians sought refuge in nearby villages, but most were eventually captured.

A few American military officials who eluded capture found the Cordillera a perfect stage for covert operations and the Igorots a promising group of guerilla fighters. One of this group's leaders, Captain Don Blackburn, had, along with Lieutenant Colonel R. W. Volckmann, escaped from Bataan and trekked back to the Cordillera (Harkins 1955:38). Once in the highlands, Volckmann and Blackburn organized a guerilla network, concentrating at first on building an organization and gathering intelligence.

The Japanese, meanwhile, had quickly reorganized the southern Cordilleran economy. They terminated all commercial gold mines while expanding the copper excavations at Mankayan (Fry 1983: 191). They also quickly established a new civilian government, staffed largely with locals; the first Igorot governor of the Mountain Province, Hilary Clapp, was appointed by the Japanese authorities (Fry 1983:194).

Buguias was little affected through the war's early months (1942 through early 1943). The indigenous leadership retained power, and life continued as before. Japanese occupation actually created lucrative opportunities for some. Many Buguias families catered to the expanded works at Mankayan, selling fruit and vegetables to the miners and managers, and a few Buguias men joined a short-lived gold rush in the Baguio mineral zone. Here they extracted high-grade ore from the abandoned American mines until poison gases began to take a heavy toll.

By late 1943, intensified guerilla actions provoked the Japanese to interfere more directly in local affairs. Earlier they had organized villages into "neighborhood associations" on the Japanese model, but these proved ineffective in curtailing partisan operations (Fry 1983:198). Military authorities now billeted soldiers in Buguias, beloved of the Japanese for its hot-spring baths. These men at first established fairly good rapport with local residents, especially with the young boys they hired to help locate edible mushrooms and other wild foods.

HOSTILITIES

The relationship between the Japanese and the Buguias people deteriorated rapidly as guerilla activity escalated in the war's later years. Soldiers had already killed a Buguias man for allegedly hiding the American manager of the Bad-ayan sawmill; now they attacked the local political structure, arresting the baknang Berto Cubangay. Executions of individuals accused of abetting the guerilla forces soon followed. By the middle of 1944, Buguias was at war.

Several dozen Buguias men now joined the fight. Inducted into the 66th (guerilla) Infantry, they were led by Bado Dangwa (the Benguet transportation entrepreneur), and Denis Molintas, who in turn were under the command of Blackburn and Volckmann (see Volckmann 1954:145). From their headquarters in Kapangan (Dangwa's home), the 66th Infantry patrolled most of the province, gathering information and laying the groundwork for the approaching battle. Civilians eagerly provisioned the troops—although as the war intensified this would not remain true everywhere.

With the American landing in Luzon (December 1944), the commanding Japanese general, Yamashita, ordered his entire occupying force, military and civilian, into the Cordillera. There he planned a prolonged last stand, designed to cost the Americans time, money, and lives, while allowing the Japanese breathing space to organize their defenses for the inevitable invasion of the home islands. Baguio now became the capital of the Japanese-controlled Philippine government, and the full force of military activity in the archipelago was concentrated in the mountains (see R. Smith 1963; Fry 1983:204).

The combined American and Filipino forces soon began their assault on Yamashita's forces, ascending the slopes from the lowlands toward Baguio City. The 66th, meanwhile, attacked the very center of Japanese power with a degree of success that some Americans could scarcely believe (see Volckmann 1954:197). Now Yamashita's position was so jeopardized that he ordered a retreat to the Magat Valley, from which he retained sway over most of the Cordillera north of Baguio. The American-Filipino army now had to take two strategic passes (Balete and Bessang), but it was clear that they would eventually fall. Yamashita thus designated a final bastion, centered in Tucucan but including Buguias and environs as well (see Hartendorp 1967).

In August, the attack on this final Japanese stronghold began. From the east, American and Filipino forces marched through Kiangan; from the west, they advanced in two salients, one across the Lo-o Valley and the other right through the center of Buguias. The ground combat was fierce, and American bombers and strafers brought extensive destruction. Yamashita surrendered in Kiangan in mid-August, just as the Allied forces were ascending, under heavy fire, the main Cordilleran ridge east of Buguias (R. Smith 1963).

SOCIAL CONSEQUENCES

It is difficult to convey the havoc wreaked on the people of Buguias and neighboring communities by the war. Quite apart from the combat, hundreds of thousands of retreating Japanese, ill-fed and desperate, presented a massive threat to the area's resources. By late 1944 and early 1945, the Buguias people had no option but to leave their homes and seek refuge in more remote places.

At first many hid in the higher country immediately east of the village. From here they could return each night surreptitiously to cultivate their fields. But this strategy proved not only dangerous but futile, since the soldiers consumed most of the crops. At this point the Buguias people sought haven with relatives living in the eastern cloud forest. But as Yamashita's perimeter tightened, even the most inaccessible refuges here became untenable; this was precisely the area of the ultimate Japanese redoubt. As hostilities approached, many refugees had to cross the lines of fire to seek new sanctuaries west of the Agno River.

The food resources of the Cordillera could not support the swollen population. Ogawa (1972) graphically describes the progress of Japanese desperation; first they had traded clothes and other items for food, but within a few months they arrogated whatever edibles they encountered. Toward the end, some subsisted on tree-fern pith. In Buguias they so thoroughly raided the dry fields that several local varieties of sweet potatoes—those that could easily be uprooted—were exterminated. Some were also allegedly reduced to cannibalism. The Buguias people also went hungry. Though few seem to have starved, many lived on banana stalks and other semi-edible foods, and some reportedly bloated to death. After Yamashita's surrender, American planes dropped fliers informing the populace that food and supplies could be obtained along the Mountain Trail, but several elders, too weak to make the climb, perished just as peace descended.

Survivors returned to a devastated landscape. The fixed capital of the prewar agricultural system, the very foundation of livelihood, was demolished. Dry fields, stripped clean of crops, had overgrown with weeds; even seeds and sweet-potato cuttings were now hard to find. Rice terraces and irrigation canals were damaged, if not destroyed, and the elaborate network of fences largely demolished. All animals had been devoured. Many individuals had attempted to conceal herds in distant places, but few were successful; what the Japanese missed the guerillas took. And although the Igorot soldiers offered receipts for the animals they appropriated, these were never honored by the United States government (a source of continuing bitterness for some). Only Paran managed to keep a small cattle herd, hidden in a cloud-forest village to the south of Yamashita's perimeter, but these animals were immediately butchered to service his own funeral; Paran had refused his grandson's entreaties to hide a second time, and thus died when American planes strafed Buguias during the final battle.

The Americans promised relief, but delivered relatively little, considering the magnitude of the damage and the depth of sacrifice made in the Allies' cause. The veterans of the 66th Infantry received small cash payments, and those disabled in combat were provided continued support. Such payments, however, could not reconstruct the prewar economy. But, as it turned out, the Buguias people did not need to rebuild their old forms of livelihood. Suddenly they had a new opportunity servicing the exploding national market for temperate vegetables.

PART II

VITALITY AND VULNERABILITY: FLUCTUATIONS IN THE POSTWAR ECONOMY, 1946-1986

INTRODUCTION

The postwar transformation of the economic and ecological bases of Buguias society was rapid and complete. Within a few years, dry fields had been marginalized, pastoralism was fading, and the livestock trade was derelict. The Buguias people had become full-time commercial farmers, buying agricultural chemicals produced overseas and growing produce for the Manila market. In tracing this transformation, the second half of this work is ultimately concerned with a question that receives increasing attention as the analysis proceeds: to whit, in what ways and to what extent was this dramatic material transfiguration reflected in social and cultural change.

In Part I, Buguias was viewed in a largely synchronic framework. For the postwar period, a more diachronic approach becomes not only possible (the texture of documentable chronological detail being much finer) but in many ways preferable (the pace of change having increased sufficiently to lessen the utility of a single-moment analysis). The shift is one of emphasis, however; as with any historical geographic inquiry, this work must illuminate not only the flow of events but also the simultaneous differentiation and interaction of distinct places.

Such dual organizational imperatives have been accommodated here by hinging the analysis on the period between 1972 and 1974, a watershed within the postwar era. Up to that point, the vegetable-producing districts experienced rising prosperity; afterward, the dominant tone became one of crisis and restructuring. The chapters concerned with the earlier period detail the establishment of vegetable culture. Because this was an expansive time, when new agricultural technologies were fitted to the local environment and when a new economy offered prosperity to most (and riches to a few), the stress here is on successful adaptation. To explicate the basis of this new prosperity, both the evolving agricultural ecology and the development of the market on which it depended are explored at length.

Social conflicts did not disappear during this period, however, and some were even exacerbated. More ominously, environmental safeguards maintained during the prewar period were gradually eroded. By the end of the 1960s, the stable economy of the prewar years had been replaced by a vibrant but precarious one. This new vulnerability, and the undercurrents of discord that had remained subdued throughout the fifties and sixties, became increasingly clear and urgent as a succession of shock waves in the global economy began to undermine the community's collective livelihood. The chapters concerned with the difficult years since the early 1970s accordingly deal explicitly with the breakdown of harmony, opening with a lengthy exposition of the market crisis before focusing explicitly on ecological deterioration and social turmoil.

6

The Establishment of Commercial
Vegetable Agriculture

INTRODUCTION

The Buguias economy transformed rapidly in the immediate post-war years. Just as the old way of life perished in the war, a new livelihood developed in commercial vegetable production. Although a few individuals sought to recreate the antebellum practices, an inherent ecological contradiction between the old and the new regimes steadily pushed the Buguias people further into market gardening. Since free-ranging cattle would quickly ruin vegetable plots, pastoralism steadily diminished. At the same time, sweet potatoes and rice were removed from the prime fertile sites, to be replaced by carrots and cabbages. By the late 1950s, virtually all Buguias residents had become market gardeners.

The transition to vegetable farming was ongoing. It demanded continual adjustments, as the changing market called for new crop mixes and as the diffusion of innovations allowed new growing techniques. The early years saw the most rapid change, and although minor improvements would continue to appear, the basic cropping system—one fine-tuned to produce a variety of vegetables in a diversity of microhabitats—was firmly in place by the end of the 1960s.

The new economy called for a new attitude toward agriculture. Previously, the Buguias people had based their planting decisions on field characteristics and family needs, guided by historically rooted agronomic precepts. They acted rationally, but not strategically; subsistence was readily attained, and households did not compete in agricultural production. But in vegetable farming, individual cultivators were forced to adopt explicit farming strategies;[1] henceforth, the market ensured that each household would succeed or fail on the basis of its decisions each cropping session. The all-important ledger balance came to depend on which crops were chosen, when and where they were planted, how much skill and attention went into their care, and last, but by no means least, on the vicissitudes of the market at harvest time. Market fluctuations, although beyond control, were not *entirely* unpredictable, and herein lay the primary terrain for strategy. Vegetable farming came to be seen as a deadly serious game, involving an elusive interplay of skill, fortitude, and luck.

As pastoralism was displaced by vegetable growing, the animal trade vanished and Buguias lost its prime economic position as a local trade hub. The previously integrated local economy was now turned inside out by the extractive power of the global exchange system. With the entire region now funneling its produce to the national capital, Buguias, poorly served by the developing dendritic (or branching) road system, was reduced to an economic backwater.

POSTWAR ADJUSTMENTS

The Aftermath of War

In 1946, the people of Buguias faced the monumental task of rebuilding their economy and society. Simply to reclaim their old fields required much labor and capital. But labor was short, and the old cash-generating system no longer functioned. And even those retaining money simply could not find livestock to purchase and thus could not rebuild their herds. Not only Buguias, but the entire southern Cordillera—and indeed much of the country—lay devastated. Rebuilding the trade circuits that formerly supported the economy would have been a project of many years.

Ultimately, the Buguias people would have been able to resurrect their old economy only if both the cloud-forest communities and Suyoc had also been able to restore their prewar routines. But both were demolished. The cloud-forest villages of Tinoc and Tucucan lay at the center of Yamashita's last redoubt, and according to census figures the population of the encompassing municipality fell from 12,873 persons in 1939 to 3,540 in 1948 (Republic of the Philippines 1960a, v. 1, pt. ii:35). The Suyoc people survived in larger numbers, but their economy was ruined; although they could reclaim their diggings, they could not counteract the relative decline in the value of gold.[2] The residents of Suyoc continued sedulously to mine their lodes, but no longer would their bullion make them the baknangs of northern Benguet, nor would it underwrite trade fortunes for the Buguias merchants.

THE RISE OF A NEW ECONOMIC SYSTEM

Although the restoration of the prewar economy was impossible, new opportunities emerged. Vegetables had provided only supplementary income in prewar days; now demand was suddenly voracious and supply short. Prices rose accordingly. In 1947, a kilo of cabbage could fetch as much as 10 pesos ($5 U.S.) on the Manila market (Hamada 1960), an astonishing price even by 1980s standards. Throughout much of Benguet, individuals with access to transport and seeds, and familiar with vegetable culture, responded quickly.

The people of Buguias were soon converting their rice terraces and dry fields to cabbage gardens. Before the war, terraces had occasionally produced vegetables in the off-season, but now a few farmers devoted them to cabbage year-round. The dry-season vegetable crop (replacing rice) brought particularly high prices since there was little competition at this time, growers along the Mountain Trail seldom being able to irrigate. Although vegetables remained for a few years a cash-producing sideline for most, a few gambled everything on the market. A boom was on, and vegetable sales brought in the capital needed to rebuild a vigorous new economy. As money became available for rebuilding terraces and extending the agricultural infrastructure, the labor shortage became more acute, and wages pushed higher than ever.

The forces behind the postwar cabbage boom remain elusive. The traditional supply zone near Baguio was once again furnishing vegetables, as were a number of new locales. Official statistics nevertheless indicate a slightly smaller production of cabbage in 1948 than in 1938, while the potato yield is shown to have tripled in the same decade (Goodstein 1962:129)—yet the immediate postwar boom in Benguet was in cabbage much more than in potatoes.

One possible explanation for the decline in the national cabbage harvest just as Benguet's yield expanded lies in a shift toward highland production. As late as 1948, according to official figures, less than half of the total cabbage acreage in the Philippines lay in the Cordillera (Republic of the Philippines 1954, v. 3, pt. ii:2944). But the mountains, blessed with far superior climatic conditions for cabbage growing, soon supplied the bulk of the national harvest. Such an account, however, must remain speculative, given the paucity and unreliability of official records; most census reports simply fail to differentiate among vegetables, and few tables designate province of origin.

On the side of demand, the American military presence was crucial. Before Japan's surrender, the U.S. Army had planned to use the Philippines as a staging ground for the assault on the home islands. In preparation, a large military force was retained in the archipelago, and in requisitioning the necessary supplies to sustain the troops, the U.S. set the Philippines awash in currency, perpetuating for a time the hyperinflation initiated during the last year of the war (D. Bernstein 1947:218). Cabbage, as one of the few available vegetables familiar to the American soldiers, was no doubt in great demand.

Through the 1950s and 1960s the demand for temperate vegetables steadily expanded with production growing apace. By 1959, the land area devoted to cabbage had increased almost sevenfold over the 1948 figure, with almost all of the new acreage being in Benguet. Official potato acreage increased at a similar rate, growing from 548 hectares in 1948 to 2,500 in 1963, and to 3,600 by 1972.[3] Davis (1973:50) ties the long-term increase in temperate-vegetable consumption to rapid urban growth and accompanying dietary changes, a convincing thesis.

THE MOUNTAIN TRAIL VEGETABLE HEARTH

The cabbage boom that transformed the economy of Buguias had little impact at first on neighboring Agno Valley communities. Along the Mountain Trail, however, the effect was massive. This cool ridge-top zone, well suited to cabbage, also boasted a road that, although narrow, unpaved, and dangerous, was passable to vehicles. The resulting advantages of climate and transport attracted thousands of settlers to the ridge. Where only a handful of families had lived before the war, a string of fast-growing market towns soon sprouted.

Among the new settlements was Natubleng, a new village sitting on a plateau only a few miles from Buguias. A handful of Buguias families had relocated here in the 1930s, but in the war's immediate aftermath many more moved up to clear small gardens in the scrubby oak. But no highlanders had the capital necessary to establish sizable farms. This would fall to another immigrant group: the Chinese of Baguio City.

Chinese and Japanese farmers had long grown vegetables in the Baguio-Trinidad area, and when the Japanese were forceably repatriated after the war, the Chinese gained financial control of the industry (Davis 1973:51). As large-scale Chinese growers prospered, they looked to expand their operations along the Mountain Trail, seeking relatively flat plateaus plentifully supplied with water. Among the best were Sayangan/Paoay in Atok municipality (formerly known as Haight's Place) and Natubleng. Backed by a shadowy financial network extending from Baguio to Manila, and relying on the wage labor of local villagers, these Chinese planters cleared gardens of 10, 20, and even 30 hectares.

Of the four or five Chinese farmers clearing land in Natubleng, one named Singa is particularly remembered in Buguias. Singa tilled his large farm with local labor bound by a variety of arrangements. During the peak season, as many as 115 persons worked for wages, on a daily or monthly basis. Those workers whom Singa came to trust were eventually set up as sharecroppers on subsidiary plots.

Laborers came to Singa's farm from throughout the entire upper Agno Valley, but especially from the smaller villages south and east of Buguias. People from these areas seldom had the wherewithal to purchase seeds, and they yet lacked knowledge of vegetable culture. But working for Singa they quickly learned the new techniques, and most were able to save the small sum needed to begin gardening on their own. Many returned home, seeds in hand, after a single cropping season. In their home villages they planted cabbage in small plots, sufficient to furnish the pittance of cash they needed. Thus the late 1940s saw the vegetable-growing frontier rapidly extend to many peripheral villages of the former Buguias economic sphere.

The Chinese may have dominated the early vegetable industry, but they by no means wholly displaced the independent cultivators along the Mountain Trail. Throughout the 1950s, highlanders with a minimum of financial backing continued to migrate to the ridge-top zone to clear and claim new lands. Most cultivated gardens of under 1 hectare, but a few grew wealthy enough to finance larger operations requiring day laborers.

While a few growers still burned brush for soil nutrients, most had turned by the early 1950s to chemical sources. The large-scale Chinese farmers, closely connected with Baguio wholesalers, doubled as fertilizer distributors. In northern Buguias municipality, however, local baknang entrepreneurs entered the chemical business. For many of the Chinese and Igorot elite, the retail selling of agricultural supplies eventually supplanted gardening as an economic mainstay.

These early postwar years saw a major reworking of the economic map of greater Buguias. A line could now be drawn down the length of the region, separating the Mountain Trail zone, with its nucleus at Natubleng, from the Agno Valley (excluding the Lo-o Basin) and points east. The former area, essentially under Chinese financial domination, supported numerous medium and large farms. The latter area, for the time being, was characterized by small market gardens still supplementing subsistence-producing dry fields. But this was only the most general of a series of fine geographical divisions that were to emerge over the next several decades.

THE ECOLOGY OF EARLY VEGETABLE
PRODUCTION IN BUGUIAS

New Techniques

The vegetable-growing techniques adopted by Benguet market gardeners were largely of Chinese provenance (Davis 1973:53). The *gabbion,* a heavy hoe foreign to the native tool kit, was now the main agricultural implement. Gardeners used this tool primarily to construct ridges, generally between and 60 to 80 centimeters wide. Once this task was completed, cabbage seedlings would be transplanted in rows of three or four plants lateral to the ridge top. Intervening furrows drained the fields in the wet season and irrigated them, where possible, in the dry. In the early years, growers watered seedlings manually, scooping moisture from the furrow and pouring it around the base of each plant.

After the year's first harvest from the dry fields, many gardeners would immediately replant, hoping to get a second crop before the rains diminished. After the second harvest they would fallow the plot. Before the next replanting, growers would dig the field again so that the furrow-and-ridge pattern would be reversed, thus incorporating any silt that had been deposited in the furrow into the cropping medium.

Vegetables in the Uma

Since few gardeners possessed terraces, most planted vegetables in their old dry fields. Since cabbage plants, unlike creeping sweet-potato vines, provided the soil little protection, erosion on sloping plots could be greatly accelerated; to counteract this, farmers began constructing narrow contour ridges. Another problem was soil fertility. Cabbage, unlike the sweet potato, languished on the exhausted soils typical of most dry fields. Farmers responded by applying ash or, if they could afford it, chemical fertilizer. Because some of the added nutrients remained in the field after the vegetable harvest, subsequent sweet-potato plantings proved quite productive. Since most Buguias residents continued in the early postwar period to grow for subsistence, many began to alternate their plantings between cabbages and sweet potatoes.

The extent of preexisting dry fields in Buguias soon proved inadequate to support both market and subsistence cultivation. By the early 1950s, gardeners began to clear new fields in pastures, using the puwal technique, and in shrub or forest land, using the swidden method. But clearing new land for permanent vegetable plots required arduous work. After burning, farmers now had to remove roots before they could create a furrow-and-ridge pattern. In the late 1950s, when carrots emerged as Buguias's main crop, this job became more difficult still, since even a small obstacle could mar the appearance of the carrot root.

Terraced Gardens

Although the Buguias people increasingly turned their rice terraces into year-round vegetable gardens, conversion was never complete. They still desired the native rice, which was yet unobtainable on the market, for beer brewing. Furthermore, even the most dedicated commercial growers would occasionally return a terrace to paddy in order to rehabilitate the soil. Where vegetable culture had compacted the earth, a season of flooding would render it again friable. But rice growing was demoted to a minor pursuit and was always rushed so that the fields could be returned to the more profitable production of vegetables. Seedbed preparation, plowing, flooding, and even transplanting were now conducted in haste, leading to low average yields.

The Buguias people constructed several new terrace systems in the early postwar years, financing them through cabbage profits. Some of the new terraces served initially for both rice and vegetables, but others were made expressly for vegetable culture. By the mid-1950s, the Buguias people discovered that simpler, less sturdy structures would suffice for the new crops, substantially reducing terrace construction costs. In the former pasturelands, several individuals experimented with sod-walled terraces, an especially cheap alternative. Although these would last ten years at most, they were so inexpensive to construct that many found the investment worthwhile. Gardeners irrigated their vegetable terraces where possible, but in general even a dry terrace was preferred over a sloped field, since the latter was both more difficult to work and more vulnerable to soil erosion.

FARMING AND RANCHING IN CONFLICT

Several of the surviving members of the Buguias elite still hoped at war's end to recreate the pastoral economy. After a few years, cattle could again be purchased in Cervantes, and several Buguias baknangs had reaccumulated enough capital to begin rebuilding their herds. In the intervening years, however, unfenced garden plots had invaded many of the best pastures. Before long the community was embroiled in a classical struggle between agriculturalist and pastoralist. The former, anxious to avoid the considerable expense of fencing, called for a change in customary law to reflect the transformed economy, while the cattlemen advocated returning to the antebellum *status quo*.

Following customary precedent, the contestants argued and settled their dispute in tong tongan deliberations. Despite the high status of the leading pastoralists, the gardeners had numerical advantage and economic logic on their side. The new rules thus called for the constraining of all livestock to fenced pastures, pens, or tethers. Whichever option they chose, would-be graziers now faced considerable expense: tethered animals had to be moved to a fresh site every few hours, and lands completely dedicated to pasture would require extensive fencing.

The few men who endeavored to enclose pastures seldom managed to mark off areas larger than 10 hectares. Since few commoners fenced their lands, the Buguias cattle barons could now lend few animals. And those who did fence their pastures had difficulty mobilizing the labor necessary to maintain grazing capacity. Soon *Eupatorium* and other noxious weeds infested most enclosed sites. Because of fencing costs, graziers increasingly withdrew into areas naturally barricaded by slope breaks, gullies, and other obstacles. They also learned to divert water to accentuate erosion in small gullies, thus creating superior barriers. Since pastoralists often skimped when they had to fence, their animals periodically escaped, and the conflict thus continued to smolder. Cattle owners and tenders were frequently assessed for crop damages, and irate gardeners who maimed trespassing animals were sometimes levied fines as well. As such incidents mounted, gardeners clamored for stricter fence regulations.

Most Buguias men still hoped to raise cattle, but this was usually possible only if one were willing to move them about on a tether. With the new labor demands in the gardens, the average household was limited to a single animal. Responsibility for the family cow now generally passed to children and the aged. Theoretically, leashed cattle could be pastured anywhere, so long as they did not damage gardens, but conflicts erupted nevertheless. Animals often pulled loose and ruined gardens, but more problematically, households sometimes quarreled when one claimed the right to pasture its cow in an area that the other sought to convert to a vegetable plot. Ultimately, securing a tax declaration would give the prospective gardener the right to determine land use, so long as he or she actually began to cultivate the site.

The new rule especially hindered hog raising, as swine could not forage effectively if tied, and they required much tighter fences than did cattle. Henceforth, hogs were increasingly confined to small houselot pens. After the transformation of customary law, the few traditionalists who clung to large scale swine raising were forced to relocate, for a household could not raise more than a few hogs unless the animals could forage. Such couples thus moved up to the higher zone east of Buguias proper, where many of the village's swine had ranged in the prewar days. Gardens and fences were still uncommon here in the 1950s, and mast-producing oak trees abounded nearby. Eventually, however, most free-roaming hogs even in these remote districts disappeared under pressure from the advancing vegetable frontier and from the steady progress of individual tax declarations.

CONTINUING AGRICULTURAL DEVELOPMENT

RECESSION AND REVIVAL

By the early 1950s, the cabbage boom in central Buguias had fizzled. Lack of quality seeds undercut Buguias growers, who were evidently outbid by more prosperous farmers along the Mountain Trail. A more serious problem was oversupply. As new land was cleared along the Mountain Trail, the cabbage harvest expanded apace. The Buguias gardeners could not easily compete with their ridge-top rivals, who enjoyed inexpensive transport and a cool climate better suited to cabbage. But as prices dropped, even the most favored areas suffered, and not a few Benguet farmers began to revert to subsistence crops. By the early 1950s, the market often glutted (*Baguio Midland Courier* May 10, 1953), and the nascent vegetable industry fell into its first recession.

Crisis was staved off in part by new crops. Unlike cabbage, other vegetables, heretofore largely limited to the Baguio region, remained fitfully profitable. Carrots especially attracted Buguias farmers, as they thrived in the moderate climate and rich soils of the Agno Valley. A sack of carrots, however, did make a heavy burden to carry up to the Mountain Trail roadhead. Lighter crops, including peas, beans, and bell peppers, were thus also attractive. Along the Mountain Trail, potatoes came to rival cabbage as the mainstay, but the market for this crop also began to reach saturation.

The real break for Buguias truck gardening came in 1958, when a branch road was pushed down the Agno Valley as far as the center of the village. Now growers could truck their produce a mere 15 kilometers to Abatan and the Mountain Trail. As transport costs diminished, carrots emerged as Buguias's prime crop. Other vegetables also proliferated, as the Agno Valley began to reap the benefits of its equable climate. By the early 1960s, the economy of Buguias rested squarely on some half-dozen temperate and subtropical vegetables.

Agricultural inputs boosted the renewed vegetable expansion of the late 1950s. Growers could now increasingly afford chemical fertilizers, and the use of lowland chicken manure spread. Although some gardeners had used DDT as early as the late 1940s, the late 1950s marked the widespread adoption of the backpack sprayer and the introduction of various special-purpose insecticides. Insecticides helped growers as much by saving labor (from the arduous task of insect plucking) as by allowing higher yields. High-quality fungicides, introduced in the same period, probably had an even greater impact, since wet-season humidity fostered vigorous fungal growth. Growers had earlier applied a copper-sulfate powder mixed with hydrated lime, but this attacked human skin as effectively as it killed fungus. With the safer new products, potatoes could be competitively grown in the Agno Valley, and the tuber crop increased approximately tenfold.

THE AGRICULTURAL COOPERATIVES

A state-initiated cooperative marketing and supply scheme also stimulated the vegetable industry in the late fifties. The co-op movement received impetus not only from the state's desire to enhance local economic development but, perhaps more importantly, from its wish to rid the vegetable industry of alien—meaning Chinese—control (*Baguio Midland Courier* Jan. 8, 1956). Local and national leaders concurred that to stabilize the vegetable market, seen as a prerequisite for orderly development, they first had to uproot the Chinese growing and marketing organization. This "cartel" was said to practice "unfair trade . . . and cutthroat competition" (Hamada 1960). The Chinese could be displaced, they hoped, by local cooperatives united under government supervision.

In 1952, the Farmer's Cooperative Marketing Association (FACOMA) appeared in Benguet (Fry 1983:220), the first of its kind. Branches of FACOMA soon sprouted in several municipalities; these in turn all operated under the aegis of the government's Agricultural Credit and Cooperative Financing Administration (ACCFA). The state directed the FACOMA to distribute subsidized fertilizers and biocides and to assist in produce marketing. In both areas, middlemen were to be eliminated, to the benefit of farmers and consumers alike. The Central Cooperative Exchange in Manila supplied chemicals, both domestic and imported. The Benguet FACOMA eventually purchased several large trucks for hauling vegetables to market and agricultural chemicals back to the farm areas, while the ACCFA financed several centrally located warehouses, from which vegetables could be shipped directly to Manila.

The FACOMA co-ops enjoyed modest success through the 1950s and early 1960s. Though perennially undercapitalized, they did provide credit to a few local entrepreneurs, nourishing a locally run agribusiness infrastructure. But early hopes that the co-ops would wrest financial control from the Chinese were soon dashed (*Baguio Midland Courier* May 5, 1963; Hamada 1960). The Chinese merchants had created a sophisticated and perennially solvent organization; where the co-ops usually worked on consignment, they could generally offer cash to the currency-strapped farmers (Fry 1983:220; *Baguio Midland Courier* May 10, 1953). They also enjoyed immediate knowledge of marketing conditions in Manila, thanks to extensive radio connections with local operatives there.

Faced with the failure of the cooperative effort to oust the Chinese, the Igorot gardeners resorted to political action. As early as 1955, FACOMA leaders trekked to Manila to protest the presence of "alien" farmers and dealers along the Mountain Trail (*Baguio Midland Courier* Dec. 4, 1955). As the political pressure intensified, then-president Ramon Magsaysay opted for direct action: in 1956, he signed into law Executive Order 180, commanding the summary expulsion of all Chinese farmers from the Mountain Trail vegetable district (Fry 1983:220).

Magsaysay's antialien policies were part of a larger program designed to aid small farmers throughout the Philippines, to ensure the ecological sustainability of highland agriculture, and to solidify state authority in rural areas. Government officials fretted over the unconstrained vegetable industry; gardens were increasingly being cleared in Mount Data National Park, erosion was accelerating, and watersheds were being denuded. By official criteria, some 94 percent of all Benguet vegetable farms were illegally occupied (*Baguio Midland Courier* Jan. 8, 1956). Magsaysay viewed the Chinese evictions as a necessary precondition before land titles could be awarded to the indigenous gardeners, most of whom were at the time considered squatters in their own homeland. Legal land ownership, it was thought, would encourage ecologically sound agriculture just as it would promote local economic development.

Magsaysay's death in 1958 cut short these ambitious plans. Much to the disappointment of Benguet leaders, the Chinese remained, although some would be expelled some ten years later. The cooperatives persisted for some years, but as government support diminished, most slowly withered; others, however, fell quickly owing to local corruption (Fry 1983:221).

CROPS AND FIELD TYPES

By the 1960s, Buguias possessed a stable and intricate system of market gardening. Diversity marked both the crop assemblage and the techniques employed; growers could now choose different crops for each microhabitat. Complex cropping schedules allowed farmers to exploit environmental variation efficiently, just as it gave Buguias an advantage over other Benguet vegetable districts where crop ensembles and growing strategies were more limited. This helped offset Buguias's higher costs of transport and labor. Since the basic system developed at this time persists to the time of writing (although with some important changes noted in later chapters), the following discussion has been worded in the present tense.

SEASONAL PATTERNS

The oscillation of wet and dry seasons shapes the basic form of Buguias agriculture. The first rains usually arrive in late April. Plantings on dry fields, especially those with clay-rich soil, can now begin, although cautious farmers wait for the more reliable rains that come in middle to late May. By July, the soil is saturated; most mornings begin with sunshine, but afternoons are usually drenching. July may also see the first typhoon. Through the wettest months good drainage is vital, especially for root crops. Fungal growths also plague most crops in this season; although these can be counteracted with fungicides, farmers avoid growing susceptible crops in damp and shady areas. Wind may also destroy certain crops in the typhoon season, although topography creates limited areas of partial protection.

The rains usually diminish in October, but typhoons can strike in November and lingering showers sometimes persist through December. This late rainy season is in many respects the ideal cropping period. Although soils are still moist enough for sowing, they are seldom too wet, and they dry gradually as the plants mature. In unirrigated fields with heavy soil, residual moisture allows cropping to continue into the early weeks of the true dry season. By February, however, all dry fields have been harvested and left fallow until the spring rains. Irrigated crops, on the other hand, thrive during the arid months. With sunshine plentiful and humidity low, fungus is minimized, and the warm weather of March and April favors even such subtropical crops as bell peppers.

Soils and Topography

Buguias has diverse soils. Before the war, dry fields had been limited to clay areas, which alone would support year-round cultivation. But the postwar transition gave all soils agricultural utility. Indeed, light soils are now often preferred during the typhoon season, since they drain readily and are always friable. Heavy soils are now disparaged as difficult to cultivate, and, since they easily waterlog, they may be left unplanted in the rainy season. Chemical fertilizers and imported chicken manure obviate concern for soil fertility, and even sterile subsoil horizons exposed by mass wasting—or on purpose—can be profitably farmed. Indeed, the very diversity of soils has allowed the Buguias growers to develop complex and flexible cropping strategies.

The main soil types of Buguias, by local classification, are as follows:

Loboy: A heavy loam found in flat areas; favored for umas. Often rich in organics.

Komog: Weathered dioritic rock; an infertile and light subsoil.

Lagan: "Mountain sand"; sterile, very light.

Tapo: Alluvial silt; very fertile, of medium weight and water retention qualities. Good for umas but previously little used because of potential flooding.

Oplit: Clay soil; good for umas, but very hard to work. Good nutrient and water-holding capacity. Usually found in flat areas and depressions.

Liang: "Red clay" subsoil. Avoided in the past; very low fertility.

(Most soils are of hybrid form. The best uma soils, for instance, are those with a high clay component, but not necessarily pure *oplit*. Many farmers favored an *oplit-loboy* mixture for their uma fields.)

Having adopted a diverse vegetable agriculture, the growers of Buguias have to consider more than just fertility, moisture retention, and drainage when selecting a cropping medium. Subsoils (*komog, liang*) are now valued because one can easily build a quasi terrace simply by removing the overburden and exposing the lower-soil horizons until a flat space emerges. Given its light, friable texture, one can harvest a good crop on a komog bench even during the wettest months. And liang, always avoided in the past, is now valued for the ruddy appearance it imparts to carrots and potatoes.

Truck farming also allowed the cultivation of topographic zones previously considered nonarable. Steep slopes are now favored for wet-season root crops, and shady northern exposures are valued for lettuce in the dry season. Even the alluvial deposits along the small streams of eastern Buguias can now be farmed, yielding especially large harvests if check-dams are constructed to trap additional sediment. But this is a risky strategy, since a single typhoon can destroy an entire field. But with the change to vegetable farming, Buguias residents became professional risk-takers; their agricultural endeavor, as they perceive it, is now one of continual gambling.

VEGETABLES

By the mid-1960s, carrots occupied the prime position among Buguias vegetables. They can be grown throughout the year and in all soils. During the dry season they are grown on irrigated terraces, and in the rainy months on inclined fields. The former crop yields larger harvests, but the latter often brings higher profits because of the season's hazardous growing conditions.

Carrots are relatively pest-free, although leaf spot demands continual spraying. Labor demands remain high through the first month, as the carrot seeds germinate with difficulty and the seedlings are delicate. Several days of dry weather can destroy a neglected field of young plants. Continual and meticulous weeding must persist through the first month. But once carrots are well established they survive many disasters, especially typhoons, comparatively well. In light soils, carrots produce long, straight roots, while in heavy soils they yield squat, bulky roots. In general, fertile soils produce larger carrots, but here they must be harvested as soon as they mature, regardless of market conditions. In poorer, lighter soils, by contrast, the roots can remain in the ground (except at the height of the rainy season) for weeks or even months without losing texture or flavor.

Buguias gardeners continue to grow cabbage, although to a much lesser extent than they did in earlier years. Cabbage grows better at higher elevations, but it is valued in Buguias for its low labor requirements and relative price stability. By the 1960s cabbage had become primarily a wet-season crop; if grown in the dry months it must be sprayed incessantly to minimize insect damage. Leaf mold, a perennial wet-season curse, is controllable with fungicides, but excessive rain can simply rot the heads, especially those of the Chinese cabbage. But some farmers still prefer Chinese over European cabbage because it matures more rapidly. And a more delicate Chinese crucifer, the flowering *pechay,* may be harvested after only five or six weeks, attracting a few growers who want an especially fast turnover.

Some growers favor potatoes for their low labor requirements and long-term storage potential. In Buguias, potatoes are cultivated in all but the rainiest months (July through September), when leaf mold and strong winds can be devastating. Gardeners avoid heavy soils throughout the wet months. Potatoes are occasionally infected with leaf wilt, which is not treatable (although crop rotation can reduce losses). Potatoes yield most heavily on newly cleared fields, especially those in the higher elevations of eastern Buguias. Buguias farmers often devote irrigated terraces to potatoes in the dry season, when many other Benguet vegetable districts lack sufficient water to produce a crop.

The edible-pod snow pea, like the carrot, is grown year-round. During the typhoon period, the slender cane trellises that support the vines are vulnerable to wind damage, so growers generally plant peas in this season in protected microhabitats. Peas are also favored in gardens far from any road, since they bring high prices per unit weight.

Snap beans flourish in the wet season, especially on sloped fields. At this time, insect pests are few, yet temperatures are high enough for good growth. Although fungus does attack, it is easily controlled. Bean plants, twining up cane poles, also suffer wind damage, but not to the same extent as the softer and more ramified peas.

Peppers, both "bell" and the "Chinese yellow," also thrive during the wet season. Gardeners sow them in seedbeds in March, the time of maximum sunshine and warmth. Transplanted as the southwest monsoon arrives, the plants fruit in the wettest months. Farmers could grow peppers for harvest during the dry season, but they would then compete with the lowland pepper crop, favored by easy access to the Manila market.

Buguias farmers also grow celery in the wet season. This most demanding of crops thrives only on highly fertile soils. Slope is also critical, for celery requires good drainage but abundant moisture at all times. Gardeners avoid shady areas that would foster fungal growth. Still, celery easily fails, and even if it flourishes, a poor market can render it virtually worthless.

Lettuce can be grown throughout the year, but in the dry season it requires careful water monitoring and in the wettest months it often rots; four days of continuous light rain can destroy a crop. Some growers favor lettuce for its fast growth (two months or less) and for the high prices it sometimes brings. But lettuce is an inflexible crop; when mature it must be harvested and shipped without delay.

The above discussion outlines a few of the considerations that Buguias farmers juggle when deciding what to plant. But it does not exhaust them. All growers, for example, rotate different crops through their fields to minimize nematode infestations. Periodic flooding of terraced fields brings some relief, but for most farmers, field rotation is the only prophylactic.

THE SURVIVAL OF SUBSISTENCE CROPPING

Buguias farmers continued to grow subsistence crops even after becoming full-fledged market gardeners. Some occasionally plant their vegetable plots to sweet potatoes, and many grow a few tubers along field margins. A few wealthier farmers continue to plant rice, and nearly every household keeps a cow, a hog or two, and several chickens. The door-yard garden, as before, supplies various foodstuffs to established families. Coffee growing persists as well, but only for home consumption. Moreover, a new source of "subsistence" has emerged in the market crops themselves. A typical Buguias meal now consists of lowland rice, an occasional bit of dried fish or tinned meat, and a "viand" of boiled vegetables from the garden's seconds.

But unlike many other peoples who have recently been integrated into the world economy (see, for example, Grossman 1984: 6), the Buguias people have not maintained a level of subsistence cultivation that either substantially subsidizes their cash-cropping endeavors or that could act as a fallback in the event of market collapse. Home-grown crops now provide little more than supplements; since the late 1950s, local agriculture has been incapable of providing the staples the community requires. Nor could the earlier ways be easily revived. Population has greatly expanded, necessary skills have vanished, the old agricultural infrastructure has disappeared, and the prewar trade network—previously vital for "subsistence"—is beyond resurrection. If the Buguias people were forced, by market conditions, to subsist directly from their own territory, their impoverishment would be drastic. No one in Buguias even contemplates abandoning commercial farming.

THE AGROECOLOGICAL TRANSITION

In recent years many geographers have linked the transition from subsistence to commercial agriculture with substantial environmental degradation (see Grossman 1981; Richards 1983; Blaikie

1985). Some have further argued that commercial farming inevitably brings a dangerous agroecological simplification, as intricate, historically rooted techniques suited to local habitats are replaced by an imported monocropping package based on massive chemical subsidies (Grossman 1981). For the Buguias people, this view represents a half-truth. Vegetable culture here is unarguably dependent on dangerous biocides and fertilizers, and it has brought severe environmental degradation. This will be analyzed in some depth below, but at this point it is helpful to recognize that it also evinces a remarkably complex environmental fit that has evolved through the detailed knowledge and ready experimentation of the farmers themselves. As deplorable as their continual spraying of poisons might be, one must applaud the Buguias farmers for their adaptation of a technically complex temperate-vegetable agriculture to the many microhabitats of their homeland.

The socioeconomic dislocations that often accompany the spread of cash-cropping into new territories may be profound enough to generate not only "subsistence malaise" (Grossman 1981:232), but, in some instances, mass starvation as well (amply illustrated for northern Nigeria by Watts [1983]). But as Watts also recognizes (1983:267), during times of "buoyant commodity prices" the living standards of even the poorest producers can substantially improve. This occurred in Benguet's vegetable districts from 1946 to 1972. Indeed, one might argue that commoditization helped *prevent* famine, for in the two decades after the war, only the less commercialized areas of the Cordillera experienced severe food shortages.[4] Varied environmental agents, including drought, rat invasions, and typhoons, caused these famines, although certainly governmental neglect must also take blame. In Buguias, however, a diverse, year-round commercial agriculture proved remarkably able to withstand such ravages; neither destitution nor even particularly lean times struck the market gardeners during these years. This is not to imply that cash-cropping represents a superior agricultural adaptation; the point is simply to recognize that, *in these years*, commercial agriculture proved instrumental to, rather than destructive of, a kind of environmental buffering. The problem is that this "safeguard" proved susceptible to secular market trends just as it brought about long-term environmental degradation. In the long run, severe new problems would appear.

STRATEGIES IN VEGETABLE FARMING

Buguias farmers must weigh many factors in choosing among cropping options. They base their choices on an intimate knowledge of field and crops characteristics as well as on their access to labor. But they also attempt to anticipate market conditions. Vegetable prices fluctuate predictably through the seasons, but erratically week by week. To some extent, market seasonality cancels environmental seasonality; when the production of a particular vegetable is difficult or perilous, its market value will usually be correspondingly high. Regional diversity adds another layer of complexity. In the dry season, for example, when cabbage can hardly be grown in Buguias, it does very well in irrigated Mountain Trail gardens.

Ultimately, the cropping strategies selected vary with the personalities and life histories of individual farmers. Some opt for conservative plans promising reasonable returns regardless of market conditions or environmental perturbations, although even the most cautious farmer cannot always avoid unprofitable crops. Other gardeners deliberately choose risk, gambling on the chance of a windfall. Precarious strategies include planting a crop during its season of maximum hazards, or sowing a dry field at the first rain, in hope that more will soon follow.

CROP VARIABILITY

The riskiest crops, lettuce and celery, are marked by pronounced price swings. This volatility reflects meteorological sensitivity, since neither crop will endure weather extremes. But the rapidity of price fluctuations, often severalfold in less than one week, baffles scholars and farmers alike. Conventional explanations cite the unfathomable machinations of the Chinese "cartels," but this is mostly conjecture.

Not uncommonly, a Buguias farmer confronted with miserable prices will allow a lettuce or celery crop to rot in the field, since harvest and shipping costs would not be recoverable. The perishability of both vegetables adds further risks; even a transport delay, common during the landslide-prone wet season, may doom a mature crop. For precisely this reason, however, a truckload of lettuce or celery brought in when the price curve peaks can bring its owner the elusive "jackpot" harvest.

A risk-averse farmer does well to choose cabbage or potatoes. These are, without rivals, the leading crops of Benguet, and their large area of supply combines with steady demand to dampen price swings. Furthermore, both crops may be stored for sale when prices rise. Cabbage remains reasonably fresh if held in a high-elevation storehouse for up to one week, whereas potatoes can last several months. Nevertheless, neither crop shows a flat price curve. Severe weather can bring on rapid changes of fortune, and a series of typhoons can block transportation, allowing those farmers retaining road access to reap extraordinary profits. Either crop, however, can be overplanted in any given season, depressing prices and leaving most growers with little if any profit.

Other vegetables generally yield reasonable returns, although all are subject to periodic gluts and shortages. Carrot prices fluctuate erratically only in certain years. In 1986, however, carrots climbed from 1.5 pesos a kilo to 7 pesos a kilo then promptly fell back to 3 pesos a kilo, all in the span of a little more than one month. At the start of this sequence farmers shipping carrots lost money, in the middle they profited greatly, and at the end they broke even. This oscillation especially perplexed local market experts, since it occurred during the dry season, a period of general price stability.

Environmental (Mis)fortune

The wild card in the gardener's deck is the typhoon. A tropical depression can destroy crops in a geographically unpredictable pattern just as it can block the market access of specific regions by triggering landslides. A storm can benefit Buguias farmers if it wreaks greater damage in competing districts than it does at home. Similarly, a landslide can be a boon or a calamity, depending on its precise location. A massive break on the Mountain Trail between Trinidad and Kilometer 73 can devastate Buguias, preventing transport for as long as one month. (Small trucks might still reach market by traveling south on the Agno Valley Road through Kabayan, but slides frequently block this road south of Buguias in the rainy season: see map 8, p. 187.) A slide on the Agno Valley Road north of Buguias is distressing, but farmers can still return to their old ways and carry produce to the Mountain Trail at Kilometer 73. A disruption of the Mountain Trail north of Kilometer 73 can actually benefit Buguias by blocking the market access of Lo-o, Mount Data, and other northern produce districts. And even what may appear to be the worst imaginable calamity can have positive attributes. Two fierce typhoons in 1989, for example, demolished the transport infrastructure throughout Benguet, but when lettuce hit 70 pesos a kilo and carrots topped 40, Buguias farmers chartered a helicopter to fly their produce to Baguio, profiting handsomely in the process.

The dry season is thus the time of relative quiescence, whereas the typhoon months are marked by unrelieved suspense. Although everyone endeavors to cultivate year-round, until the late 1970's, arid-season cropping was constrained by a lack of irrigation facilities. Accordingly, during these years the wet months formed the main cropping period. But the Buguias farmers have never shied away from the risks so entailed. Indeed, many have welcomed them, pinning their hopes not so much on steady income as on a jackpot. Their belief that the flow of luck is largely controllable promotes this attitude; the new economic realities only affirm traditional ideology on this score.

INSURANCE STRATEGIES

Buguias farmers employ several tactics in anticipating the vagaries of price. Some simply observe what crops others are planting, especially in the premier vegetable districts along the Mountain Trail, and then try to avoid whatever seems currently popular. But information is always too limited to make this strategy truly effective; only a fraction of Benguet's farms are visible from the road between Buguias and Baguio. Buguias farmers also watch the arrival of the first rains with great interest, since most Benguet gardeners depend on rainfall. If precipitation comes late, harming dry fields on the Mountain Trail, cabbage planted on Buguias's irrigated fields may be more remunerative than usual. Farmers even try to anticipate typhoons; if they foresee a large storm they will quickly harvest any relatively nonperishable crop, such as cabbage, and ship it forthwith to a storehouse in Baguio or Trinidad. If the typhoon indeed strikes, these prescient farmers will profit; if not, they will incur a loss, since their now-wilted cabbage will command a reduced price.

Many farmers would ideally cultivate a mix of crops in all seasons to spread their chances. But those with small gardens (0.2 hectares or less) have limited options. Wealthier growers are able to cultivate more diverse assemblages, and a few large growers living elsewhere in Buguias municipality even maintain widely separated garden plots located in different climatic zones—a strategy that provides calamity insurance without diminishing the possibility of a jackpot. Outside development experts have advised farmers to stagger their plantings even in individual fields to gain security against market drops (FAO 1984:22), but this practice has not spread to Buguias. Such serial plantings complicate labor scheduling, and, more importantly, they decrease the chance of superprofits.

Cropping strategies also vary because of partial specialization. Each crop requires specific techniques that are unevenly known by different farmers. Some individuals devote more time than others to mastering the culture of demanding vegetables such as celery. These semispecialist growers hope to gather at least above-average yields, if not extraordinary profits. Crop periodicity adds still another dimension. Young farmers especially seek to maximize their jackpot chances by squeezing in as many crops as possible. By concentrating on fast-growing vegetables and by carefully timing seedbed planting and transplanting schedules, they can harvest four or even five crops from a single irrigated plot. Such frenetic work, however, discourages most farmers.

THE SPATIAL REORGANIZATION OF EXCHANGE

After its economic transformation as before, Buguias depended on trade for its livelihood. But whereas the community had once formed the hub of an essentially local circuit, it was now reduced to an outlying production zone for the national market. For centuries, Buguias had been tenuously linked to the international economy through the Suyoc gold trade; now it was directly dependent on global resource flows.

As the position of Buguias and neighboring communities shifted vis-à-vis larger economic structures, the spatial patterns of the local economy reformed. This process manifested itself, in part, in the emergence of distinct agricultural regions, one of which was coterminous with the territory of Buguias Village. But for local exchange, it was the road network, connecting the vegetable districts with the Baguio and Manila markets, that emerged as the organizing framework.

The Displacement of Buguias Central

The immediate postwar years saw the rapid rise of Buguias Junction (Kilometer 73 of the Mountain Trail) as the new trade center of the greater Buguias region. Before the Agno Valley Road reached Buguias in 1958, all local vegetables had to be ported to this site. A number of Buguias residents soon moved to Kilometer 73, both to farm and to take advantage of the emerging market. As commerce began to settle in place, the tradition of peripatetic trade withered.

On market days (Thursday and Sundays), those Buguias farmers with produce to sell would begin their strenuous hikes to the Mountain Trail hours before dawn, lighting their way with pine torches. The habitués of the market at Kilometer 73 included many others as well; since few Buguias traders now ventured into the cloud forest, its residents also began to trek to this emergent entrepôt.

As its marketplace grew, Buguias Junction displaced Buguias Village as the center of the regional meat trade. The Agno Valley no longer produced many animals, nor did its traders procure meat in the eastern oak woodlands. But demand persisted, even strengthening in times of high vegetable prices. The few Buguias residents who had purchased trucks for vegetable hauling now began to import animals directly from the lowlands. But within a few years, Ilocano entrepreneurs discovered this profitable trade, and before long lowlanders all but monopolized the transport of livestock.

The Rise of the North

Buguias Junction's ascendancy proved short-lived; by the 1960s exchange had jumped to other centers. Buguias itself reclaimed a minor commercial role as it gained road access and as the cloud-forest people began to hike to the village for their needs. But this did not last long either, since Buguias was soon far overshadowed by two new mercantile villages in the northern part of the municipality: Abatan and Bad-ayan.

Abatan, situated on the junction of the Mountain Trail, the Agno Valley Road, and the Mankayan-Cervantes Highway, had long been a natural market site. A few permanent businesses clustered around the crossroads in the prewar period, to be joined by several more following the armistice. But Abatan developed slowly. Some attribute its retarded growth to the arrogance of certain Lo-o baknangs who had established the first stores. These early merchants would reportedly intimidate any potential competitors, in some instances simply expelling them from town. Not until Northern Kankana-ey and Ilocano merchants arrived—people not so easily bullied—did Abatan flourish. The northern traders first dickered in a new periodic market, but gradually a number of them constructed permanent stores. By the early 1970s, Abatan reigned as the premier trade depot of northern Benguet and as the new *de facto* seat of the Buguias municipal government.

Lo-o, only a few kilometers east of Abatan, did not suffer as the latter town rose. Rather, the two communities were close enough to form something of a single trade hub, and a number of small businesses also emerged in central Lo-o. Lo-o also benefitted from its thriving agricultural high school and from the Buguias Town Fiesta, celebrated annually on the school grounds.

Bad-ayan, while never rivaling Abatan, gradually emerged as the second trade center of the Buguias region. Exchange gravitated here during the early 1950s, when Bad-ayan marked the terminus of the Agno Valley Road, and it expanded when a periodic market was established in 1957. Permanent stores were soon built by Bad-ayan residents, and two of them evolved into fully stocked agricultural supply houses. By the 1960s, road extensions to the east gave the village a growing hinterland of its own. Now Bad-ayan was the most accessible town to the cloud forest of western Ifugao province.

Gradually a stable periodic market system developed, linking the various old and new commercial centers of northern Benguet. David Ruppert (1979) discovered in the 1970s that just over half of the market vendors in Abatan were Igorots (mainly Northern Kankana-ey), the others being largely Ilocanos and Pangasinanes. Virtually all were women. By the mid-1980s, many vendors rotated

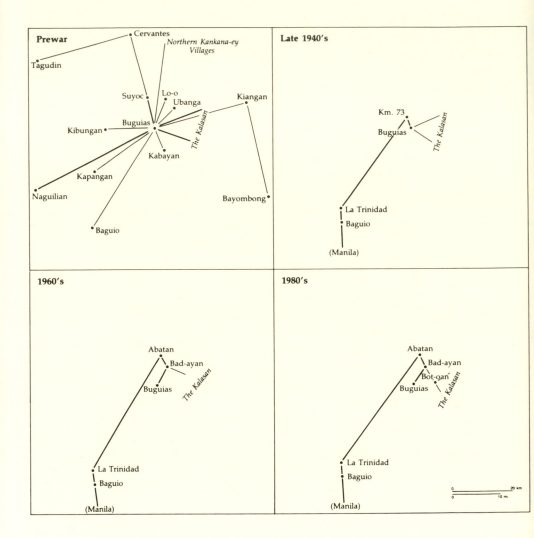

Map 7.   *The Changing Spatial Structure of Buguias Trade.*

from Lo-o on Wednesdays, to Bad-ayan on Thursdays, to Abatan on Fridays and Saturdays, and finally to Mankayan on Sundays before journeying to Baguio or even Manila to purchase new supplies.

THE MARKET IN BUGUIAS CENTRAL

When the Agno Valley Road was finally pushed south to Buguias, local trade temporarily revived. Thursdays and Sundays were designated market and produce-shipping days; vegetable traders would then drive their large trucks to the center of town, where they would be greeted by growers descending from the surrounding farmlands with their harvests. After selling their vegetables, farmers would shop in the periodic market and in the half-dozen or so permanent stores that had recently opened. But the shops of Buguias offered fewer goods at higher prices than their rivals in the northern towns, and the market was a local affair, unable to attract the professional peripatetic vendors.

When marketing innovations in the 1970s permitted farmers to ship their vegetables on any day of the week, the Buguias market withered to virtual extinction. Most farmers continued to devote Sundays and sometimes Thursdays to socializing in the center of town, but by the mid-1980s only a single used-clothing trader offered any substantial goods in the marketplace.

CONNECTIONS WITH THE GLOBAL ECONOMY

The Benguet vegetable farmers became entangled in the world economy not primarily as producers for a global market, but rather as consumers of agricultural supplies produced in the metropolitan states. Certainly international economic ties are implicated in vegetables sales—the tourist hotels of Manila and the American military bases are large and steady produce customers—but little is exported. By contrast, most of the industry's inputs are imported. Russell (1983) has argued persuasively that the companies supplying these goods extract a substantial surplus from the vegetable growers.

The transport systems of economically subservient regions often assume a dendritic pattern, in which roads effectively channel resources from the interior to an export entrepôt without developing corresponding internal connections (see C. Smith 1976). Benguet is no exception. Here too a dendritic pattern is readily discerned in the still-developing road network. Internal transport remains tortuous, for almost all trunk and feeder routes culminate in Baguio, from which point a busy highway leads directly to Manila.

The agricultural inputs employed by the Benguet farmers fit into three major categories: fertilizers, biocides, and seeds. Each developed its own pattern of supply and distribution, in which one can trace the global geographic patterns underlying the vegetable industry. As of the later 1980s, Benguet is linked to all of the world's centers of economic strength, including several emergent ones.

Approximately 40 percent of the typical farmer's fertilizer budget goes to chicken manure. This input is domestic, produced on poultry farms in central Luzon. Tagalog merchants truck manure into the mountains, often delivering it (sometimes on their backs) to very remote locales. Chemical fertilizers are of two major kinds: ammonium sulfate, providing nitrogen, and so-called complete, a balanced plant food. Although the Philippine government has made efforts to foster a domestic fertilizer industry, most supplies are imported. At present, the largest suppliers, especially of ammonium sulfate, are Taiwan and South Korea.

Biocides (including insecticides, fungicides, and herbicides) are largely manufactured offshore by multinational corporations. As of 1986, four companies predominated, two German (Hoescht and Bayer), one Anglo-Dutch (Shell), and one American (Union Carbide). While their products are sold by local distributors, these companies maintain a strong presence in the vegetable industry, particularly through their advertisements and other competitive activities.

In the early days of vegetable growing, American companies supplied most seeds. Gradually they have been supplanted by Japanese competitors; today only lettuce seeds are routinely imported from the United States. Seed potatoes have been generally procured from western Europe, but local supplies (developed largely by a Philippine-German cooperative project on the slopes of Mount Data) are becoming increasingly available. Quality seed procurement has long been a bane of the Benguet farmer. The demand for seeds of early maturing cultivars especially is often unsatisfied (FAO 1984). Moreover, several Buguias farmers complain that they cannot grow several potentially profitable crops, such as scalloped squash, because they are simply unable to obtain seeds.

The multinational agrochemical companies dispense much self-serving information to Benguet farmers through their field agents. Indeed, these agents, rather than government extension personnel, are the main source of new technical information (Medina n.d.:2). Many, if not most, company operatives are local residents, usually graduates of the agricultural college in Trinidad. These agents organize meetings for growers when they have a new chemical to sell, selecting "demonstration farmers" who receive the product free in exchange for cultivating "test plots." The typical recipient is a successful farmer who possesses an easily visible roadside garden. Other farmers then inspect the experiment to judge whether the new input is worthwhile.

Such advertisements often prove successful for the sponsor. Farmers use substantial quantities of chemicals, although applications have decreased somewhat since the crisis of the early 1970s. Previously, many growers used biocides prophylactically and to great excess (Medina n.d.:2). But despite the recent decline, the spraying of biocides is incessant, and the environmental and medical consequences appalling.

In short, the postwar transformation both reordered Buguias's agrarian ecology and repositioned the community within the global economy. In so doing, it undermined the old bases of social hierarchy: pastoralism and Cordilleran trade. But at the same time, the new order presented abundant opportunities for the elite—both old and new—to (re)assert dominance. Here one may find both striking discontinuities between the prewar and the postwar eras and profound carryovers as well.

1. *Headman of Buguias, 1901.* Courtesy, Worcester Collection, University of Michigan. *Themeda* pasture is visible in the background, with scattered young pines in the higher areas. On the far left, several fence lines may be distinguished.

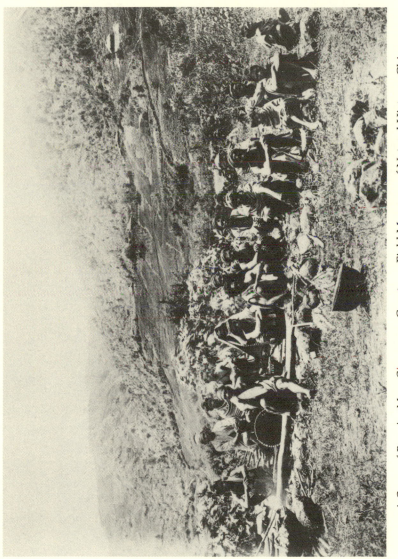

2. *A Group of Buguias Men, Circa 1900.* Courtesy, Field Museum of Natural History, Chicago. Intensively cultivated *uma* fields, stone walls, and small houselot gardens are visible in the background.

3. *Puwal Cultivation, Circa 1900.* (Originally titled "Igorots breaking ground with pointed sticks, Baguio, Benguet.") Courtesy, Worcester Collection, University of Michigan.

4. *Southern Cordilleran Traders, Circa 1900.* (Originally titled "Igorot carriers on the trail.") Courtesy, Field Museum of Natural History, Chicago. These merchants have likely just returned from the lowlands, where they would have purchased the dogs. In Buguias, women seldom joined such expeditions.

5. *Buguias Village in 1986.* Only the central part of the community is visible.

6. *Sloped Fields and Pine Forests near Buguias, 1986.* This area, just south of the village, has experienced rapid field expansion and forest retraction in recent years. Note the roadway in the foreground.

7. *Carrot Harvest, Buguias 1986.*

8. *Bulldozing "Mega-Terraces," East of Buguías, 1986.* The bulldozer cuts deeply into the subsoil, a nutrient-poor but friable material that will make an adequate cropping medium once fertilizers are applied.

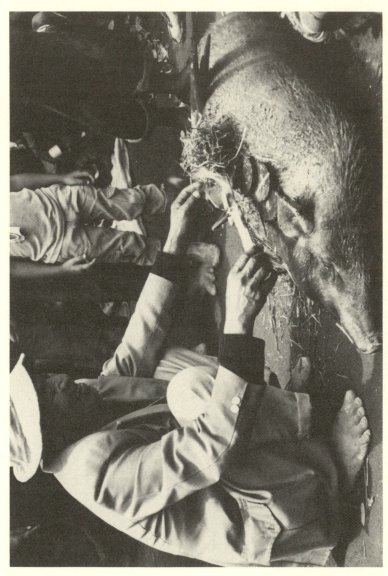

9. *Manbunung (Pagan Priest) and Sacrificial Hog, Buguias 1985.* The blood-soaked taro slices on the animal's back symbolize cash.

10. *Ritual Dancing in Buguias, 1985.* Wearing a death shroud, the dancer is performing in the stead of one of his ancestors.

7

The Sociology and Economics
of Vegetable Production, 1946–1972

INTRODUCTION

The postwar agrarian transition reformulated social relations in
Buguias. In the old days, commoners acquired livestock from their
wealthy confreres by entering a pastol contract. When these same
commoners switched to vegetable growing after the war, their capital requirements ballooned. Now they needed cash both to purchase agricultural inputs and increasingly to buy subsistence goods
imported from the lowlands. To meet this demand, new forms of
credit emerged to take their place alongside the old.

Labor recruitment was also transformed in the poastwar period.
Previously, most commoners had relied largely on family labor,
augmented with reciprocal labor exchange (ogbo) for the occasional heavy task. The elite, for their part, could also entice workers through the payment of meat (dangas). After the war, the bases
of both ogbo and dangas eroded. Commoners now found themselves needing additional hands regularly, but no longer could
they readily promise their own labor in return. For related reasons,
the elite found their meat offerings inadequate to attract as many
workers as they required. Both parties now had to pay cash wages.

Class and gender relations in Buguias responded to the new
economy's pressures with subtle and overt adjustments. The preexisting class structure, although temporarily upset, soon restabi-
lized more or less as before, with one critical difference: for the first
time, a handful of regional vegetable merchants and farmers tran-
scended the local economy and established themselves as provincial elites. Relations between the sexes changed even more dramatically. In the new economy, women and men suddenly carried
the same tools and toiled at the same jobs. Moreover, a small set of
women traders emerged as wealthy entrepreneurs, an unprecedented development.

RESTRUCTURED SOCIAL RELATIONS

CLASS STRATIFICATION

The postwar economic transformation initially acted to level class positions in Buguias, but the old system of stratification was soon reestablished, albeit in modified form. In the early years, vegetable growing presented an economic opportunity for the common people unmatched in earlier days. The local baknangs continued to seek laborers in the traditional dangas fashion, but as the going wage increased, their attempts were increasingly frustrated. In response, real wages paid for agricultural and pastoral work doubled in a few years. But despite the higher potential wages, most commoners now wished to act independently of the elite, and the very term *baknang* began to carry pejorative connotations in some quarters.

Yet Buguias remained a stratified society. Immediately following the war, many wealthy families coasted on paybacks for loans they had extended before the conflict began; others exhumed the cash reserves they had buried before the final devastation. More importantly, a handful of families retained ownership of most terraces, and if they were slow to plant them to cabbage, they were quick to lease them to willing experimentalists. By the second postwar decade, the elite had discovered the profitability of farming their own extensive and well-watered lands for themselves. Meanwhile, the Buguias baknangs continued to lend money, usually at 5 percent interest per month, allowing them to reap an additional harvest from the vegetable boom. Berto and Apisa Cubangay even managed to perform a *second* pedit at the stratospheric level of "25" in the late 1940s. But after Berto's death in 1951, there were no longer any true baknangs in Buguias. But the vegetable economy continued to present opportunities for accumulation, and by the late 1960s a new group of wealthy people, primarily from nonbaknang lineages, had arisen.

This scenario was played out only in Buguias proper. The traditional Lo-o elites maintained and even augmented their positions by leasing their extensive terraces to Chinese entrepreneurs and by establishing businesses in Abatan. In contrast, the new communities of the Mountain Trail, having no traditional elite class, experienced *de novo* stratification. There the most successful farmers

rapidly amassed money and land, soon joining the Chinese planters in the local "aristocracy." In some areas the first migrants were
able to assume the position of "lead family," but continued success
depended on access to capital, usually through family connections
in the valley communities.

LIVING STANDARDS

By the 1960s, the lot of the average person in Buguias had improved markedly from prewar standards. People recall this melio-
ration primarily in terms of diet. With the rise of market gardening,
lowland rice became a staple food, while sweet potatoes were demoted to a supplementary position. Now the common farmer could
also purchase dried fish, an occasional tin of meat or seafood, dis-
tilled liquor, and kerosene for cooking and lighting. Clothing and
housing standards also improved; most couples replaced their
thatch roofs with galvanized iron sheets, which, although unap-
pealing to the (Western) eye, are locally regarded as far superior to
thatch.

But the populace did not share equally in this new bounty. Some
had inadequate lands to support their often sizable families in the
new style. The poorest fifth of the population could not afford
boiled rice as their mainstay; instead they subsisted on a watery
rice gruel supplemented with sweet potatoes. But as before, the
poor received community subsidies; they ate high-quality food at
communal feasts, they could gather fruit on the waysides, and now
they could glean the remains of harvested vegetable fields.

Many of the wealthier couples continued to live in much the
same style as their poorer contemporaries. As before the war, they
devoted the bulk of their riches to religious ceremonies. But the
very rich—those who traded vegetables on a large scale—rose to a
new level of consumption. Several couples built large, modern
houses in both Buguias and Trinidad, filling them with a variety of
consumer goods.

Despite the common academic notion of "subsistence affluence"
(Sahlins 1972) giving way to "commercial deprivation" in the global
periphery, the rise in living standards that accompanied agricultural commercialization in Buguias is paralleled in many other peripheral societies. While many scholars still hold to a view that

William Clarke (1988) has felicitously labeled "edenism" (a recurrent myth, once popularized by Rousseau and later spread with the countercultural impulse of the 1960s), it is now clear that many subsistence economies were anything but prosperous. As Dennett and Connell (1988:281) say of one group of New Guinea highlanders, "They have no wish to retreat to the 'subsistence affluence' and nobility that have sometimes been thrust upon their ancestors." Whatever the costs of commercialization have been, the Buguias people unanimously voice the same sentiments.

Gender Relations

More permanent than changes in class structure was the postwar transformation of gender relations. Before the war, most agricultural tasks were strictly segregated by sex. Although husbands and wives occasionally worked together, women usually toiled in the dry fields while men tended livestock and conducted trade. Moreover, each gender previously possessed its own distinctive tool kit, although there was little stigma attached to, and sometimes even genuine admiration for, individuals competent in using the implements of the other sex. But the tasks of vegetable gardening were never divided by sex. True, most men continue to avoid tedious tasks, such as weeding, in preference for more strenuous chores, but such choices have devolved into family matters, no longer arbitrated by cultural expectations.

Vegetable trading allowed for a different restructuring of gender roles by opening a new window on the larger world. One of the central jobs of vegetable trading, namely vehicle driving and maintenance, remained firmly in the male domain. But this is a special assignment that few men ever hold. Of much greater consequence was the opening of trade itself to women. Before the war, women had conducted local barter, but none engaged in professional long-distance commerce. Yet by the 1960s, women came to dominate the much-enlarged retail sector in Buguias, while several female traders reached the highest level of prominence in the profitable vegetable business. Although these merchants have generally worked with their husbands, in several notable cases it is no secret that the genius lies on the distaff side.

Before the war, women had worked extremely long hours, while men had enjoyed relative leisure. This too changed in the reconstruction; vegetable culture demanded continual applications of labor, much of which could only be drawn from men. In the vegetable economy, most Buguias residents agree, men toil in the fields just as hard as women do. But women still work longer hours, since they are also responsible for more domestic tasks. Moreover, fathers no longer supply the childcare they once did; children now are likely to be taken into the fields, or entrusted to an older sibling, cousin, or grandparent.

One could argue that the rise of female-run businesses reflects not so much a change in gender relations as a reconfiguration of economic spheres that elevated the traditional female activities to a higher level. Women had always bartered vegetables; now the vegetable trade was the community's economic pivot. Yet other indicators suggest a more fundamental transformation. For the first time, for instance, a few women entered the animal trade—just before the entire endeavor vanished. More significantly, women could now aspire to political office. Although this has yet to occur in Buguias, in 1986 the barangay, or village, leader of Suyoc, as of several other Benguet villages, was a woman.

Beyond a doubt, the men of Buguias still control the community, continuing to dominate the tong tongan and other political forums. Women are also still socially constrained; Bridget Hamada-Pawid (personal communication) argues that in all of the Cordillera, only among the Ifugao do women drink, gamble, and socialize freely with their male peers. Nor can women in Buguias hold the high offices of religious authority, those of manbunung and mankotom. But overall, the position of women is undoubtedly higher than it had been in the prewar period.

CAPITAL AND LABOR

In the early postwar years, virtually all Buguias residents made tax declarations on their vegetable fields. Land availability was no problem; in fact, arable land was more abundant than before, now that light soils could be cultivated. Nor did the average farmer suffer labor constraints. Family workers sufficed for most tasks, and in the few bottleneck periods, such as time of harvest, neighbors would usually assist. Since growers now planted on different schedules, no longer were there periods of concentrated work throughout Buguias. But if land and labor were reasonably abundant, capital was scarce. And in the new economy, capital had become vital.

SOURCES OF CAPITAL

Throughout the postwar period, most young couples have been strained to purchase the seeds, fertilizers, and biocides needed for a successful farming venture. Many turn to their wealthier neighbors and relatives, or to vegetable traders, to acquire a stake. In the usual arrangement, called "supply," the backer purchases all inputs and the borrower provides all labor with net profits divided equally. A typical supply contract covers only a single crop cycle; the financing of the next planting depends on the success of the first. A single highly profitable harvest can often cover the expenses of the subsequent crop, provided the increase is not set aside for a feast. A low price at harvest, however, can force the laboring couple to negotiate a new supply agreement, and perhaps even to borrow extra money to purchase necessities before the next crop is due.

Caught between price fluctuations and religious obligations, most farmers have fallen deeply into debt. If desperate, they can "mortgage" their land in a *salda* arrangement. As Davis (1973:60) explains, salda differs from the Western mortgage in that the borrower theoretically loses claim to the land until he or she repays the principal. In actuality, the original holder usually retains control in exchange for a share, often one-fifth, of the harvest. After a stipulated period elapses, the borrowing couple can retain ownership only if they pay off the interest and the principal. If they default, as was not uncommon during the early vegetable-growing years, the land passes permanently to the creditor. Again, the original owners may still cultivate it, but now as outright sharecroppers. A "bankrupt" couple wishing to avoid sharecropping can declare and clear new lands, but this is an expensive, labor-consuming ordeal—and increasingly so as the more accessible lands have been progressively claimed.

As virgin land grew scarce in the 1960s and 1970s, the practice of salda declined; few farmers now wished to risk their properties. Still, during emergencies (often religious), this could be a poor couple's sole recourse. On a ritual occasion, a parcel might be mortgaged, not for money but for sacrificial livestock.

Most vegetable dealers have long doubled as agricultural input suppliers, advancing fertilizers and biocides to cash-short farmers in exchange for a guaranteed sale of the prospective crop *at a discount.* Such deals are often extended, since a poor market at harvest time can quickly send the farmer deeper into debt. Dealers find this consistent with their own interests as well; it ensures them a steady supply of vegetables, and they can always recoup some of their losses through the discounts they receive. The farmers also benefit from the perennial refinancing that does not jeopardize their lands. Davis (1973:208, 209) finds this system mutualistic, as it provides both parties with a measure of security in a capricious business, while Russell (1987) counters that it allows the trader to control the relationship to his or her own benefit. Vigorous disputes do arise when a farmer, encumbered with years of outstanding debt, suddenly dies. In this eventuality, the vegetable dealer might try to collect from the heirs, who in turn may argue that these matters should have been settled years earlier and that the dealer deserves a loss for letting the debt persist indefinitely. Such arguments can only be settled on an individual basis in *tong tongan* deliberations.

Two additional sources of capital emerged in the late 1960s. The first, local credit cooperatives, played a relatively minor role. The second, a government-backed program of bank loans, proved almost revolutionary. The land boom it precipitated, as well as the subsequent vegetable bust, will be discussed in chapter 8.

SHARECROPPING

Even though most farmers in Buguias own land, many have inadequate holdings. Land-hungry couples usually look to sharecrop subsidiary plots owned by neighbors and relatives. As a general rule, poorer families sharecrop the fields of wealthier villagers, but household demographics as well as temporary turns of luck also influence tenancy arrangements. Young couples with many children often take on the fields of others, only to graduate from sharecropping later in life. If their children leave Buguias, such a couple might even find themselves with a surfeit of cropland. On a shorter time scale, two households can experience widely divergent fortunes depending on their cropping strategies; a couple might let out some of its land to sharecroppers in one year, only to lose some of its own fields (through salda) the next and be forced itself into sharecropping.

Unlike other villages in the region, Buguias Central has not had a single family that has been able to accumulate such expansive tracts of land as to necessitate the extensive use of sharecropper labor. Those couples who garnered great wealth preferred investments other than Buguias land. In Buguias, tenancy and labor arrangements most often link farmers who, despite disparities of wealth, are essentially of the same social class, and often closely related as well.

The population of Buguias mounted rapidly during the postwar period. As the inner village became increasingly crowded, many young couples chose to clear new lands on the higher slopes east of town. Relying at first on a "supply" sponsor, the fates of these gardeners depended on their luck at market, their farming strategies, and their ceremonial expenditures. But farming in any remote area presents heavy demands, since even after the plots are cleared, both supplies and vegetables have to be ported to and from the road. Many young adults therefore have preferred to relocate on the Mountain Trail where they can work as sharecroppers for large-scale growers. Most hope to return eventually and acquire land in Buguias, a reasonable expectation only if they harvest a jackpot crop.

WAGE AND COOPERATIVE LABOR

Even farmers cultivating modest plots often hire wage labor at harvest time. Growers rush their harvests, especially if prices are high and the crops perishable. Most farmers turn to neighbors and relatives with a loose expectation of eventual reciprocation. Wage agreements actually came to be preferred over work exchanges since the implied finality leaves both parties free from future commitments that could conflict with their own schedules. Of course, poorer couples disproportionally rely on wage work, especially after opportunities diminished in the 1970s and 1980s. Nevertheless, wages in Buguias have remained much higher than those along the Mountain Trail, in part because no outside workers (Ilocanos and Northern Kankana-eys) lodge here. In 1986, when a full day's labor earned 15 to 20 pesos in Natubleng, workers in Buguias could earn as much as 35 pesos.

One specialized task has been particularly well rewarded with cash, namely the portage of vegetables from field to road. This job requires great strength and stamina, and is usually undertaken by adolescent boys and young men. Growers pay by weight and distance, with some variation for competitive bidding. Those strong enough to carry a number of sacks in quick succession receive ample rewards, and the best can reportedly earn 75 pesos in less than a full day.

Traditional labor exchange, ogbo, has rarely been applied to vegetable harvesting. Davis (1973:58) argues that hired labor is more efficient, a reasonable position considering the complex individual schedules that would have to be meshed as different growers reach hurried decisions on harvesting dates. Voss (1980) sees informal reciprocity in wage-labor agreements and argues that it is a modified form of labor exchange. This view is reasonable when applied to the few remote villages east of Buguias that have formed a semicooperative system of wage-labor exchange to bypass what would be excessive levies for vegetable portage.

Pure labor exchange does persist in select situations. Ogbo is still applied, for example, to the non-urgent but laborious task of new field preparation. Cooperative work parties are also organized along village or hamlet lines for road and trail maintenance, and for the construction of new traditional-style houses. And finally, irrigation system maintenance is performed jointly by all water recipients. Dangas, the prewar system of meat and beer "wages," also survives in attenuated form. Today farmers occasionally hire young men to clear brush or perform other heavy tasks in exchange for meat (often a cow's head) and—equally essential—San Miguel gin.

The clearing of new fields can be accomplished through one's own painstaking labor, through ogbo, or through dangas, but the more prosperous farmers usually hire outsiders on a contract basis. As in the old days, Kalanguya men predominate. Prosperous Buguias growers also commission contract workers to build new terraces, to saw boards, and to perform other skilled or tedious jobs. The worker's daily emolument depends on his rapidity of work, but it often reaches nearly twice the average daily wage. Contention not uncommonly erupts, however, as contract laborers are tempted to rush through their tasks, leading many employers to complain about the quality of the finished work.

LABOR AND CREDIT ELSEWHERE IN BUGUIAS MUNICIPALITY

Along the Mountain Trail, in Lo-o, and in Bad-ayan, very different linkages between labor and capital have developed. In these areas, a small number of large-scale farmers, many of whom also sell inputs and deal in vegetables, came to dominate their communities. Such growers have managed to raise considerable capital on their own, and many acquired finesse in tapping governmental and other exterior sources. Large-scale farmers have always secured bank loans more readily than have small-scale growers (Russell 1983:96), and the Chinese among them have enjoyed ample financing through their far-flung ethnic networks.

Along the Mountain Trail, in Lo-o, and in Bad-ayan, poor Ilocanos and migrant Igorots (from beyond the vegetable frontier), anxious for even exiguous wages, have provided inexpensive labor. Farmers in these areas accordingly devote only a small percentage of their outlays to their workers; C. DeRaedt estimates that labor accounts for only 15 percent of the average Sayangan farmer's production costs (1983:11), while an FAO report concurs that labor is the least costly "input" for the large agricultural holdings along the Mountain Trail (1984:21).

THE VEGETABLE TRADE

THE EARLY VEGETABLE TRADERS

As discussed earlier, one Buguias entrepreneur, Pokol, traded vegetables before the war. Pokol died in the conflict, but after liberation several young men of moderate circumstances emulated his career. Purchasing produce both at Kilometer 73 and from small farmers along the Mountain Trail, they transported it at first on buses or in rented truck space to Baguio where they could sell it to Chinese agents.

The most successful of the early postwar vegetable traders, Hilary Camas, soon hired several "commissioners," underlings who would haggle deals with individual farmers. This position served as a stepping-stone for a new set of dealers. One of them, Ernesto Simion, first transported vegetables on the tops of lumber trucks headed to Baguio from the sawmill at Mount Data. Soon, Simion was leasing trucks to haul larger loads. As his business grew his attention shifted to Trinidad, where he contracted to build housing units and warehouses for vegetables. In Buguias, Simion employed subordinates to handle the vegetable trade; several eventually graduated to the position of independent dealer.

Bisna and Stafin Olsim

One of Simion's protégés, Bisna Olsim, eventually surpassed all other vegetable traders of Buguias. Mrs. Olsim was born to a poor couple and was fatherless from an early age. In 1956 she married into a relatively well-off family, but her husband, Stafin Olsim, sojourned through the early years of their marriage as a gold miner in Mindanao. After learning the vegetable trade from Simion and others, Bisna established her own "buy and sell" business. She received some help from family members, who, by her own account, pitied her for being without a father or, temporarily, a husband. Stafin's uncle lent her a truck at favorable rates, and other relatives provided vegetables to her on consignment.

By the time her husband returned, Bisna had saved a respectable sum and had purchased, on credit, a large truck. This proved to be a timely investment; as the FACOMAs collapsed, new opportunities arose for local transporters. Between 1965 and 1970 the Olsims' ascent was meteoric. Soon they needed better market access, which they attained by purchasing property and building a house and storage facility in Trinidad. Twice a week they would now make the six- to eight-hour drive to Buguias to buy vegetables, returning to Trinidad the following day.

By the mid-1970s the Olsims began to ease out of the vegetable trade and to experiment with new lines of business. Several endeavors were not successful. For a number of years they owned and managed a bus company, but the high cost of repairs and the formidable competition from Dangwa Tranco proved discouraging. Similarly, a supply store in Buguias could not compete against the independent traders and the large supply stores of Bad-ayan and Abatan. But the Olsims' other dealings have more than compensated for these losses. Several land investments in Trinidad proved quite remunerative, and by the 1980s a road contracting business brought excellent returns. They are now fully established as the one truly wealthy family of Buguias—an identity they cultivate despite spending most of their time in the provincial capital.

The other Buguias vegetable traders were less fortunate. Although several attained prosperity, few have approached, and none has maintained, true baknang status. Several suffered business calamities, commonly the loss of a truck or two over a Mountain Trail precipice. Another followed the Olsims in running a bus company, but two disastrous crashes in the 1980s brought financial ruin. Several found misadventure in gambling, usually in the Baguio casino.

Ritual practice has been a two-edged sword in the rise and fall of prominent Buguias families. In one story, often repeated by Buguias Christians, a certain trader's decline appears to have been accelerated by ritual; after each setback he conducted elaborate propitiatory rites, which further consumed his dwindling resources. Those who practice the traditional religion, however, counter by pointing to other instances where a family's imminent downfall was averted, they say, precisely by staging the proper ceremonies.

THE PRACTICE OF VEGETABLE TRADING

Vegetable trading in Benguet has taken on many forms, confounding generalizations. Individuals holding a small business operate differently from those with larger concerns, while those who continue to farm face different economic circumstances from those who do nothing but trade. Russell (1983:91) suggests a clear-cut taxonomy of Benguet produce traders: the full-time trader is an agent, the farmer-trader is a dealer, the trader who does not own a vehicle is a buy-and-sell, and persons who rent vehicles to traders are transporters. In Buguias, however, these distinctions are not clearly developed. Until recently, most persons working in vegetable commerce were full-time traders. Because conditions changed markedly after the crisis of the mid-1970s, when smaller vehicles became available, the following discussion focuses on the practices of the full-time vegetable agents as they existed in the heyday of the 1960s.

To prosper in the vegetable business, a trader must keenly forecast price trends and competently manage credits and debts. The ambitious trader must also master the exacting practice of *pakyao*, or the advance purchase of unharvested crops. If prices are high, or if the trader anticipates a sharp rise, he or she may wish to secure a large future supply. Growers are often amenable, as they may be anxious to obtain cash as early as possible, declining to speculate on the possibility of a future price upswing. To profit on such a deal, the trader must accurately assess the future yield of a given field. And even if the prediction of the harvest volume should prove accurate, the trader could still be crushed if the market were to fall in the interim.

Other hazards can also sink the unwary trader. The vegetable business can be very competitive (despite the fact that farmers are often beholden to specific traders), and it offers thin profit margins. Furthermore, growers do not always repay their debts. Vegetable trading is a social endeavor, and successful agents must maintain good relations with employees, buyers, and sellers (see Anderson 1969). They must also maintain their vehicles against the grinding wear of the rough mountain roads. Fortitude is equally vital; when prices are high, dealers and their crews must work feverishly, often forgoing sleep for several days.

The advance purchase system, and vegetable trading in general, can generate enmity between farmers and dealers. An unscrupulous grower, for example, might resell a standing crop for which he or she has already received payment. A dealer, in contrast, may take advantage of a consignment sale by remitting to the farmer less money than promised, justifying the action through reference to a lowered price or to spoilage. Davis (1973) argues that such potential discord reinforces the tendency for dealer-farmer connections to develop along kinship lines. In Buguias, the deeply embedded genealogical and "co-villager" relationships extending throughout the community have to a great extent safeguarded against these corrupting tendencies.

Since the 1960s and early 1970s, large-scale vegetable traders from Buguias have sent produce to their own storehouses in Trinidad, from which they can sell directly to the Chinese (and, increasingly, Tagalog) merchants who control the Baguio-Manila trade. Smaller traders have usually sold directly in the wholesale section ("New Market") of the Baguio market. The largely Igorot wholesalers of the New Market, numbering some 350 to 400 (Russell 1987:142, 143), offer competitive bids on incoming produce. After cleaning and sorting the produce, they sell it to Chinese or Tagalog traders, who then ship large truckloads to their marketing agents in Divisoria, the vegetable emporium of Manila.

A few of the large agribusiness concerns in the greater Buguias region presently ship vegetables directly to Manila. This requires both a dependable supply of vegetables and a fleet of large trucks. But even those who transport their own vegetables to the capital still have to deal through Chinese middlemen. One wealthy Bad-ayan family, for example, sells produce to their Manila partner for a price somewhere between the Baguio and the Manila wholesale figures. Many large-scale farmer-traders do not find these marginally superior prices worth the effort, and thus continue to deal in Baguio. Several powerful traders, including the Olsims, have attempted to eliminate another rung of intermediaries by acquiring a wholesale stall in the Divisoria market, but so far all such attempts have failed. Most highland observers attribute their ill success to the machinations of Chinese "cartels."

Agribusiness Reconsidered

The most successful indigenous entrepreneurs in Buguias municipality have been those who have integrated farming, trading, and input sales. A prime example is the Maliones family of Bad-ayan. Mrs. Maliones began her career shortly after the war by cultivating a few experimental cabbage patches on soils that local residents had regarded as sterile and worthless, and by selling fertilizer out of a tiny shack. Since then her fields and her sales have expanded continuously. By the 1970s she owned several large trucks suitable for hauling produce directly to Manila, had purchased additional lands on the Mountain Trail, was developing commercial property in Trinidad, and managed one of the best-stocked input and hardware stores in Benguet.

Successful business people like Mrs. Maliones have in many respects been able to thrive precisely because of earlier successes in gardening. Big farmers with integrated concerns enjoy economies of scale, just as they are buffered from economic and natural disasters. Indeed, one study (Lizarondo *et al.* 1979) has shown a direct relationship between the size of a farm and the profit per unit area that the grower can realize. This advantage is amplified when one also considers the other aspects of vegetable agribusiness pursued by most large-scale farmers.

Yet in Buguias proper, no large agricultural combine has emerged. While the Olsims' businesses have grown, they have not invested in Buguias agriculture. This is partly because they have seen few opportunities in a district characterized by small owner-occupied farms; yet their very decision to invest elsewhere has contributed to the divergent social and economic evolution of the village. Some locals regret the absence of big growers in Buguias, feeling that this has redounded to the economic marginalization of their once-central place. But while the Olsims have located most of their endeavors in other areas, they nonetheless continue to play prominent roles in the political and ritual life of their natal community. And considering the environmental and social problems that have increasingly impinged upon the Buguias landscape in the past two decades, the Olsims' decision to invest their profits elsewhere may well prove to have been prescient.

8

Economic and Ecological Crisis

INTRODUCTION

The health of the Benguet vegetable economy in the 1950s and 1960s masked an underlying environmental deterioration. Soil erosion and exhaustion, water-table depletion, deforestation, and pesticide contamination threatened the sustainability of commercial agriculture from the beginning. During periods of prosperity such problems were not apparent, as nutrient subsidies and imported substitutes allowed continued expansion. But when the vegetable industry suffered a partial collapse in the mid-1970s, environmental degradation began to form an economic constraint. Unable to obtain adequate supplies of commercial fertilizers, farmers could not easily coax crops from the depleted soils. Furthermore, the economic trauma deepened the ecological wound; when the price of petroleum-based fuels suddenly exceeded the means of most farmers, deforestation accelerated.

The Benguet farmers have not, however, merely allowed themselves to be buffeted by adverse economic winds, nor have they succumbed to environmental calamities. Rather, they have responded with a series of innovations, permitting them to continue farming, and, in some instances, to prosper. In the language of human ecology, they have adapted to their precarious condition through continual readaptation, based on opportunistic responses to ever-changing circumstances. But their very solutions have sometimes made matters worse. A few well-off growers, for example, have derived great profits in clearing the high-elevation eastern oak forests, but in so doing they have diminished the water supplies of many lower and older farm districts.

Environmental deterioration puts Benguet farmers in a wrenching bind. To survive they must jeopardize their futures. And with the national economy unable to absorb many rural migrants—at a time when local population is mounting rapidly—human pressure on the land lies heavier every year. And the growing ecological debacle should not be considered in human terms only. As chemically intensive agriculture expands, natural areas are diminishing and a number of species face extinction.

If one were to seek culprits, both wealthy agriculturalists and certain powerful government officials would have to be named. Large-scale farmers, both Chinese and Igorot, have financed the poorly graded roads and the wastefully bulldozed gardens in the cloud-forest highlands, while military and other high officials have underwritten the illegal clearing of the diminishing pine stands. But to lay all blame at the feet of these individuals would be to obfuscate larger social and economic processes. Almost all local residents approve highly of road and farm development in the cloud forest and they have consistently encouraged it. Most consider the responsible entrepreneurs as the *progresso* benefactors of the larger community. The denudation of the pine lands is also problematic; Cordilleran residents need fuel and construction lumber, and the profits made here help support a segment of the community.

The conjunction of economic movements and environmental effects presents a seemingly inescapable bind, a tragedy as classically defined. This becomes evident in studying government policy, where actions designed to abet the vegetable industry consistently exacerbate land degradation, while those formulated to protect the environment deepen the farmers' economic plight. As a result, official policies have been ineffectual at best, and occasionally calamitous.

Despite this gloomy prognosis, I am not ready to conclude that the Benguet farm economy is doomed. Nature is surprisingly forgiving; wildlife may be exterminated, but gardening will likely struggle along as farmers devise solutions to each new ecological impasse. And a more fundamental release, based on a complete agroecological reorientation, is not unimaginable. Some farmers are now experimentally cultivating tree crops in hopes that they might support a more economically secure and environmentally benign agriculture for the future. The success of this project, however, depends as much on the well-being of the Philippine economy as on the health of the trees; at present it is hard to say which looks more vulnerable.

BOOM, BUST, AND READJUSTMENT

Boom

In the mid-1960s, most observers agreed that the Benguet vegetable industry would continue to thrive. The Philippine economy was expanding, vegetable consumption was increasing, and the escalating American presence in Vietnam presented a new market. In 1964, the Mountain Province Development Authority (MPDA), an agency patterned after the TVA (Fry 1983:228), inaugurated its development program by declaring that vegetable production had not yet reached half of its potential. The MPDA leaders held up Benguet, with its market gardens, mines, lumber mills, and hydroelectric dams, as a model of economic growth for the rest of the Cordillera (MPDA 1964:5).

Because farm expansion was still thwarted by the scarcity of capital, development agents turned to new sources of funding. MPDA planners looked to government functionaries (especially those with the Development Bank of the Philippines) to facilitate new bank loans. As with other Benguet economic schemes, the goal was not merely to assist farmers but also to displace the Chinese, thus "nationalizing" the industry (*Baguio Midland Courier*, Oct. 9, 1966). In the late 1960s, many Buguias farmers were financing garden expansion through bank loans. Although collateral was necessary, a land claim—through title or tax declaration—proved sufficient. This prompted a minor land rush, as gardeners hurried to declare the remaining open lands in order to qualify for loans.

Development authorities also encouraged the forming of local credit unions, and by 1969 mutual loan associations emerged in both Buguias and Bad-ayan. Official rules limited loans to two times the amount of an individual's savings, and placed a cap of 3 percent on monthly interest payments. Through the early 1970s, these two credit unions operated successfully.

Bust

But the optimism of the late 1960s vanished rapidly in the early 1970s as the vegetable industry suffered two destructive blows: the imposition of martial law in 1972, and the energy crisis of

1973. Soon after assuming dictatorial powers, Ferdinand Marcos attacked Benguet's political leaders and seized the local news media. When oil prices skyrocketed the following year, the Manila government used its new powers to "guide" the country's agriculture through the crisis. Unfortunately for Benguet, it considered vegetable growing an expendable luxury. Fertilizer was now scarce, and authorities earmarked the available supplies for lowland rice and corn, attempting even to prevent delivery to the highlands (*Baguio Midland Courier* Nov. 25, 1973). The official view was that the world now faced a food crisis, and that the Benguet people should respond by cultivating sweet potatoes and other staples (*Baguio Midland Courier* Sept. 29, 1974).

The Benguet farmers, of course, continued to grow vegetables. Desperate for fertilizer, they soon resorted to extralegal methods of procurement. The leaders of the Buguias Credit Union were at one point arrested after returning from the lowlands with a truckload of ammonium sulfate; political opponents of the co-op leaders had evidently informed the local military.

The vegetable industry languished through 1974 and 1975. The state eventually allowed fertilizer sales, but supplies remained inadequate. Moreover, fewer persons in the cash-strapped Philippines could now afford temperate produce. On November 2, 1975, the *Baguio Midland Courier* reported that massive quantities of Buguias vegetables were rotting in the fields. Although many farmers blamed the industry's middlemen, some community leaders began to attribute their dilemma to state policy and international oil-market manipulations. Local government suffered too; by August 1975, the Benguet treasury had lost some 1,000,000 pesos of tax revenue (*Baguio Midland Courier* Aug. 29, 1975).

The vegetable industry also had to endure "crony capitalism," Marcos's practice of helping companies that supported his regime at the expense of businesses owned by individuals perceived as enemies. Thus the Philippine Planters Company, a quasicooperative that both manufactured and distributed agricultural inputs, nearly expired when it was ordered to deliver supplies below cost. The main beneficiary was the rival Philippine Phosphate Company, owned by a friend of the president.

The state did not entirely abandon the vegetable industry, however, and as the food scare abated it again devised new credit schemes. Development authorities futilely attempted to revive the marketing cooperatives, but most farmers now regarded any government meddling with suspicion. Once again, economic planners looked to bank loans. In 1974 the Development Bank of the Philippines put forward a new scheme by which groups of five farm families could receive credit in common, each household acting as a guarantor for the others (*Baguio Midland Courier* Sept. 22, 1974). And in 1976, the same bank established a branch in Abatan, further facilitating credit procurement in Buguias (*Baguio Midland Courier* Nov. 30, 1976).

But all such loan programs eventually failed. Even after the vegetable industry partially recovered, few farmers could pay their interest charges. When the banks threatened foreclosures, gardeners lobbied successfully for easier terms (*Baguio Midland Courier* Aug. 2, 1976). But this only delayed the reckoning; by the late 1970s, some 59 percent of loans to Benguet farmers were delinquent (Buasen 1981:22).

Ultimately, the inability of the Benguet farmers to repay their loans proved disastrous only for the lending institutions. Despite their powers of foreclosure, the banks could not recoup their losses. For delinquent loans secured with titled property, a bank theoretically could sell the land after the borrower had failed for a given period to make payments. In the resulting auctions, however, no one would offer adequate bids; in essence, the growers maintained solidarity against the outside financiers. Land titles thus passed to the banks as "acquired assets," but as assets of no utility. The banks could only hope that the original owner would eventually want to regain the title, necessary if he or she were to sell the parcel legally. But even here the borrowers held the advantage, since the original loans had been greatly devalued by inflation. The banks lobbied for a retroactive inflation index, but with no success.

By the end of the 1970s, official lending institutions refused to extend new credit to the average Benguet farmer, a person now considered an unacceptable risk. Wealthy growers still managed to qualify, but sometimes even they would first have to bribe the responsible loan officer.

The other new font of capital, the local credit unions, have had mixed histories. A few co-ops, notably Bad-ayan's, have continued to thrive, helping local farmers expand their fields and weather unfavorable markets. The Buguias Central Credit Union, however, crumbled in the mid-1970s. Some former members allege that its officials were too lax and disregarded loan regulations. By the 1980s, capital in Buguias was again scarce, and wealthy farmers and traders again reclaimed the financial structure of the local vegetable industry.

READJUSTMENTS

By the late 1970s the Benguet vegetable industry had only partly recovered. Input costs remained stubbornly high relative to the price of vegetables. Moreover, the entire Philippine economy had stagnated, and the market for temperate produce no longer expanded at its previous pace. Growers lived on thinner profits, and suffered losing seasons more frequently.

But a series of agricultural innovations ameliorated the beleaguered vegetable economy. In Buguias, several new crops, notably beets and summer squash, provided some farmers with healthy gains for a few seasons. Beet culture diffused in the late 1970s after a dealer discovered a small but unfilled culinary niche in the festive dishes of the Chinese New Year. Beets brought jackpot harvests for the early adopters, and they came to be the favored crop for a number of fields along Asinan ("salt") Creek that are too salt-impregnated for other vegetables. Summer squash first appeared in Buguias fields after a Chinese wholesaler advised a local dealer of a potential market. Growers soon discovered in squash an ideal crop for the warm months; planted in the early dry season it yields abundant fruit by March. Once the heavy rains arrive, however, the vines wither from fungus infestations. But zucchini squash remains a seasonally important crop in Buguias. Other nearby vegetable districts do not produce it; higher elevation areas, such as Lo-o and the Mountain Trail, are too cold, and farmers in Kabayan (according to Buguias sources) simply do not realize the value of this crop.

Improvements in irrigation technology overshadowed the introduction of new vegetables. In the late 1970s, Benguet farmers discovered that they could efficiently transport water in garden hoses or PVC (polyvinyl chloride) pipes, and that they could use water pressure to power simple sprinklers, known as rainbirds. A rainbird can effectively irrigate any field, regardless of slope. Although expensive to install, sprinkler systems offered overwhelming advantages, and within a few years they had been adopted by a large majority of farmers in Buguias and neighboring villages.

As gardeners adopted rainbirds, the available water supply effectively doubled, for in the old ditch delivery systems as much as half of the flow had been lost through seepage and evaporation. Furthermore, the rainbird's gentle sprinkling was found to be more effective than flooding and discouraging to a variety of pests as well. (This same period marked the spread of thrips, small insects troublesome during the dry season but sparing crops that are regularly sprinkled.) Its greatest advantage, however, was in allowing sloped fields to be cultivated year-round; this significantly increased the annual harvests of most growers. As a result, cropping schedules became more flexible, and water conflicts diminished for a period.

Not all Benguet farmers benefited from the rainbird revolution. Many poor growers could not afford hoses, while most farms along the Mountain Trail simply lack water during the dry season. In several favored Mountain Trail locales springs allow some irrigation, but even with rainbird delivery the water supply along the ridge is presently insufficient and is rapidly declining.

Transformation of
the Vegetable Trade

Vegetable traders also changed their practices after the economic crisis. In the mid-1970s, the large-scale traders essentially abandoned Buguias. They continued to buy and sell vegetables in Trinidad, but now they purchased from small dealers rather than from individual growers. Russell (1983:93) argues that the introduction of light utility vehicles allowed a new group of small-scale traders to insert themselves between growers and wealthy dealers. As these small traders struggled among themselves, long-term dealer-farmer obligations gave way to more competitive bidding. The large traders then found it more profitable, and less risky, to retreat to Trinidad where they could remain one step removed from the vegetable growers.

Although this scenario partly accounts for the transformation

of trade in Buguias, it must also be noted that the large-scale traders' abandonment of Buguias coincided with the rise of the New
People's Army in the local hinterlands. Local interpretations of this
timing vary considerably; while some claim that the wealthy capitalists feared imposition of a "revolutionary tax," others argue that
the two developments were coincidental.

In any case, by the mid-1980s, a new and diverse system of vegetable trading had emerged in the upper Agno Valley. To this date,
the large agribusinesses of northern Buguias municipality continue
to transport produce in large trucks, but for the most part they haul
only what they grow on their own farms. In Buguias Village, however, almost all vegetables are now carried in light utility vehicles.
Of the twelve such trucks present in the village in 1986, five were
owned by full-time traders, the others by farmers who transported
their own crops and, for a small fee, those of their neighbors.
These part-time traders increasingly sell their produce not in Baguio but rather along the Mountain Trail. Tagalog traders, recognizing the trend, now drive up the highway to flag down passing
trucks, hoping to haggle a better deal from the road-weary farmers
than would be possible in Baguio.

The five full-time vegetable dealers of Buguias presently operate
on a local scale and drive small vehicles, but otherwise their practices mirror those of the large-scale traders of the precrisis days.
Farmers often sell to the highest bidder, but many are again in debt
to, and thus tied to, a specific trader. In some respects farmer-
dealer obligations were strengthened in the mid-1980s when traders
began to sell rice. They can undersell (or, as is more usual, "under-
lend") store owners, both because they subsidize their own transport costs (it is inefficient not to carry a backload), and because
they do not pay as much tax as a store proprietor. As this has deprived shopkeepers of their most profitable commerce, many now
devote most of their time to their own fields, opening their businesses for only a few hours a day.

Despite the adverse economic climate, an ambitious and re-
sourceful individual may still prosper in the vegetable trade. At
present, one dealer in particular runs a thriving business, and he
may well reach the position of baknang in the space of a few years.
This man had been an ordinary farmer when an injury forced him
to seek another line of work. Beginning as a commissioner (pur-

chaser) for another trader, he soon graduated to full partner. Not long afterward he bought his own small truck (soon to be joined by a second) and established an independent business. Some observers have attributed his initial success to a simple but clever (and exhausting) tactic: he would tour the Baguio market each evening to discover which vegetables were short, rush back to Buguias to secure a supply, and then return to Baguio in time for the next day's sales.

THE PRECARIOUS STATE OF THE
VEGETABLE INDUSTRY

Just as the vegetable industry began to recover from the debacle of the mid-1970s, it received another blow: the assassination of Benigno Aquino in 1983 and the attendant round of inflation and economic decline. Once again, the prices of agricultural chemicals, fuel, and consumer goods increased faster than did those of vegetables. Rice especially escalated in cost, and by 1985 many families could scarcely afford their staple food.

The Buguias people had long since adjusted to an inflationary environment by such means as tying salda mortgages to the price of hogs. But inflation eroded their living standards nonetheless. This is evident by viewing wages in swine equivalents. In 1970, thirty ten-hour days brought in enough money to purchase a large hog (at 10 pesos a day for labor, 300 pesos for the animal); by 1985, nearly twice as many days (fifty-seven) were required to obtain the same hog (at 35 pesos a day for labor, 2,000 pesos for the animal). Fuel provides another index of decline. In the late 1960s, most households living in the village center cooked with kerosene or liquid petroleum gas; by the mid-1980s, the majority had returned to wood, an increasingly scarce and expensive commodity itself.

The current economic standing of Benguet's commercial vegetable farmers vis-à-vis other Igorots who have retained subsistence agriculture is another question, and one on which evidence is mixed. Although market gardeners undoubtedly enjoyed greater prosperity prior to the early 1970s, several scholars claim that they are losing ground to, and may well have been surpassed by, subsistence growers. Carol DeRaedt (personal communication) argues that while vegetable farmers are often perceived as wealthy, mostly because they handle large sums of money and often own vehicles, this is, in fact, belied by their hopeless debt and ever-declining returns. An anonymous contributor to the First Cordillera Multi-Sectoral Congress (Cordillera Consultative Committee 1984:167) states this in more certain terms: "[The Benguet vegetable farmers] have become poor relatives to their sisters and brothers who have not adopted cash crop agriculture."

Other evidence suggests that such pronouncements are premature. Beyond doubt, all Buguias residents prefer to risk market participation rather than return to subsistence. Elders remember the prewar days as a time of hardship, for which they voice little nostalgia. Indeed, several elderly individuals refused even to discuss the prewar days, saying simply, "Life was bad—we only ate sweet potatoes." Furthermore, communities previously excluded from market participation for lack of infrastructure have readily adopted commercial growing—even if it entails sharecropping—as soon as road access is gained. Of course, one may argue that local people suffer false perceptions here, but I would prefer to trust their judgments. After all, they have in many circumstances proved themselves keen observers of economic opportunity.

In any case, even if Benguet vegetable growers remain the envy of their subsistence-farming neighbors, the good times will not necessarily persist. Many seemingly intractable problems confront the commercial economy. Most of these are environmental, and will be discussed at length in the following pages. But one specifically economic threat is worth considering briefly here: the growth of a competing temperate vegetable industry in central Luzon.

A good measure of state-supported research has recently been directed toward breeding cultivars that can tolerate the lowland climate, at least during the low-sun season. Some success has been achieved with cabbage and cauliflower. Not only does this contribute to a potential oversupply, but the generally inferior lowland vegetables are often intentionally mislabeled as "Baguio produce," undercutting the market for the genuine product. More significant, perhaps, is the emerging vegetable center of Tagaytay, a few hours drive south of Manila (see Figoy 1984:37). Here a cool ridge top blessed with excellent highway connections to the capital offers an ideal environment for temperate crops. But the Philippine economy is not expanding quickly enough to absorb the increased supply, and the Benguet farmers may well suffer as a consequence. Despite both declining living standards and the precarious state of the entire industry, the growing of vegetables still presents a strong lure. Many farmers can easily weather economic turmoil and change. In frontier zones, new opportunities for accumulation continually emerge, drawing ever more villages into the commercial network. But the biggest attraction is the jackpot. As long as it is still possible for a lucky farmer to realize great profits on a single crop, few will resist the temptations of the vegetable economy. But as the local population quickly expands, the possibility of a major jackpot harvest will be open to ever fewer farmers.

DEMOGRAPHY

POPULATION TRENDS

Demographic growth has been a crucial component of recent environmental degradation in Buguias. Although the exact pace is impossible to gauge, given the unreliability of early census data, it is clear that the local population grew at a rapid rate during the American period. The available figures show Buguias municipality more than doubling in two decades, rising from 2,611 inhabitants in 1918 to 5,691 in 1939 (Republic of the Philippines 1960a, v. 1, pt. ii:35–2). Not surprisingly, the war interrupted this expansion; the 1948 figures show a gain of only 203 persons during the previous decade.

After the war, when statistics—although still suspect—improve, a demographic boom is clearly evident. By 1960 the municipality had swollen to 8,658 persons; ten years later it had reached 12,402; and in 1980 the figure stood at 17,556 (Republic of the Philippines 1960a, v. 1, pt. ii:35–2 and Buguias Municipality 1983:12). The rate of increase is presently diminishing, and stability in the near future is not likely; even assuming a decline in natality, government statisticians expect Buguias municipality to hold 23,819 individuals by the year 2000 (Buguias Municipality 1983:13). The barangay (village) of Buguias repeats this pattern in miniature; its 1960 population of 869 had increased to 1,300 by 1970 (Republic of the Philippines 1960*a*, v. 1, pt. ii:353, and Republic of the Philippines 1970, v. 1(10):1,2), and by 1986 local officials estimated the community's population at well over 2,000.

The social and ecological consequences of this rapid demographic expansion are palpable. Since the national economy does not easily absorb rural migrants, the growing population requires an expanded agricultural base. New gardens must be cleared and existing ones cultivated more intensively. Yet intensification is already advanced; after the "rainbird revolution" most fields produced year-round, and increased labor or chemical inputs yield exceptionally low marginal returns. New irrigation systems could expand dry-season production, but the potential here is also limited. The most feasible option in recent years has rather been the expansion of the garden area, entailing the cultivation of ever more marginal sites. A second option is migration to new agricultural areas, including both the eastern cloud forest and the few frontier zones remaining in the lowlands of Nueva Vizcaya.

LOCAL ATTITUDES AND POPULATION GROWTH

The Buguias people are well aware of the problems arising from their quickly growing population. Even the ancestors are sometimes asked to intervene; during one recent ritual a manbunung chanted a prayer that might be loosely translated, "We have become many but the land does not become wide, so please help our children who have gone to the lowlands to make their gardens." According to almost all local observers, today's average nuclear family is larger than that of prewar days. While they partly attribute this to decreased child mortality, women generally concur that the birth interval has shortened. Some facetiously conclude that whereas in the prewar period couples required three years to conceive their first child, many today can seemingly produce an infant in only three months.

In exploring these changing fertility patterns, attention must be paid both to cultural attitudes and to the economic role of children. The data here are curious. As in much of the world, Buguias parents generally prize large families, and many saw the postwar fertility increase as a great boon. But, in contradiction to some influential demographic theorists, the high value the Buguias people accord to numerous offspring is not easily attributable to economic calculations. According to several scholars (Mamdani 1972, Caldwell 1978), one should expect high birthrates where children confer more to the domestic economy than they consume. Under such conditions, the more children a couple have, the more they may hope to prosper. Low birthrates, in contrast, are expected in societies in which children are an economic drain. Yet in Buguias, children are abundant even though they cost much and contribute little.

Young children in Buguias do occasionally labor in behalf of their parents, but school and play consume most of their time. They do, however, care for younger siblings; this does not directly add to the family budget, but it does free their parents. Adolescents, especially young men, often devote themselves to gainful labor, but the money they earn is their own, and few accord significant sums to the family account. Although children as young as six may carry vegetables, even at this age they retain their own wages; parents usually must ask for a part of the earnings, but not all children agree to share. Indeed, young men even in their twenties commonly remain a net financial drain on their parents, supporting themselves periodically but returning home when in financial straits. Education beyond the sixth grade is also a significant cost for those who continue. In short, virtually everyone in Buguias agrees that children are a net expense. It is the few *basig* couples—those without charges to support—who enjoy unexpected prosperity.

Cain's (1981) demographic thesis focuses in part on social security; couples often have numerous children, he claims, in the hope that at least one will be able to give them adequate care should they become ill or when they reach old age. This theory also fails in Buguias. Here the few elders who are too infirm to work are always supported by their extended families.

The high birthrate in Buguias is perhaps, in contrast, linked to the peculiarly local *cultural* value of children. Buguias religion revolves around ancestor worship, and most persons believe that the ancestral spirits maintain their power through the actions of their descendants. The more numerous one's progeny, the greater one's chance of attaining a high afterworld position. Childless predecessors—even wealthy ones—are eventually forgotten, excluded from genealogical reckonings. As one elder phrased it (in English), "If you have no children you are erased from the map of Buguias."

Nevertheless, a demographic sea change may be near. Worry about the future availability of farmland is widespread, and some individuals openly question the value of having large families. Parents with inadequate land to support their children properly now endure quiet censure. Women educated up to the high school level, and especially the college level, generally desire only three or four children. Young men, however—especially those without an education—often hope to raise, as they put it, as many children *as they can afford*.

In accordance with the Philippine national population program, subsidized contraceptives are available from the barangay clinic. Although some couples make use of them, artificial birth control is not a standard practice. Both devout Pagans and Christians feel moral qualms, and many women fear the side effects of certain methods. Contraception may one day be accepted, but as it now stands even couples who (claim to) desire ending their reproductive careers often continue to have children. And regardless of future changes in attitude, the present age structure ensures that the population will continue to expand. Given the economic conditions of the Philippines, social and ecological strains will increase with it. One casualty will certainly be Buguias's forests.

DEFORESTATION

Pine and Oak Forests: 1930–1980

Although pine is vital for local subsistence, government policy under both the American and the Philippine regimes has always favored industrial users, especially the large mining corporations. The state long ago awarded the pines of greater Buguias to the Heald Lumber Company, which constructed two sawmills in the vicinity (at Bad-ayan and Sinipsip on the Mountain Trail) before the war. Not all of the region was logged, however, and several healthy stands survived in and near Buguias Village. To ensure an adequate supply of mine supports, the state has, at various times and with variable success, attempted to prevent the Benguet people from cutting trees in the concession areas. But through the American period timber was plentiful and most forestry agents were lax in the enforcement of official rules.

By the late 1950s, however, the Buguias people and the government foresters came into sharp conflict. Forest guards were now ordered to require official approval for every pine cut. Furthermore, local residents could no longer make new tax declarations unless their plots were certified as containing no pines. Since agriculture had to expand, gardeners were forced to clear new plots surreptitiously, uprooting all potentially incriminating pine seedlings before the inspection teams could arrive. Although this entailed needless destruction, farmers felt they had no alternative.

Foresters classify the high-elevation oak woodland as non-economic, since its stubby and gnarled trees are worthless as lumber. They do consider it vital watershed, however, a function that became particularly important after two hydroelectric dams were installed on the middle Agno in the 1950s. Most recent government forestry reports have accordingly advocated cloud-forest preservation (see, for example, MPDA 1964). Yet no safeguards have been implemented. The cloud forest of Mount Data, for instance—the source of the four major rivers of the Cordillera (the Agno, Chico, Abra, and Ibulao)—officially lies within a national park, yet most of it has long since been abandoned to cabbage fields. Benguet conservationists, led by Sinai Hamada, publisher of the *Baguio Midland Courier*, fought hard to protect the Mount Data forests, but to no avail.

Through the late 1960s, the pine forests of Benguet continued to dwindle under pressure from both corporate and indigenous logging. Even when National Power Company agents joined the foresters in pressing for conservation the state could not act effectively; as with other environmental issues, conflicting interests demanded contradictory actions. For example, in January 1969, Marcos banned all cutting in the upper Agno watershed, but Heald Lumber Company protested and within a few days he rescinded the order (*Baguio Midland Courier* March 9, 1969). In 1975 a more far-reaching ban protected all pine trees within 50 kilometers of Baguio, but a year later, when lumber ran short in the gold mines, Heald again received special exemptions (*Baguio Midland Courier* Sept. 12, 1975).

Although the Marcos regime could not thwart corporate logging (if indeed it had ever intended to), it could harass Igorot farmers and woodcutters. During the early martial law period, forest guards often arrested decree violators. This period witnessed a renewal of purposeful seedling destruction by local farmers resisting forestry interference. By 1976, however, the enforcement power of the state simply began to evaporate; with the New People's Army (NPA) on the rise, forest guards rapidly retreated. Although the NPA later withdrew from the Buguias region, the state did not attempt to re-assert its forestry authority.

Meanwhile, through the 1970s the novel oleoresin industry seemed to portend the salvation of the Benguet pines. The insular pine produces copious, high-quality resin, long used by the Igorots in the form of *saleng*. When forest researchers discovered that resin extraction would not harm the trees (Veracion 1977), development agents began to encourage local tapping. If the Igorots could tap commercially, foresters reasoned, they would protect old trees and nurture saplings. On February 1, 1970, the *Baguio Midland Courier* hopefully announced that the solution to the *"kaingin* problem" (Tagalog for swidden field) had at long last been discovered.

The Buguias people quickly moved into the naval-stores industry. Individuals who had been instructed in the proper tapping techniques obtained licenses; these persons invited others to tap under their permits in return for a percentage of the profits. For a few years a number of residents of the higher reaches of Buguias extracted a substantial supplementary income. But the practice soon proved to be unsustainable; few tappers followed regulations closely, and most trees were over-drained. The fire threat was also heightened since resin often continued to dribble out of the tap scar, and the accumulated deposit would easily combust during a grass burn, in turn igniting the entire tree. Moreover, the tappers seldom realized the desired profits. By the early 1980s, the oleo-resin industry lay in ruins.

RECENT FORESTRY PRACTICES IN BUGUIAS

Although the state's withdrawal from the forests of Buguias allowed the local inhabitants to develop the resource as they wished, the community government has been unable to reconcile the inevitable conflict of interests within the village. A few entrepreneurs have discovered great profits in cutting, hauling, and selling wood, both for lumber and fuel, to outside interests. This small-scale commercial logging owes its existence to the chainsaw, an expensive but profitable investment. By the early 1980s, the buzz of chainsaws emanated daily from the slopes above Buguias, seeming to foretell the demise of the remaining pine stands.

Few Buguias citizens are pleased when the sawyers sell local wood to outsiders. But firewood is in strong demand, especially in Lo-o, where large-scale farmers must provide meals for their many hired workers. Even more profitable is the traffic in construction lumber. The same chainsaws used to fell trees also mill them, and the boards thus crudely produced fetch a high price in the expanding metropolis of Baguio. Four men working half a day can (in 1986) reportedly earn as much as 1,000 pesos, provided they cut a timber stand with good road access. Even under less favorable conditions, saw owners commonly pay their workers 50 pesos for half a day, an impressive wage by Philippine standards. Because of community opposition, commercial loggers usually work surreptitiously, often at night. But this does not substantially limit their operations. In 1983, one particularly valuable stand located on the northeastern border of Buguias Village yielded an estimated 50,000 board feet over a three-month period.

Such profiteering demands protection over and above the cover of dark; usually it entails the complicity of government agents, especially military officials. In exchange for a share of the profits, officers of the Philippine Constabulary have ensured black-market loggers uninterrupted felling and safe transportation. In a few instances, military men have instigated cuts, contracting for lumber that they then sell through their own networks. Barangay officials have lodged protests with the Bureau of Forest Development (BFD), but the foresters are powerless to challenge the military hierarchy.

Conflicts have also erupted between professional sawyers and tax declaration holders. Although some individuals declared pine stands precisely with an eye to their potential timber harvests, in other cases woodcutters have descended on stands without the declaration holder's knowledge. Some woodsmen willingly placate angered declaration holders with cash payments, but others argue that a tax declaration gives only cultivation rights, and that the plot's trees should be free for the taking. With the rapid rise of such conflicting claims, even tong tongan proceedings have difficulty resolving the contentious issues surrounding local commercial logging.

Yet in a few other Cordilleran regions pine forests have expanded in the postwar period. This is particularly true in Sagada (in Mountain Province), where villagers have assiduously planted seedlings in abandoned swiddens (Preston 1985). But in Benguet, and especially in Buguias, pine stands are in retreat. A few villages in the Buguias region have established communal forests to protect the diminishing resource, but even here removal outpaces growth. Thick stands remain only in the few rough and roadless areas; wherever soils are fertile, gardens encroach and road development follows. Knowledgeable individuals predict that few if any sizable pines will be left near Buguias by the year 2000. Seedlings continue to sprout vigorously, but few seem likely to reach maturity.

The cloud forests face less immediate threats. Valueless for lumber and disdained as firewood, oaks are cleared in large numbers only for garden expansion, or occasionally for speculation. Although the Mount Data forest is now gone and the oaks of eastern Buguias municipality are falling fast to expanding gardens, along the main Cordilleran ridge and eastward into Ifugao province wide expanses of cloud forest remain virtually untouched. They too may disappear as roads push eastward, but not for some years into a very uncertain future.

Development Plans: Social and Agroforestry

Benguet foresters despair over current forest trends. Their daunting challenge is to design programs that at once protect watersheds, ensure timber availability, and yet do not interfere with the Benguet farmers' livelihoods. With this in mind, officials of the Bureau of Forest Development have attempted to foster local participation in arboriculture.

Several Cordilleran scholars have excoriated the very notion of "social forestry," claiming that it represents yet another attempt by outsiders (or by capital, more generally) to gain control of local resources (see Parpan-Pagusara 1984:59). While this may well be true for some projects, the recent plans implemented by the BFD office in Abatan and forwarded by the scholars at Baguio's Forestry Research Institute (FORI) seem neither so ambitious nor so threatening.

For many years forestry officials have touted the Japanese alder (*Alnus japonica*), a fast-growing species that both protects slopes and fixes nitrogen. At various times they have distributed free seedlings, which school children were required to plant in the early 1970s. Yet the program has enjoyed only marginal success. As of 1986, seedlings were scarce, and since alders do not regenerate spontaneously here, they are at best maintaining their position. Another social forestry program of the 1960s encouraged farmers to plant pine seedlings around their gardens, but this could not help but fail. Pines shade crops and extract nutrients, while, at the time, the mere presence of trees could jeopardize a land claim. This is the kind of project rightly denounced by Baguio activists, but such approaches have by now been largely abandoned.[1]

More recently, development agents have begun promoting fruit crops. Orchards would not replenish wood supplies, but they could protect watersheds, minimize erosion, and provide an alternative income should the vegetable industry again falter. In 1976, Benguet planners unfortunately gave top priority to coffee and mango culture (*Baguio Midland Courier* March 28, 1976). Although coffee is an old Cordilleran crop, disease and market fluctuations have kept it from fulfilling its early promise, and mangoes thrive only on the lowest slopes, where they are still out-competed in the market by the lowland groves.

Temperate fruit offers another possibility. Although winters are not cold enough for true dormancy, Bauko municipality in Mountain Province is able to produce meager crops of both apples and pears, and a team of development workers has suggested temperate fruit culture in the Lo-o basin as well (Duhaylungsod n.d.; Dar 1985). Citrus is another option; several farmers near Baguio have derived excellent returns from small plantings of improved orange and lemon varieties, and one Buguias resident is now nurturing a small orchard. Viral diseases, endemic in indigenous trees, pose a threat, but a joint Philippine and German development program now provides resistant root stocks and advises participants in control methods.

Even if diseases could be eradicated, most Buguias farmers would probably resist fruit growing. The single annual harvest would translate into fewer jackpot opportunities, and growers find the prospect of waiting several years before the first harvest as disconcerting. New orchards also require substantial amounts of capital, and Buguias farmers fear predatory children would deprive them of the long-awaited harvest. Nevertheless, the one citrus grower persists in seeing tree crops as Buguias's hope, a possible substitute for the imperiled vegetable industry. That the community at large could be persuaded to make such a drastic change cannot be ruled out. It would not be the first time the Buguias people had completely reoriented their production system.

WATER SHORTAGES, EROSION, AND BIOCIDES

WATER SHORTAGES

The loss of forest cover has reduced dry-season stream and spring flow throughout northern Benguet, a problem that has become acute along the Mountain Trail. Only the high semiplateaus (Sayangan-Paoay, Natubleng, and Mount Data) have ever had adequate water for dry-season cultivation, but as their vestigal woodlands are gradually cleared, even previously dependable springs have desiccated, leaving farmers desperate for water. Hoses and PVC pipes have allowed some to tap more distant flows, but as the water table continues to drop, many farmers have been forced to abandon cultivation during the dry months.

Lying deep in the Agno Valley, Buguias enjoys a relatively abundant water supply. The Agno still flows strongly and dependably, and the waters of the larger side streams (Toking and Capuyuan) are plentiful. Numerous springs and seeps in the lower valley augment the supply. In the village's higher reaches, however, the dry season is increasingly a time of water stress.

Water scarcity is nothing new to Buguias. Before the war, poorly irrigated rice fields often withered toward the end of the growing period, for it was simply too difficult to bring water out of the deeply incised creek beds or from the main river. As new irrigation

systems were built, terraces expanded, consuming all new deliv-
eries. Growers achieved partial rationing, but disputes could not
be avoided.

Vegetables demand less moisture than do paddies, and as carrots and cabbages replaced rice on most terraces, water was temporarily abundant once more. But as new vegetable terraces were
built, demand again outstripped supply. Garden hoses and PVC
pipes brought another spell of relative plenty—until subsequent
garden expansion brought on a new round of water scarcity.

As of the mid-1980s, only specific areas of Buguias experience
severe water shortages. In general, the lower valley is still abundantly supplied. On the higher slopes, however, only select fields
located near springs or seeps could produce dry-season crops before the spread of rainbirds. When hoses and sprinklers were diffused, the numerous hillside rivulets could also be tapped. But as
these are mere trickles in the dry months, gardeners soon quarreled
over the scanty seasonal supply. Some hamlets have instituted informal rationing, but gardeners still argue heatedly when water
runs low. Some individuals even disconnect their neighbors' hoses
at night in order to reconnect their own to the dwindling flow.

Lacking an adjudication precedent, Buguias elders cannot easily
mediate the growing number of water disputes. Some irrigators
strongly adhere to a local version of the doctrine of "prior appro-
priation," holding that the individual who first tapped a source
should have superior rights. Other water users (generally those
who started irrigating later) argue for communal (hamlet-level)
control. One party to a recent water conflict became desperate
enough to engage a lawyer, a rare and distinctly antisocial move.
The attorney allegedly informed his client that neither side had any
legal rights whatsoever, and the conflict had to be settled within
Buguias. Eventually, in this case, a compromise was reached in
tong tongan.

In the dry season of 1986, water quarrels intensified. As gardens and irrigation facilities have spread, many springs and small
streams have steadily diminished. Finally, in March 1986, several
formerly perennial brooks ceased to flow, destroying a number of
standing crops.

Large-scale irrigation systems, tapping the waters of either Toking or Capuyuan creeks, could eliminate water scarcity through large areas of Buguias, but this would require assistance from the National Irrigation Authority (NIA). So far, only one Buguias hamlet, Tanggawan—traditional home of the elite—has managed to secure such governmental aid.

Erosion

In increasingly large areas, erosion exacerbates water shortages. On Buguias's eastern slopes, many small streams are entrenching, making water delivery even with hoses ever more difficult. Near Asinan Creek the problem is compounded: as the stream has cut downward the salt spring has migrated headward, forcing gardeners to extend their hoses ever further upstream to find fresh water.

Topsoil loss more directly threatens many gardens. Scattered throughout Benguet are former vegetable fields now abandoned for lack of soil (Dar 1985:136). Typhoon-generated erosion, taking the forms of sheet wash, gullying, and slope failure, can be extraordinary. Terracing mitigates the danger, but even the best-engineered terraces occasionally fail. Moreover, most farmers purposefully keep some fields sloped for wet-season drainage. And landslides, slumps, and debris flows may strike regardless of agricultural engineering; a massive flow in central Buguias in the late 1960s devastated several tens of hectares both in its source area and in its deposition zone. Neither place has yet been reclaimed. Farmers usually rebuild small slump scars, even if it takes several years. But even a small slope failure can financially devastate a family if it destroys an entire crop.

Buguias's climate and geology conspire to generate frequent and severe slope failures. Intense and prolonged rainfall periodically saturates a deeply weathered and unstable mantle. Human practices compound the problem. Deforestation and road construction are obvious culprits; many private roads are severely gullied in a single season, while all roadways channel runoff and thus contribute to gullying in nearby fields. Even more destructive is the purposeful diversion of water during floods. When a typhoon strikes, farmers often dig ditches and build embankments to protect their own fields. This funnels the flow into their neighbors' gardens, who must then redouble their own efforts. A frantic battle ensues, as each grower tries to protect his or her own fields even at the expense of those adjacent.

In the late 1970s the bulldozer appeared as a new agent of erosion. Where agriculture is rapidly expanding, wealthy farmers find it expedient to bulldoze fields of several hectares. Many of the resulting "cut-and-fill terraces" erode severely after a single rainy season. Equipment operators often do not even save the topsoil; instead they merely push it aside to provide a foundation for the terrace fill. This does not usually concern the farmer. Supplied with enough fertilizer, the subsoil yields adequately. And even those agriculturalists who do strive to conserve often find their newly bulldozed fields ravished. One wealthy Buguias couple spent over 30,000 pesos for plastic drain pipes and stone retaining walls for a new field bulldozed near Baguio, but lost virtually the entire investment in a single storm.

With the deforestation of surrounding hillsides, typhoon-induced erosion seems to have become more severe in recent years. The worst disaster to date occurred on July 15 and 16, 1989, when typhoon Goring devastated Buguias, causing fifteen deaths in the municipality. After the storm, the *Baguio Midland Courier* reported one Buguias elder as saying, "Maybe the gods are angry, there are no more trees on Mount Data."

Many vegetable districts along the Mountain Trail are more susceptible to erosion than is the Agno Valley. Soil loss along the ridge was aggravated, according to most local observers, by careless Chinese farmers who were more concerned with fast profits than with sustainable practices. By the early 1950s, development agents began to focus on erosion control. The state soon insisted that only farmers who had constructed terraces and planted grass or trees on steep slopes could gain land titles. In the 1960s, the Mountain Province Development Authority, with funding from the UN and USAID, initiated a more ambitious bench-terracing project (*Baguio Midland Courier* July 9, 1967). The irony of teaching some of the world's preeminent terrace engineers how to construct simple earth benches was apparently lost on the sponsors. Moreover, many farmers, particularly sharecroppers, have resisted making the necessary investments for financial reasons, while much land is purposefully kept in slops for wet-season root crops.

BIOCIDES, HUMAN HEALTH, AND
FAUNAL DESTRUCTION

The biocides continually sprayed on the Buguias landscape have poisoned many farmers as well as entire aquatic ecosystems. Farmers occasionally use officially banned poisons (Medina n.d.); many more overapply legal pesticides and dispose of the residues improperly. In earlier years, growers often washed their backpack sprayers directly in streams, even those providing drinking water. Local ordinances now prohibit this practice, and barangay officials continually warn of pesticide hazards. Buguias residents will not even eat their own cabbage grown in the dry season because they know it is highly contaminated. Few warnings are forthcoming, however, from company agents, the individuals who provide most new information on chemical-intensive agriculture.

Few Buguias streams have potable water, owing both to chemical residues and to amoebic and bacterial pathogens. In the center of town, several spring-fed domestic water systems were installed shortly after the war using the steel pipes supplied as war reparations by the Japanese government. These frequently clogged pipes spew rusty water, but more worrisome are the contaminants entering the spring-boxes in runoff from adjacent fields. In the dry season, desperate farmers often tap the community's drinking water supplies to irrigate their gardens; when the domestic systems are reconnected, the water runs brown for several hours. Barangay officials have battled to maintain and even to improve local drinking water, but funds are limited, and farmers upslope are reluctant to jeopardize their own livelihoods for the benefit of those living in the center of the community.

The effects of pesticide and fertilizer ingestion, derived from field exposure and from eating and drinking, are impossible to evaluate without a medical study. But indirect evidence suggests adverse impacts on human health. Virtually all Buguias residents argue with conviction that people die younger today than they did before the war, despite the much-improved postwar diet. Although this probably results from age-related memory distortion (old people seem much older than they are to children), the community's intellectuals, persons of critical and discerning bent, agree that average longevity may have declined. (A few elders, however, actually blame the supposed life-span shortening on the varied postwar diet: people today are no longer "preserved by sweet-potato vinegar.") A more plausible culprit would be agricultural chemicals. But regardless of actual mortality trends, acute pesticide poisoning is not an uncommon diagnosis in local clinics.

Pesticides, fertilizers, and silt have destroyed most of the aquatic life that once spiced the local diet. Eels have been virtually extirpated, and other species are now rare. In Lo-o, the surviving river life is simply too contaminated to be edible (Figoy n.d.). In Buguias, sculpins, tadpoles, and water bugs are still avidly consumed, although almost exclusively by the young men who value highly such *pulutan* (rich snacks that complement gin).

But agricultural chemicals are not the sole cause of faunal destruction. Many land animals have been locally exterminated through habitat destruction and overhunting. In Buguias, the only remaining "game" mammal is the rat, although a few civets may still dwell in the thickets along Toking Creek. Deer survive only in the steep pinelands between Natubleng and the Agno, and although wild hogs still roam the cloud forest of eastern Buguias municipality, they are now rarely seen. Humans long ago drove monkeys out of the Agno Valley, and they now seem to be doing the same in western Ifugao. Snipes, herons, and wild chickens, formerly abundant in Buguias, are gone, victims of overhunting, rice-field conversion, and garden expansion. Song birds are rare and diminishing in number, and such as remain are still avidly pursued by young boys. The migratory birds caught seasonally along the mountain crests continue to return annually, but even they come in smaller flocks than in past years.

A few officials, both local and national, have endeavored to save the Cordillera's wildlife, but all actions have been futile. In 1970, the state declared a large part of the upper Agno basin a game refuge, evidently an empty gesture (*Baguio Midland Courier* Oct. 4, 1970). Some conservationists saw in martial law a potential wildlife reprieve, since most guns were confiscated (*Baguio Midland Courier* July 22, 1973); indeed, Kabayan residents credit this move for the survival of the deer herd below Natubleng. But habitat destruction and population expansion join as an inexorable force against which wild animals cannot stand.

Within recorded history, the Cordillera has not supported abundant wildlife; the scarcity of large fauna is repeatedly noted by nineteenth-century German travelers. But this does not make the current destruction of wildlife any less tragic. Nor is faunal extinction the only concern; many of the cloud forest's numerous endemic plants may well be exterminated within the next few decades. While most local residents decry this loss, they, like the Bureau of Parks and Wildlife, cannot prevent it; to do so they would have to counteract enormously powerful forces, cultural as well as economic. For even if agricultural expansion could somehow be contained, the young men of the community show no inclination to abstain from hunting any animal, however rare it might be.

THE VEGETABLE FRONTIER

Beginning in the late 1960s, and accelerating through the following decades, the high-elevation region of eastern Buguias municipality was opened to commercial agriculture. Although a few vegetables had been grown here since the 1940s, large-scale production was initially held back by poor transport. When feeder roads finally penetrated the pine-oak border zone, gardening was suddenly very profitable; soils were fresh, waters abundant, and weeds and other pests uncommon. But the local inhabitants could not easily harvest the rewards, as they lacked the capital needed both to clear the land and to farm it intensively. Entrepreneurs from the Agno Valley realized the bulk of the profits in most eastern villages.

Geographical Patterns of Expansion

The southern Cordillera's vegetable zone has gradually projected outward in several different salients over the past twenty years. As the road network has been extended, ever more communities have been able to take up commercial farming (see map 8). In the 1960s and 1970s, several projections pushed westward from the Mountain Trail heartland. But further movement to the west is uncertain. In much of Bakun municipality, for example, progress is impeded by steep and rocky slopes and by the locally active New People's Army.

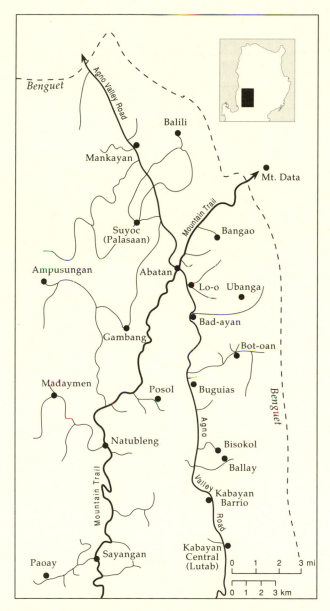

Map 8. *The Road Network of Buguias and Nearby Locales.* Some of the
smaller and more recent roads are not indicated. Note also that the Agno
Valley Road north of Kabayan Barrio is seldom passable during the rainy
season.

Northward, the vegetable frontier has recently enveloped several Northern Kankana-ey villages in Mountain Province. Here local residents who had previously labored on Mountain Trail farms introduced commercial production. Yet these communities essentially retain subsistence orientations, with vegetables forming subsidiary cash crops (see Voss 1983). The same is true in several Ifugao villages in the Kiangan region, where vegetable gardens are presently increasing in acreage.

In recent years, the main thrust of expansion has been eastward from the Agno Valley, particularly in Kabayan (Calanog n.d.) and Buguias municipalities. In greater Buguias, development in the 1960s and early 1970s was concentrated in the north. Contractors gradually extended feeder roads east from Lo-o and Bad-ayan into the oak-covered hills. In 1976, however, the main frontier shifted southward after the Buguias–Bot-oan road was inaugurated. Intended as the first leg of a proposed highway into western Ifugao, this route terminated at the then insignificant hamlet of Bot-oan. Within a few years, Bot-oan had become a major agricultural and commercial center, and the seat of the new barangay of Catlubong, carved out of the territory of Buguias proper.

Bot-oan, sitting on the pine-oak border, is ideal for most temperate vegetables. Here a relatively flat saddle is endowed with abundant water and unusually light and friable soil. Yet the local inhabitants had little interest in vegetable culture before the mid-1970s. A few had grown and sold peas, but most still raised swine for their minimal cash needs. Hog raising no longer yielded much profit, however, in large part because hogs could no longer roam free.

The Bot-oan people, considered the least "progressive" of all the residents of greater Buguias, lacked both the knowledge and the capital necessary to exploit the new opportunities the road provided. But several prosperous couples quickly moved up from the Agno Valley to develop the land. Before long, they composed a local elite, whose exogenous origins their poorer neighbors did not forget. Only one local resident ascended into the elite stratum, a rise made possible by many years of work in the Saudi oil fields.

The outside developers first hired workers, both locals and Kalanguya immigrants from Ifugao province, to clear new gardens. But by the 1980s most had turned to bulldozers. Usually they would turn the newly made plots over to local sharecroppers. Many sharecroppers later cleared their own tiny gardens, giving Bot-oan today a mixture of large and small holdings.

Not long after the road arrived, other entrepreneurs opened a number of stores and a periodic market emerged as well. Impetus for retail expansion came from both the growing local economy and from Bot-oan's newly strategic position vis-à-vis western Ifugao. The village now occupied the closest roadhead to Tinoc and Tucucan. By 1985, several hundred Tinoc residents were making the trek to Bot-oan twice each week, returning home the same day heavily laden with goods ranging from rice and gin to treadle sewing machines and iron sheeting.

More profitable than stores are transport vehicles. During the long wet season few trucks can negotiate the steep climb out of the Agno canyon; the three Bot-oan entrepreneurs who own powerful International Harvesters able to make the climb form an effective, if seasonal, transport oligopoly. Nevertheless, Bot-oan retail prices are on average lower than those of Buguias. Buguias residents find this perplexing and infuriating, and most attribute it to the noncompetitive environment of their own increasingly marginal community.

The Bot-oan road has also allowed the Kalanguya people of Tinoc and nearby villages greater participation in the market economy. Tinoc now lies at the far eastern fringe of the vegetable empire, the position previously occupied by Bot-oan itself, where high-value, lightweight crops can be grown profitably. Peas in particular have made inroads into local swiddens. Physiography itself contributes to pea culture, Tinoc being somewhat protected from the typhoon winds that frequently destroy fragile trellises farther west. After a severe storm, Tinoc growers can reap high profits in the inflated pea market. Lately, a few growers have gambled on other crops; by early 1986, young Tinoc men were carrying fifty-kilo sacks of carrots to the Bot-oan market during price peaks. To date, however, seldom are such vegetables valuable enough to bear the cost of portage over the tortuous, muddy, and leech-infested trail linking the two villages.

In southern Buguias and northern Kabayan municipalities, contractors pushed two other feeder roads to the edge of the cloud forest in the 1970s. Here, in contrast to Bot-oan, almost all local residents had been cultivating small commercial plots since the 1940s, carrying their produce first to Kilometer 73, then to Buguias Central. Road development allowed some to expand their gardens, but most have remained small operators. Outside entrepreneurs have not found these areas attractive, in part because their slopes are steep and their water insufficient. Furthermore, since the locals already had gardens of their own they have been reluctant to accept sharecropping arrangements.

Continuing Road Development

Eastern Buguias municipality's road development in the 1970s was financed largely by the national government and by the United States, whose motivations were mainly military. At the time, Botoan formed an NPA stronghold. By the early 1980s the NPA presence diminished, and state funding evaporated. A road extension into western Ifugao—a remaining NPA refuge—was still planned, but this proved too expensive and dangerous. After the 1984 legislative elections, politicians seemingly abandoned the road, much to the consternation of the Kalanguya people of western Ifugao province.

Through various creative financing schemes, feeder-road construction continues. Wealthy farmers, especially those living in the Bot-oan area, occasionally build private roads. Road developers sometimes convince the barangay to assume maintenance costs, effectively passing all burdens to the public sector. Barangay roads are usually maintained through cooperative work parties, with some communities occasionally purchasing bulldozer time.

Less prosperous farmers sometimes jointly finance road construction in their hamlets. In a typical case, each farmer directly benefitting will donate something on the order of 500 pesos, with wealthier growers usually contributing severalfold more. One such project in Buguias was unsuccessfully negotiated for several years; the interested farmers all sought different corridors, since all wanted close access but none wished to lose any land. Although they finally reached a compromise, one barangay official fears that erosion safeguards were discarded in the process. A similar road in another Buguias hamlet had eroded so quickly that it was downgraded to a buffalo-cart path after several years.

The municipal and provincial governments share responsibility for major roads, generally those entailing construction costs of over 50,000 pesos. Funding is politically charged, as villages compete for road access. In 1985, the Buguias municipal council released funds to extend the Bot-oan road southward toward the upper Ca-puyuan drainage. Southern Buguias municipality marked this as a victory, since in their eyes the more powerful northern interests usually monopolize road funds. This project also generated some unusual local opposition, as a few elders argued that it would only bring in more gin and associated social ills.

Land Speculation

The new roads east of Buguias have provided opportunities for speculators as well as gardeners. Local land speculation dates to the credit schemes of the late 1960s; bank loans had to be secured with real estate, whether titled or declared, and the only broad areas still available lay in the eastern reaches of the municipality. While property claims were officially limited by one's ability to pay tax (as determined by the assessor), even persons of moderate wealth could obtain tens of hectares of undeveloped land.

Although these lands were initially declared as loan collateral, a few individuals realized their development potential should a road reach the area. By the early 1970s, a handful of speculators rushed to stake out lands along the planned transport corridor between Bot-oan and Tinoc. One wealthy Buguias couple even claimed a plot on the highest pass, intending to build a cafe there to service the buses that they thought would soon ply the Tinoc route. Such explicitly speculative declarations were largely held by residents of Buguias and nearby valley communities, but a few locals also claimed large plots, in part to protect themselves from the out-siders. By the mid-1970s, virtually all lands of any agricultural po-tential had been declared.

A tax declaration is difficult to define in the cloud forest. Land-marks are rare, visibility through the dense forest is low, and move-ment is constrained. Some speculators thus cleared their plots of all woody growth. Although most cloud-forest trees readily stump-sprout, continued recutting has reduced these parcels to a low scrub. This needless degradation has prompted some resentment, but no one is powerful enough to contend with the economic interests involved.

Few of the Buguias speculators reaped the profits they had anticipated. The Tinoc road stalled and the general pace of transport development slackened. When the vegetable industry stagnated, many could not afford their taxes, and therefore allowed their declarations to pass into delinquency. As feeder roads were slowly built, most declarants sold their remaining parcels piecemeal, sometimes at a fair profit, to the wealthy Bot-oan farmers.

But when the municipality initiated extension of the Bot-oan road in 1985, several declaration holders finally made good. It is of interest that the most successful was not a speculator but rather a local ritualist. Many years earlier, this modest man had declared several hectares of relatively flat and rich land near his home and exactly proximate to the future roadway. He managed to pay his taxes, while leaving virtually the entire plot in virgin oak forest. When the road pushed through, his parcel suddenly gained value, and when a wealthy Bot-oan farmer offered him 20,000 pesos a hectare, he happily sold.

In 1975, before even Bot-oan had road access, a hectare of land in this area could hardly have sold for 200 pesos. The following years saw fierce inflation; by 1985, the price of a large animal had increased some tenfold. Yet as this case shows, prime land on the cloud forest fringe could appreciate as much as a hundred times. Clearly, land speculation *could* yield spectacular gains.

By early 1986, this particular plot had already been bulldozed clear of vegetation and topsoil. The new owner had hired several local residents, who had earlier raised hogs for their cash needs, to sharecrop the land. Potential tenants are not lacking here; the market is a strong lure, and most residents prefer to begin gardening by working for a successful entrepreneur rather than by cultivating a tiny and underfinanced private garden.

Agricultural development in eastern Buguias municipality has primarily benefited three parties: wealthy farmers, a few lucky land speculators, and bulldozer owners.[2] For most local residents, the results are mixed. Although now more prosperous than before, they must share the risks and the dim future of the vegetable industry. Nor is expansion itself without economic contradictions;

the overall vegetable harvest grows faster than demand, lowering profits elsewhere.

But the eastward march of the vegetable frontier is most threatening ecologically. As the cloud forest of eastern Buguias municipality vanishes and as new irrigation works are installed, stream flows gradually diminish, undercutting Agno Valley irrigators. In several areas of the municipality, formerly verdant rice terraces are now dry, most likely because of water development upslope. As their natural endowment deteriorates, farmers in the lower valley may find it exceedingly difficult to compete with those who have recently developed rich, new lands. And as economic and ecological problems mount, social and political turmoil grows apace.

9

Social Conflict and Political Struggle

INTRODUCTION

Although downplayed by classical social theory, conflict is increasingly recognized as a vital force for effecting social transformation. More complex in origin than is suggested by the organic or systems view (where conflict is often little more than the intrusion of discord into a preexisting idyll), and more diverse in its effects than is allowed by the standard Marxist portrayal (as the force behind a preordained historical progression), social friction is highly variable in intensity and outcome, and it must be examined afresh in each setting. Its historical development, social configuration, potential for resolution, and role as an agent of change all vary enormously in differing empirical circumstances.

In Buguias, the lines of fracture are several. Struggles over rights to farmland are especially fierce, occasionally even pitting sibling against sibling. Families are also torn apart by generational rivalry, as the young men of Buguias increasingly withdraw into a subculture of their own. Political battles split the municipality into geographically based factions, just as they reveal hamlet-based cleavages at the barangay level. Class divisions, for their part, pervade all arenas of contention.

The dramatic transformations of the postwar period have raised new forms and objects of discord within the community. This comes as no surprise, for conflicts are generally expected to intensify in times of rapid change (both as cause and effect of said change), and to become particularly acute when economies stagnate or decline. But the relationship is far from simple. Uncertainties can in some circumstances enhance rather than undermine social solidarity, as individuals seek mutual support. Such a seemingly contradictory response is evident in contemporary Buguias, where the pressures of a perilous economy have provoked bitter rivalries, yet where social cohesion and cultural identity have in several ways intensified.

The pivotal ideological dispute structuring both contention and the making of peace in Buguias in recent decades has pitted Pagans against Christians in a complex and ongoing debate whose contours are explored in chapter 10. Meanwhile, a new language of conflict is emerging in political philosophy. In the 1980s, radical Cordilleran activists were increasingly setting the terms of a very different ideological debate, one that may yet redraw the map of the mountain provinces. And revolutionary fighters, both Igorot and lowlander, are attempting not merely to reconstitute the Cordillera's lines of power, but rather to capture the very Philippine state.

LAND CONFLICTS

Contradictions in land law, including discrepancies both within the Philippine land code and between official and customary law, have generated an extraordinary legal quagmire. Property disputes at present form the primary focus of social tension. The roots of these conflicts extend back to the early American period.[1]

COMMUNITY AND PRIVATE LANDS

Within Buguias, only a few small plots are under community management. It is interesting that these represent not a survival but rather a new form of communal tenure, one devised to protect dwindling forest resources. When the Americans established the Cordilleran Forest Reserve, they "awarded" each community a small woodlot for common use, that of Buguias covering some 70 hectares. These forests were not respected. They had no indigenous roots, and the larger "public" reserves, although formally ceded to lumber and mining corporations, were still considered village property. Eventually the entire "Buguias Communal Forest" was cleared for gardens. But by the late 1960s, a perceived need to stem forest clearing prompted the reinvention of the communal forest at the local level. Within Buguias, the residents of Demang, the hamlet to the west of the Agno, grew concerned over the use of their wood to support a building boom in the center of town. Realizing that their pine stands would soon be exhausted, the local elders argued for partial closure and communal control. The hamlet accepted their proposal; henceforth outsiders could obtain firewood and lumber only if first granted permission by the elders. To date, no other hamlet of Buguias has established a common forest.

The Americans designated a few communal lands, but the thrust of their land policy was to privatize indigenous holdings in order to facilitate the expropriation of all "unclaimed" land as public domain—which could in turn be consigned to corporate interests. But the colonial government lacked the wherewithal to carry out the requisite surveys, and the hurried examinations they did conduct assured a discordant future.

The first major postcolonial change in land policy came during the Magsaysay era of the mid-1950s. Magsaysay supported a partial land reform as part of his strategy to stanch rural unrest in the lowlands. His Executive Order 180 of 1956 allowed cultivators to claim certain lands within the public domain. Benguet gardeners could now theoretically acquire title to their plots, even if they lay within the Forest Reserve. To guard against soil erosion and watershed destruction, however, the state required each farmer to obtain a release from several government agencies (*Baguio Midland Courier* April 8, 1956). Such bureaucratic maneuverings proved formidable; each farmer had to negotiate with the Bureau of Forests, the Bureau of Land, the Bureau of Soil Conservation, and several other agencies as well. Later administrations strengthened and extended the rights established under Executive Order 180, but the titling procedure remained cumbersome, while new natural resource laws actually erected additional hurdles.[2]

The Marcos regime continued to make vain promises and to pass unenforceable laws. In signing Executive Order 87, Marcos only raised new hedges in the maze; now deed-seeking farmers had to gain clearance from the Bureau of Forestry, the Mountain Province Development Authority, the Bureau of Parks and Wildlife, the Reforestation Administration, the Bureau of Highways, and the National Power Corporation. Two years later, Proclamation 548 placed 182,000 hectares of the upper Agno drainage—including virtually all Buguias—into a watershed protection zone (Tauli 1984:82); new titles were to be prohibited here and indigenous forestry and cultivation severely restricted.

After Marcos declared martial law in 1972, the state again tackled the Cordilleran land issue. Presidential Decree 410, signed in 1974, provided for the parceling of all Philippine "ancestral lands" into 5-hectare private plots (Lynch 1984). Although Benguet was expressly excluded, this act would have threatened the territorial integrity of most Igorot communities had it been enforced. Then in 1976, seeking to combat erosion, the state mandated that no lands of more than 18 percent slope could be titled. This act officially excluded most of Buguias from title application.

Not surprisingly, few farmers have found their way through the land titling labyrinth. Lynch (1984 : 195) tells of one man who moved through twelve certification levels before abandoning his quest. Most farmers found the necessary journeys to Manila too expensive and baffling. But a few growers persevered, and in so doing eventually learned to move smoothly through the halls of government. This knowledge enabled them to become legal entrepreneurs of sorts: individuals who could secure titles for others in return for a part of the newly legitimated property.

Legal entrepreneurship required a thorough understanding of Philippine land policy. To title a parcel located within the Forest Reserve, for example, one had to process papers at a series of agencies in the correct order, at each step convincing the responsible officials that the mandated conservation measures had been adopted. To title a plot already classified as Alienable and Disposable yet never before registered, a court order was also necessary.[3] Unclassified lands presented a different challenge; here the entrepreneur had to use political channels, including Imelda Marcos's Ministry of Human Settlements, to gain reclassification. And presidential caprice could undo successful work; lands in Tuba municipality along the "Marcos Highway," for instance, had been reclassified after years of local activism to allow prepatent titles, but in 1982 Marcos decreed that a 5 kilometer strip on either side of his eponymous road should remain a watershed preserve.

The several legal entrepreneurs have provided a valued service for Benguet farmers. They are perceived as acting in the common good, and their fees are generally considered to be deserved. Their strategy contrasts markedly with that of a more rapacious group of property law operators discussed below under the rubric of "land pirates."

Government policies allowing land titling have been aimed primarily at Mountain Trail growers. Now the center of vegetable culture, the Mountain Trail area was largely untouched by the prewar

American surveys since it was virtually unsettled at the time. In the Agno Valley, by contrast, much prime agricultural land was titled, or at least declared Alienable and Disposable (and thus eligible for titling), during the first years of American rule. As a result, land controversy here often revolves around disputed "real" ownership of long-titled land.

LAND CONFLICTS IN BUGUIAS CENTRAL

Property disputes in Buguias hinge largely on conflicting interpretations of the shoddy American surveys. The first such survey (made in 1903) has generated the most intractable litigation. Since most community members supported the later property examination of the 1930s, and since the subsidiary oral agreements devised at that time are still remembered, it has proved less contentious. But some of the best agricultural and commercial lands in Buguias remain under fervently disputed 1903 titles.

Land pirates, individuals who attempt to arrogate private parcels through legal conniving, cause the most serious property conflicts in Buguias. Their legal standings derive from colonial blunders; ancestors of the pirates were the compliant dummy owners of the large tracts titled in 1903. At the time, numerous individuals cultivated these plots, and since their holdings passed down and were subdivided during the intervening generations, an even larger group now tills and claims them. That a descendant of the original title holder would go to court seeking the entire estate represents a betrayal of community trust. Not surprisingly, the several land pirates reside not in Buguias but in Baguio City. If they succeed in gaining control, they plan to sell or lease the land back to the present cultivators, making a tidy profit in the process.

A descendant of a dummy owner won the first major case, the court ruling that both the original title and its inheritance were valid under Philippine law. But this individual has not realized his victory, since the occupants have simply resisted the order, hoping that a presidential review will overturn the ruling. A similar case has remained in court, undecided, for ten years. Community leaders fear that another unfavorable decision could endanger the existing unofficial community authority. But the court itself is seemingly stumped by the issue's complexity; the parcel in question has been divided, subdivided, and partly mortgaged and resold on many occasions. Moreover, this involves the delicate and politically charged issue of indigenous land rights, raising questions the jurists may well find daunting.

The most important property struggle in Buguias has a somewhat different origin. The parcel in question, located in the village's very heart, was originally, and correctly, listed as the property of Danggol. It passed through customary inheritance to one of his sons, who, since he did not wish to pay taxes, simply relinquished his claim. One of his brothers then assumed the tax burden in return for the title. When this man subsequently married into a powerful family in Kabayan he lost interest in his Buguias property. But his son (whom I will call "E. K.") decided to press the claim, and he has engaged virtually the entire community of Buguias in court battle.

This struggle is especially significant because of E. K.'s expertise in indigenous land rights. As an officer in OMACC (Office of Muslim Affairs and Cultural Communities), he has traveled to many areas where tribal peoples have been victimized by outside land-grabbers. Although his duties there involved protecting the victims of land piracy, he has used his knowledge and position to enhance his own acquisitions in Benguet.

While E. K.'s actions may at first glance seem hypocritical, at a deeper level they are fully consistent with his official duties. State agencies such as OMACC (and its predecessor PANAMIN [Roccamora 1979]) have endeavored not so much to protect indigenous land rights as to privatize community territory. In so doing, to be sure, they have sought to "give" each indigenous family an allotment. But when land is made fully private, individuals become free to accumulate property through any *legal* means. E. K. has now set himself to do precisely this, arguing that the Buguias people cling to an outmoded land system that impossibly combines customary and state law. What they must do, he insists, is discard all oral agreements and henceforth work through official channels.

While his case lingers in court, E. K. has met repeatedly with the Buguias people in tong tongan. He is willing to relinquish some claims, but he steadfastly demands rent on all commercial properties. The store owners fear that he may be powerful enough to

force an unpleasant outcome, and most would reluctantly compromise. But as of 1986, no reasonable offer had been made.

The American land-survey system ensured the present-day
property conflicts. Customary land rights were too complex to be
accurately represented by a simple survey using Western categories of land ownership—even if the survey teams had been trustworthy and adequately funded. As it was, while the Buguias people
could only comply with the colonialists on the surface, they had to
retain oral agreements to apportion actual land control.

As memory decays, oral agreements are revised retroactively
through self-interested reinterpretation—but land titles retain so-
lidity. Yet the Buguias people cannot afford legalities. The mere
cost of surveying exceeds the budgets of most farmers. Land titles,
even if undisputed, must therefore pass to a single offspring, who
must then be trusted by his or her siblings; moreover, this trust
must pass into subsequent generations. Some persons have attempted to sidestep such problems by attaching notes to their titles
detailing all relevant oral agreements, but these are of questionable
legal validity.

Many contemporary land disputes are indeed settled in tong
tongan, a testament to the institution's flexibility and to the diplo-
matic skill of the Buguias elders. But indigenous conceptions of
property rights have changed since the war, and aspects of the imposed Western system have been adopted for specific circumstances. As a result, even if the clogged Philippine legal system
could be entirely bypassed, customary law could not immediately
handle the existing backlog of cases.

TAX DECLARATIONS AND
CONFLICT SETTLEMENT

Western land law has failed in Benguet. As the tax-declaration system reveals, the government has reverted to a system of state ownership. In most parts of Benguet, private parties acquire only use-
rights through the payment of a fee—a "tax" on property that is
not "owned."

This system is replete with contradictions. Municipal governments, hungry for revenue, accept most declarations offered, even

where claims overlap. And at the municipal level it is meaningless that a given parcel may lie within the Forest Preserve, or be designated for watershed protection. This "blindness" does help protect indigenous land rights, but only in a backhanded manner. Yet tax collection and land allocation proceed surprisingly smoothly, as most individuals respect the declarations of others. Controversies arise most commonly over speculative holdings. Neighboring farmers may slowly expand their own gardens into such idle properties, and then claim "ownership" through occupancy.

Since three property legitimation systems (customary agreements, tax declarations, and official titles) intermesh in Buguias, any one couple may hold a staggeringly complicated estate. They may claim different kinds of rights to several dozen parcels. Some of their land may be inherited titled property, the title to which may be held under their own names, in trust by a sibling or a cousin, by a "land pirate" seeking to expel them, or by a bank. In addition, they may have tax declarations located in sectors not classified as Alienable and Disposable. Some of their holdings may be mortgaged by salda, while they may hold the plots of others through the same arrangement. Similarly, they may let out some land to another for a share, while at the same time they may themselves sharecrop another's parcel. Still another lot may have passed unofficially from them to a less prosperous sibling with no expectations of return.

It is thus hardly surprising that land disputes consume so much time and effort. But despite all complexity and contradiction, most conflicts are resolved in the traditional tong tongan forum. The tong tongan participants are entrusted to make peace, and if both disputants are Buguias residents this invariably occurs. The key is compromise, which the elders facilitate by the use of a series of flexible precepts. In land debates the primary considerations are length of occupation, actual land use, and the inheritance wishes of the parcel's previous holders. Elders may also weigh relative wealth, slightly favoring the less prosperous party. Disputed plots are usually divided, and if this is impossible the household receiving the land may be required to give its rival a cash payment. Neither party loses completely. The final agreement is always verbal, and although this leaves an opening for future conflict, it also dispenses with any suggestion of legalism, signifying instead that the settlement was agreed upon mutually.

THE RISE OF YOUTH CULTURE

Vegetable portage has provided the young men of Buguias with unprecedented cash incomes. At the same time, the decline of the vegetable industry and the growing scarcity of land have provoked pessimism among many. Enjoying easy money in the present but uncertain about the future, they have developed a distinct youth subculture marked by values variant to those of adult society. According to their parents, the typical bachelors not only lack proper respect for their elders, but are altogether unambitious, embodying the antithesis of the traditionally desired qualities. Many adults find this recently emerged subculture simply appalling. As one elderly man stated, "In the old days we wanted sons, but now we think it is perhaps better to have daughters, since they don't cause as much trouble."

The young men (and women) of Benguet group themselves into informal cliquelike groups (*barcadas*), structured primarily by residential groupings and voluntary association. The male barcada presses its members to conform to the bachelor culture and to oppose the ways of the adult world. A few boys chart independent courses while avoiding ostracism, but most remain under the heavy influence of their peer groups.

Boys begin the bachelor's life as soon as they have the strength to carry heavy sacks of vegetables. Many begin to avoid school in the second or third grade to earn portage fees. Even at this age children control their own earnings, often spending them on candy or in gambling. By the higher elementary grades many boys abstain from regular schooling, and by the age of fourteen most are professional vegetable carriers, fully identifying with the bachelor subculture.

The young men usually spend their nights together in the houses of older bachelors. Their work (when they work) is extraordinarily strenuous, but they usually pass many idle hours each day waiting for labor calls, giving rise to their English-derived nickname, "standbys." For supper they usually eat bread and canned foods; few bother to cook the standard fare of rice and vegetables. On leisure days (generally Thursdays and Sundays), they play basketball or volleyball, socialize in the municipality's markets, or scour the riverbed for the rich morsels used to complement San Miguel gin. To a great extent, bachelor culture revolves around drinking; as one young man phrased it, "Every night is a party for us." Not surprisingly, they enthusiastically attend all prestige feasts held in the community, despite the fact that many regard both Pagan and Christian religiosity with cynicism.

If no work is available, young men may be forced to return home temporarily. Most parents readily consent to the return, but familial turmoil not uncommonly follows. American visitors are often asked whether parents in the United States really insist that their sons support themselves once they reach eighteen; as one adult lamented, "We wish we could do this, but it is against our *ugali* [culture]—no matter how old our children are, we must care for them if they are in need."

The bachelors' worst sin, in the eyes of their parents, is their bellicosity. In normal circumstances most youngsters are irenic and bashful; young men often say that when sober they are too timid even to speak with their elders. But when intoxicated they not uncommonly fight among themselves. Most quarrels stem from geographically based rivalries or family feuds, but on at least one occasion an inebriated youth punched a barangay official who had restrained him, an unthinkable breach of social order. In response, the barangay council attempted to restrict the sale of alcohol at night, but this proved unenforceable.

The apolitical rebellion of the young is not entirely explicable in economic terms. Although many boys may join a subculture that offers a prosperous if brutal present because they face a possibly dismal future, the sons of the truly elite, young men whose careers are secured by doting parents, are not uncommonly the most obstreperous of the bachelors. Furthermore, the current economy is not so weak that any youngster could not build a base for future prosperity by accumulating rather than squandering his earnings. This is, of course, what the elders claim they would have done in the same position.

Many young men do begin to cultivate gardens before they marry, but most have access only to marginal sites. But even the most ambitious are hard pressed; if they do manage to obtain a decent plot they must also convince a wealthier farmer or trader that they are mature enough to be trusted in a "supply" relationship. Since few save any of their earnings, self-financing is not possible. Often their only gardening opportunity is to clear new land in the village's remote upper reaches, entailing much labor and few initial returns. Vegetable portage thus continues to lure, for its rewards are both abundant and immediate.

With marriage, the bachelor lifestyle is no longer tenable, and full-time gardening becomes both possible and attractive. Marriage often brings inherited property (from either side) and thus a chance for decent profits without the arduous task of land clearing. Furthermore, most young women are considered more responsible than their male peers, and wives often coax their husbands toward stability. Finally, the wedding itself usually saddles a young couple with considerable debt, which in itself is said to instill a sense of duty. After marriage, most men begin to heed their elders.

Youngsters eventually abandon the bachelor lifestyle, but some parents find the phase so destructive that they try to shield their sons from it altogether. This is best done by moving to another village where the generational split is less pronounced. The bachelor counterculture is strongest in Buguias, owing mainly to the community's agrosocial environment; vegetable portage, the subculture's economic underpinning, has developed significantly only where small, independent farms are poorly served by roads and where communal work-exchange groups have atrophied. According to some, the cloud forest provides the best refuge; here teenagers are said to be naive, and traditional values persist. Several Buguias couples have accordingly moved up-slope, in part to protect their children from peer groups. Others have sent their sons to distant schools, and a group of Buguias students attend secondary school in Tinoc for this reason.

CONTEMPORARY POLITICS

BENGUET AND THE PHILIPPINE GOVERNMENT

Relations between the people of Benguet and the Philippine state began to deteriorate in the 1950s and 1960s, and by the depression years of the mid-1970s crisis was fermenting. The 1950s brought territorial dispossessions; several whole villages were displaced by two hydroelectric dams constructed on the Agno River, while other communities lost their lands in the 1960s and 1970s to the Loakan airport near Baguio, to the "Marcos Park" (infamous for its giant hollow-headed bust of the former dictator) in Tuba, and to the Baguio Special Export Processing Zone. The national government lost credibility as entire communities were summarily deprived of land and livelihood (Anti-Slavery Society 1983; Cordillera Consultative Committee 1984).

The increasingly poor quality of government services also disturbed Benguet residents (Solang 1984). The foremost issue here was the condition of the roadways, lifelines of the vegetable economy. While the Marcos government laid extravagant concrete highways throughout the Ilocano-speaking lowlands, the Mountain Trail remained a rough dirt track. The Buguias people were also galled by their lack of electricity, despite the high-voltage lines passing through the municipality, and by the minimal attention given to irrigation development.

The state agency overseeing indigenous groups has been another major irritant. This bureau, known in 1986 as OMACC (Office of Muslim Affairs and Cultural Communities), has been reformed every few years, but state policies toward "national minorities" or "cultural communities" have changed little. Several scholars have accused the bureau of intentionally undermining traditional cultures (Roccamora 1979; Anti-Slavery Society 1983) or, at best, of "preserving" them only for the tourist trade. Indeed, in earlier years state agents readily admitted their desire to submerge the "non-Christian" peoples into the single "Philippine Nation" (see Tadaoan 1969:247). In Buguias, a relatively powerful community, such policies have been ineffectual, but they have added another level of bureaucratic interference. If a Buguias farmer seeks a bank loan, for example, he or she must first obtain OMACC permission. Even the charitable OMACC projects are often considered fraudulent.

LOCAL POLITICS

Political rifts take different forms at the local level. Buguias municipality is unofficially divided into two rival parts: the north, centered on Abatan and Lo-o, and the south, focused on Buguias

Central and, to a lesser extent, Natubleng. The northern district, home of the largest farms and businesses, is more powerful. Buguias Village, despite its several wealthy families, is now a depressed barangay relative to its northern neighbors.

The Buguias people complain that the northerners dominate municipal politics. They accuse mayors from Lo-o and Abatan of refusing to support road projects in the south, instead shunting the available funds northward. National political rivalries are also implicated here; in 1984 and 1985, Buguias's barangay captain was staunchly oppositionist (i.e., anti-Marcos), whereas all the municipal officials supported the dictator and his KBL party. This, according to some, prompted an even greater pinch on the southward flow of municipal funds. Many Buguias residents also remain indignant over the transfer of the municipal seat from their village to Abatan.

But the rivalry between the north and the south is still generally friendly. A series of informal compromises includes an agreement to the effect that northern mayors should be paired with southern vice-mayors, and vice versa. Less easily realized is the corollary notion that mayors should come alternately from the north and the south.

The mayor, more than any other municipal office holder, must intercede between his constituents and state institutions, and it is crucial to have a mayor who will be sympathetic to one's own village's needs. To serve effectively, he must cultivate personal relations with powerful individuals in the provincial and even national governments. For the people of Buguias, Stafin Olsim has long fulfilled this role, first as a private citizen, and after 1988 as the mayor of Buguias municipality. A continual stream of supplicants has long passed through his Trinidad home. Such assistance is invaluable at both the personal and the community levels; as one woman living in a remote Benguet village told me: "Our problem here is that we have no one like Stafin Olsim who can help us with the government."

Pagans comprise the majority of the municipality's population, and virtually every mayor has been of that persuasion. Since most persons agree that a Christian cannot hope for this position, religion plays little role in municipal elections. Indeed, in 1989, following the election of a strongly traditionalist mayor from Buguias proper, Paganism was virtually institutionalized when the Buguias Town Fiesta included within its celebrations a pedit of "13." At the lower barangay level, however, religious politics may be significant. Some barangays are divided evenly between the two faiths, and campaign rhetoric often has a religious flavor. But other issues may be overriding. Candidates' personalities and positions on specific issues, as well as the rivalries between different hamlets within a single barangay, strongly influence local elections.

Class plays a major yet ambiguous role in local politics. A mayoral candidate must be wealthy. Campaigns themselves are expensive, and, once elected, a mayor must play host at a continual series of negotiations and rituals. Only a wealthy man would command the prestige necessary to consider standing for office in the first place. Yet prosperity alone will hardly ensure political success. An unpopular baknang, one who stints on feasts or who gives no quarter to debtors, cannot expect popular support.

In Buguias, class divisions also reflect an inchoate philosophical divide. Two vague camps have recently emerged. The first, identified with the Pagan traditionalists, supports the prerogatives of wealth—if validated through feast performance; the second, composed of both Pagans and Christians, argues for the rights of poorer persons. But both camps wield similar rhetoric, centering on the necessity of redistribution and accepting class divisions so long as the elite act in the spirit of noblesse oblige. The "traditionalists," however, restrict redistribution to ritual occasions while their rivals call for a more generalized practice.

The intellectual leader of the latter camp is an expert on Pagan ritual and is the village's foremost negotiator. He frequently advises politicians (both Pagan and Christian) and pedit aspirants on protocol, and he conciliates individuals embroiled in intrafamilial religious disputes. When counseling the rich, he reminds them of their obligations to the community (on both sacred and secular occasions) and of their responsibilities to forgive, on occasion, their debtors. Adhering to the tradition of Buguias "spiritual empiricism," he holds as exemplars a certain baknang couple who he says has been scrupulously honest in all business dealings, has offered minimal-interest loans to needy persons, and has celebrated every ritual occasion unstintingly—and who has prospered tremendously in the process.

MARTIAL LAW AND REVOLUTION

After Marcos declared martial law in 1972, the state began to interfere more directly in local affairs. Individuals were then summarily arrested for tree cutting, and fertilizer delivery was temporarily banned. Acting under a questionable sanitary theory, local military forces demolished pigpens located underneath houses and destroyed all swine fed on human waste. These actions devastated many households living in areas too remote for commercial farming.

Such arrogant policies prompted a quick reaction; by 1972 the revolutionary New People's Army (NPA) started recruiting local students. Shortly thereafter, economic collapse bolstered the budding rebellion. Several knowledgeable Buguias residents estimate that some twenty local students hiked to the eastern mountains to join the mixed Ilocano, Kalanguya, and Ifugao guerilla bands already established there.

Under the leadership of a man from northern Buguias municipality, one guerilla band established an informal base at Bot-oan. In these early years the rebels regularly hiked through Buguias, sometimes asking for food and lodging, on their way to purchase supplies at Kilometer 73. By 1975, NPA territory had expanded to include the whole of eastern Buguias municipality.

The presence of an NPA contingent in Buguias prompted the state to establish a Philippine Constabulary camp north of Lo-o. Soldiers were also billeted in Buguias, where they frequently quarreled with the local youths. Road construction formed another anti-insurgent policy; the major roads east of Buguias were primarily designed for military operations and financed through military channels. The U.S. Air Force, Camp John Hay, and the 206th Home Defense Team together financed the Bot-oan road (*Baguio Midland Courier* April 27, 1975). The largest battle in the Buguias region marked this road's opening; the inaugurating committee, which included several high-ranking military officers, was met by a well-coordinated, although not entirely successful, ambush (*Baguio Midland Courier* Feb. 14, 1976).

The increased pressure of the Philippine military, the building of roads, and even the rapid clearing of forests, gradually weakened the NPA's position in Buguias municipality. The rebels also encountered personnel difficulties. The Benguet recruits supposedly found life in the mountains, characterized by the dull diet of sweet potatoes that their parents had so happily abandoned, to be a trying ordeal. The partial recovery of the vegetable industry in the late 1970s also helped lure the locally born guerillas back to village life. Popular support for the rebels, never overwhelming, also began to evaporate as Buguias citizens increasingly came to see rebellion as more of a threat to their remaining prosperity than as a promise for a more just regime. Meanwhile, the local cadre retreated out of the municipality and into the oak forest fastness of western Ifugao Province.

But the NPA did remain strong in the Tinoc district. This region has been neglected and victimized more than any part of Benguet. Here a mixed group of Kalanguya, Ifugao, and Ilocano guerillas has enjoyed much local support. In the early 1980s they temporarily seized Tinoc, disarmed its police, and imposed a curfew. This guerilla band appears to support itself in part by cultivating marijuana, much of which is supposedly sold ultimately to the American servicemen of Clark Field and Subic Bay.

Since all attempts to construct a road between Tinoc and Buguias have failed, military actions in western Ifugao have been limited. Airborne parties have, however, destroyed *Cannabis* patches and strafed suspected guerilla bases. Such actions have further turned the locals against the Manila government. In September 1987, NPA fighters raided a munitions supply near Tinoc, and in early 1988 guerillas were again seen in the hinterlands of Buguias.

The CPA

Since the late 1970s, Igorot intellectuals have been increasingly drawn to radical and *indigenista* thought. They argue that the Cordillera should be locally controlled, and that outside incursions, whether through state interference or capitalist penetration, should be firmly resisted. Following the outline established by the World Council of Indigenous Peoples, many have stressed territorial rights (CPA 1984). Considering the dispossession and exploitation suffered by the Cordilleran peoples, this movement's rapid growth is not surprising. In 1984, several dozen Igorot interest groups joined together under an umbrella organization called the Cordillera People's Alliance, or CPA. CPA leaders sought to establish a measure of political and economic autonomy for the mountain peoples and to revitalize old cultural patterns in forging a new polity.

The CPA agenda was widely embraced by students in Baguio and by the inhabitants of the northern Cordillera. Few Benguet residents, however, accepted these radical proposals eagerly. To politicize the Benguet people, the CPA initiated in 1986 a student-run educational program; during their summer vacations, groups of students from throughout the mountains visited various Benguet villages (including Buguias) to discuss politics and to circulate a petition calling for Cordilleran autonomy.

The Buguias people reacted to the CPA students in a decidedly mixed fashion. When the discussion focused on control of local resources, land rights, and governmental neglect, consensus readily followed. But more specific points encountered skepticism. Here the CPA was disadvantaged simply by the ages of its representatives; a number of community leaders did not think it proper for such young persons to propose a political course. More substantially, the CPA agenda continually snagged on the issue of intercultural relations; several Buguias leaders expressed fear that any autonomous region would soon be dominated by the northern peoples. As a corollary, they argued that the Benguet farmers would pay a disproportionate share of the region's taxes, just as they had under the old unified Mountain Province.[4]

A few Buguias residents also found offense in one student's off-hand comment that taxes, private property, and monetary interest should be abolished. To a Buguias Pagan, an attack on interest could be construed as a salvo aimed at the very heart of his or her culture, since the entire prestige feast complex rests on interwoven debt relations. Ultimately, the meeting of the CPA youths and the people of Buguias proved frustrating for both parties. It was a clash between two discordant philosophical perspectives; one determined to effect radical change, the other pragmatic and deliberate.

THE 1986 ELECTION AND BEYOND

In 1984, Benguet elected Samuel Dangwa, nephew of transport entrepreneur and war leader Bado Dangwa, to the Philippine legislature. Dangwa ran as an oppositionist (i.e., opposed to Marcos), but soon transferred his allegiance to the KBL. According to rumor, he did this to extract a promise that the Mountain Trail would be paved. Once Dangwa aligned himself with Marcos, the Buguias municipal elite followed. Several politicians stated (for public consumption) that the entire municipality, except the errant barangay of Buguias Central, would heed their words and vote for Marcos in the 1986 election.

This prediction proved to be grossly unfounded. All but two of Buguias municipality's barangays favored Aquino, most by margins of two to one. When the Marcos family fled the Philippines, spontaneous celebrations erupted everywhere—although several leaders, concerned that their political futures were now jeopardized, were notably absent. Yet it was soon evident that such fears were unfounded when, in 1988, the municipality voted these same men back into office.

The larger arena of Cordilleran politics since the fall of Marcos can only be described as convoluted, if not bizarre. Conrado Balweg, the (in)famous "rebel priest of Abra," soon left the NPA, denouncing it as lowlander-dominated, anti-Igorot, and totalitarian. Balweg's troops then joined forces with the Aquino government in attempting to fashion an "autonomous" Cordilleran government. Meanwhile, the CPA leaders accused Balweg of acting on behalf of the CIA and the still-repressive state; he, in turn, inveighed against the covert Marxist agenda of his attackers. Eventually the government as well turned against Balweg. Moderate Igorot intellectuals, for their part, saw only danger in both camps; most would like local autonomy, but they fear both the revolutionary furor of the left and the largely invented "traditional" communalism of Balweg's group. Most of Benguet's local politicians, for their part, have desired only a continuation of the status quo. Apparently many citizens agree, since in January 1990 the only Cordilleran province to vote in favor of autonomy was Ifugao (on recent Cordilleran politics, see Finin 1990).

As has been alluded to above, virtually all levels of political discourse in Buguias, from barangay campaigns to the contentious relationship between the Cordillera and the Philippine state, involve religion to some degree. Rituals continue to affirm communal solidarity, but with part of the village having converted to Christianity, the community affirmed has become that of believers rather than that of the village as a whole. As a result, Paganism—the cultural linchpin and economic fulcrum of Buguias life—has become at the same time a focus of contention. It is in this ideological sphere, to which we now turn, that some of the most emotional conflicts within the community occur.

10

Religion in Modern Buguias

INTRODUCTION

The economic, ecological, and political life of prewar Buguias was guided by a strong community consensus in religious ideology. That consensus has been sundered since the war by a growing Christian presence, the full import of which has yet to be reckoned. Christian converts today account for roughly a third of the village's population, and their continued proselytizing has made religious belief a primary axis of controversy.

The following discussion opens by introducing the central tenets of Pagan thought, a metaphysics in which earthly fortune is firmly tied to ritual performance. Many of the practices based on this belief were described in detail in the discussion of prewar prestige feasts. In this chapter, additional rituals concerned with "capturing luck" are introduced, and the implications of the whole set of Pagan practices for the community's social structure are analyzed. The remainder of the chapter recaps the relatively brief history of Christian missionizing in the area, presenting in detail both sides of the subsequent ideological debate, and exploring the social and geographic contours of the present standoff between the two groups of believers and their numerous syncretic offshoots.

THE "BUGUIAS PAGANISM SYSTEM"

The pivot of Pagan thought and practice in Buguias is the capturing of luck through ritual. Fate is believed to be in the hands of the ancestors, who bestow it differentially upon the living in accordance with the rectitude of the latter's propitiations. This tenet has, if anything, been strengthened by the transition to commercial agriculture, entailing as it does a continuous gamble.

OMENS AND RITES

The cultivation of good fortune begins with marriage. Once a couple has a child, "their blood is out and their luck runs with it." A feast must therefore precede the first birth; if it does not, the union is jinxed. The newlyweds must watch for supernatural signs; if, for example, they spy near their house a lizard facing east, they may rejoice, but a reptile turned to the west will force a short period of separation. Other favorable omens may be encountered at any time throughout one's life; those associated with dreams, insects, or other natural signs (*sangbo*) call for expert interpretation so that the promised luck can be captured. Since predicted good fortune can sometimes be expropriated by another more aggressive person, action must be prompt.

Having performed the required rites, a family may not realize the sangbo's promise for some time—occasionally for several generations. Nor will luck ever appear as a mere windfall. Usually it must be activated by undertaking new economic endeavors, or at least through diligent work. But the reception of a sangbo is often motivation enough to strive. As one Buguias resident put it, "I must work hard in my garden because my grandfather had a sangbo, and I am waiting for its manifestation."

Arduous labor alone will not ensure that the sangbo will be realized. While awaiting fortune, one must fulfill all ritual obligations, lest the luck should seek a more worthy beneficiary. If a couple neglects the ancestors their luck will simply "come and go." It is only by supporting sangbos with ritual action and diligent labors that prosperity may be achieved.

Stories of sangbos, both realized and lost, reinforce Pagan ideology by demonstrating the efficacy of ritual. One tale, recounted as far away as Kapangan municipality, tells of a momentous sangbo received by Stafin Olsim; after he was pestered repeatedly by a large, red-striped bee, the elders determined that this presaged success in the truck, bus, or heavy equipment business (the ubiquitous Dangwa buses are red and black). Although Olsim's bus company failed, his family has dramatically prospered in trucking and bull-dozing, apparently fulfilling the prophesy.

Other stories recount the foolishness of ignoring supernatural signs. A swarm of bees, for example, once entered the house of a newly married couple who, being Christians, declined to capture the fortune. The bees then moved to a Pagan household, but one too poor to perform the necessary *dawat* ceremony. Finally the swarm settled with a couple who, willing and able to seize the promised luck, subsequently rose to become top vegetable traders. Even those already wealthy must heed such messages; one prosperous trader supposedly refused to butcher a pig after consulting a medium over a troublesome dream, arguing that the recommended procedure only reflected the ritualists' greed for meat. Soon thereafter his fortunes reversed, and one by one he lost his trucks and his friends.

To cultivate good fortune, Buguias Pagans perform several rituals other than those concerned with omens or designed specifically to honor the ancestors. Prayers for specific business endeavors cultivate momentary luck and ward against misfortune. Such rites, performed in the prewar period before trading expeditions, were readily adapted to commercial farming. In *buton*, a ritualist determines the promise of a proposed venture through chicken gallbladder divination; if it is positive, the individual may perform *bunat* to garner additional luck. Buton and bunat may serve for any risky occasion, including political contests, card gambling, court battles, and, of course, the vegetable trade. Several local manbunungs have even found a lucrative market in the cockpits near Baguio. This has engendered priestly conflict, however, for the more conservative Pagan leaders feel that cash payments (often 250 pesos per cockfight), rather than the traditional emoluments of meat, threaten to undercut the power of the ritual and to discredit Paganism in general.

FEASTING AND SOCIAL STRATIFICATION

As in the prewar period, ritual expenses do not level class distinctions. Certainly wealth is redistributed during rituals, and the ability of the elites to accumulate is hampered by their continual ceremonial obligations. But couples of modest means must also celebrate, and although their expenses may be smaller, they often entail a greater proportion of their wealth than do the grand feasts of the baknangs. In prewar days the powerful sometimes took advantage of the financial plight of poorer celebrants to acquire their lands, but this practice seems in abeyance at present, possibly because the Christian challenge has forced greater caution.

Several writers have recently argued that Benguet prestige feasts no longer effectively redistribute resources because the elite can avoid participating (Voss 1983:230; Russell 1983:239). In Buguias, at least, this is not true. None of the wealthy in Buguias is a Christian, and no well-off Pagan can shirk ritual obligations. Along the Mountain Trail, traditional observances are more lax; yet even there, social pressures as well as religious beliefs motivate most baknangs to continue celebrating ritual feasts. The expectations of reciprocity and of noblesse oblige—as mediated by the council of elders and by the mankotoms—remain at the center of what one resident called (in English) "our Buguias Paganism system."

Beyond a doubt, the pedit series has attenuated since the war, even in the traditionalist stronghold of Buguias. In earlier days, the richest continued escalating the scale of their feasts until they reached the level "twenty-five"; now, few surpass "nine," the point at which baknang status is conferred. Yet because of population increase, a modern pedit of "nine" may well entail the same expenditure as a prewar celebration of "twenty-five" (see map 9). In April, 1986, an Abatan couple performed "thirteen," feasting an estimated 5,000 persons at a total cost of some 300,000 pesos (U.S. $15,000)—an outlay unthinkable before the war. Nor do a wealthy couple's ritual responsibilities end with pedit. Memorial and other services for the dead also consume more money than they did previously. The most powerful individuals, those who aim for political careers, also find themselves burdened with numerous minor feasts, as well as with the expenses incurred as negotiators.

If prestige feasts fail to level wealth in Buguias today it is because the poor continue to celebrate beyond their means. Both worldly and spiritual rationales contribute; ritual performance is needed to secure the goodwill not only of the ancestors but of the wealthy Pagans as well. Russell (1983:238) is on track in arguing that ritual expenditure in Benguet may be "a way to increase bargaining power vis-à-vis the village elite through status enhancement," but in Buguias, this is often a matter less of enhancing than of merely maintaining one's position with kinspeople and covillagers.

Nonelite celebrants sometimes find themselves in uncomfort-

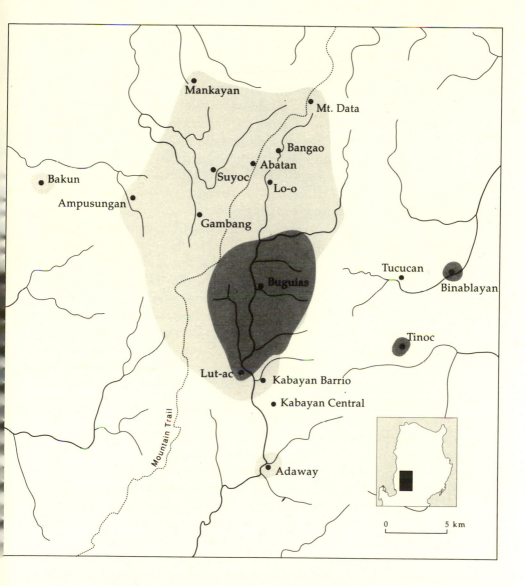

Map 9. *The Spatial Dimension of Pedit Feasts.* The dark zone indicates
the area invited to a pedit of "nine" held in Buguias Village; the larger,
lightly shaded zone (which fully encompasses the former zone except for
the outliers of Tinoc and Binablayan) indicates the area invited to a pedit
of "thirteen" held in Abatan. The larger the feast, the larger the area
invited. Determination of the villages included depends on their
proximity to the host village as well as the residence locations of close
relatives of the celebrating couple (hence the presence of "outliers").

able positions. In May of 1986, for example, a couple in desperate debt was convinced by relatives to perform a memorial ceremony (*otong*) for the man's deceased mother combined with a lim-lima, or level "five," pedit. Although both spouses professed Christianity, they felt obligated to perform otong, having promised as much to the dying woman; they however wished to avoid the pedit, but they simply could not withstand the pressure. The husband was from a prominent family, and his relatives argued that backsliding could imperil the entire lineage. The feast thus thrust upon them worsened the couple's financial straits dramatically. Since they still had outstanding debts from previous ceremonies, few neighbors were willing to lend, and loans from relatives fell far short of the 60,000 pesos ($3,000) required. They managed to obtain the requisite sum a few days before the ceremony began, but throughout the proceedings their countenances reflected unrelieved gloom.

The wealthy give feasts in part to enhance their power and prestige. Having reached the level of "nine," a man can expect a position of honor at all public occasions, and can gain a powerful voice in tong tongan councils. Yet if such a man does not continue to meet community expectations, the elders will begin to prod, reminding him of his parents' and grandparents' actions, of the need to balance getting with giving, and of the dangers that lurk for those who ignore the dead. If a wealthy couple fails to legitimate their wealth, people will insult both husband and wife behind their backs, and some may move business dealings to competing elites.

In a recent example, a very wealthy couple living on the Mountain Trail had performed only "seven," and this many years previously. Such stinginess, combined with a reputation for unsavory business dealings, cost the family much of its respect. In 1986, a health problem prompted the husband to seek guidance, and when the elders advised pedit—at a level several jumps ahead of their prior celebration—the couple agreed. Once they completed the ritual, negative feelings began quickly to evaporate.

Feast observations are necessary to legitimate wealth, but they are not always sufficient. Individuals who come into wealth quickly face special problems; they may be dismissed as having merely discovered hidden treasure (a fragment of Yamashita's legendary hoard perhaps), or even condemned for having exploited the poor. Here ritual expenditures are but the first step; the nouveaux riches must also take on the social responsibilities of wealth. Foremost among these is lending money to poorer villagers who wish to observe their own feasts. This too could potentially act as a hidden form of redistribution, if the capital involved could be more profitably invested elsewhere. But the structure of debt relations ensures that in the long run it is the elite who benefit.

CHRISTIAN CHALLENGE AND
PAGAN RESPONSE

The Spread of Christianity

Although Christianity is relatively new to the area, Paganism has not gone unchallenged in Buguias. Spanish missionaries made little progress in Benguet, in part because "nuevo Christianos" were obligated to pay higher tribute. Catholic priests did missionize several large villages, but they ignored Buguias, by one account because the dispersed settlement pattern made missionizing difficult (Perez 1904 : 191,192). American proselytizers also bypassed Buguias, according to local Christians, because the new colonists rushed to convert the headhunting peoples of the north. Only after the war did Christian missionaries arrive in the village.

In the early postwar years, the Catholic Church greatly increased its missionary activity in Benguet. Following a pattern established in the American period, Flemish priests staffed most new missions. In thoroughly Pagan areas, such as Buguias, newly arrived priests sought to understand indigenous beliefs, commonly attending local rituals for a time. Such activities were suspended in the late 1950s, following the establishment of a Catholic church and a high school in Abatan. A satellite church soon followed in Buguias, where the Abatan-based priest would visit for monthly masses.

Protestant missionaries also arrived in Buguias shortly after the war. The Jehovah's Witnesses enjoyed early success along the Mountain Trail after an American missionary reached Natubleng in 1948. When converted laborers returned from the Natubleng farms to their home villages, the religion spread. Its members now constitute a distinct minority in many communities; the congregation in Buguias includes a handful of families. The mainstream Protestant churches began to proselytize in greater Buguias a few years later. They spread in a geographically discontinuous pattern, each church assigning missionaries to a few specific villages. The Assembly of God established a firm base in Buguias, the Wesleyans set up outposts to the north and south, and the Anglicans attracted a strong following in Lo-o. The Lutherans built a hospital in Abatan but made few converts in the region.

The early missionaries gained converts from a variety of social backgrounds. In the 1950s and early 1960s, Catholicism attracted many college students in Baguio, some of whom saw Pagan practices as thwarting economic development and sometimes as threatening their own educations.[1] Several students later returned to Buguias to form the community's initial Catholic nucleus. Protestants more often came from poorer families; many saw in their austere new doctrines an escape from the burdens of Pagan ceremonials. But Protestantism attracted a few others also; one fairly wealthy woman joined the Assembly of God after numerous, expensive Pagan rituals failed to relieve her of extreme pain during pregnancy.

Conversion has often followed family lines; this has joined with the usual spatial congregation of kin to form a distinctive geography of religious affiliation in present-day Buguias. One hamlet is predominantly Catholic, whereas others, especially those more remote *and* those wealthier than average, have remained largely Pagan. Gender also plays a role, since more women than men have converted to Christianity. Men sometimes follow their wives into the church, but not a few remain reluctant Christians.

Members of the three Christian sects of Buguias differ in their relations with the Pagan majority. The Jehovah's Witnesses remove themselves from most aspects of village life. Assembly of God members avoid any activities that smack of Paganism or that call for drinking alcohol, but they do interact with their Pagan neighbors on other public occasions. Roman Catholics are yet more ambivalent, as they are not necessarily prohibited from attending Pagan feasts. While objecting strenuously to the religious content of such rites, the Catholic Church leaders recognize that indigenous ceremonies cement family and community ties. A good Catholic may attend a relative's pedit, but he or she is discouraged from joining in ritual dancing or other sacred activities.

Even among its leadership, however, the Catholic community is divided in its appraisal of Paganism. According to some observers, the local church has waffled considerably over the past thirty years, depending largely on the convictions of the priest stationed in Abatan at any given time. The official position at present advocates toleration and hopes for the eventual "Christianization" of public feasting. Thus, community-oriented redistributive feasts receive favor so long as they are undertaken in a Christian context, such as occurs at a house blessing.

Those most at odds with the Abatan church are the so-called *"Chrispas,"* or Chris[tian]-Pa[gan] syncretists. Members of this group, consisting largely of the metropolitan elite, are Pagan when in Buguias but Catholic when in Baguio. Buguias Christians usually view such heteroclites as true Pagans who only feign Christianity to gain acceptance in the city. The self-styled Chrispas, however, see no inherent contradiction between their two belief systems; each has its own *place* and each covers its own sphere of activity.

RELIGIOUS RIVALRY:
THE CHRISTIAN POSITION

A few Buguias residents appear to have converted to Christianity primarily to avoid ritual expenses. Devout Christians disparage this motive, and they were not surprised that several economically moved converts returned to Paganism on discovering that their new faith did not bring them wealth. Some persons formerly argued that Christians, being unencumbered by rituals, would become more prosperous than their Pagan neighbors, but this view is no longer tenable. Yet the economic debate continues. The most sophisticated Christian thinkers claim that whereas mass butcherings sensibly disposed of excess livestock in the past, today they only consume scarce capital. Moreover, they argue, a couple that saves in order to educate their children—rather than to feast the community and enhance their own prestige—should be respected as self-sacrificing rather than denigrated as self-serving.

The Christian judgment against Paganism aims squarely at the religious-economic linkage the traditionalists expound. They accuse Pagans of subordinating their religious practices to the base desire for worldly riches. Christians point to the silver coins over which manbunungs chant prayers as evidence that their Pagan neighbors actually worship money. Similarly, in pedit, taro slices soaked in hog blood symbolize coins, naked evidence of Pagan materialism. Christians accuse traditional priests of asking the ancestors to deliver the wealth of Christian outsiders into the hands of feast celebrants, or to send diseases from Buguias to other communities. Some Christians, most notably the Belgian priest, argue that Paganism is based on fear: fear of the ancestors and spirits, and fear for one's afterlife position. Christianity offers an escape from this fear, they say, through its assurance of love, joy, and salvation for all believers.

Christians also censure fervent Pagans for abusing their bodies by working too hard. Elderly men and women in the Pagan community often continue to toil in their fields even when they are ill, a pattern the Christians interpret as further evidence that they value money above all else. Some also disparage certain devout Pagans for wearing tattered clothing, quipping that one can easily distinguish an elderly Christian from an elderly Pagan at some distance. They also claim that the poor Pagan is effectively more impoverished than a poor Christian because the Pagan has to reserve much of his or her money for religious contingencies.

At least one individual converted to Christianity because he felt betrayed by Pagan practitioners. This man, who was studying to become a Pagan priest, noticed at his father's funeral that the corpse was wrapped in a woman's burial blanket, a grave insult to the dead. He convinced himself that this "error" was actually a deliberate move to anger the ancestors and thus withdraw favor from his family line. Pagan leaders insisted it was an honest mistake, and unsuccessfully urged him to consider his advanced age and investment in traditional learning.

The refusal of the Pagans to allow traditional cultural practices to be unlinked from their religious content has created a final arena of conflict. Unlike their counterparts in most other Cordilleran areas, Pagan leaders in Buguias allow no ritual actions to take place in secular contexts. If one wishes to dance to the gongs and drums, one must mark the event with sacrifices. Buguias schoolchildren's annual community performances thus feature dances from other Cordilleran regions rather than those of their own ancestors. Christians point approvingly to the northern Pagans for their less hidebound attitude in this regard.

Pagan Responses

Pagan rhetoricians are quick to counter the criticisms brought against them, and to level their own charges against what they see as the contradictions of Christianity. Christians are hypocritical, they argue, for while claiming that their faith is based on sharing and love, its real hallmark is selfishness. Pagans feed everyone, even dogs and rats, in their holy ceremonies, but Christians feed only themselves. Pagans sacrifice continually to ensure communal prosperity, but Christians work only for their own families. Several Pagan thinkers go so far as to argue that Pagan ritual embodies true Christian charity, enacting the injunction to love one's neighbor as one's self.

These apologists see no problem in their faith's materialism. Indeed, they point proudly to the intimate connection between the spiritual and physical realms as the cornerstone of their religion, citing empirical evidence to prove that proper ritual performance brings economic prosperity. Their religion, they argue, is based on nature and local tradition and is verifiable through observation; Christianity, in contrast, is supported merely by a foreign book.

Since Buguias Pagans see material fortune as the manifestation of spiritual integrity, they must explain how some Christians become prosperous. The usual explanation for the wealth of the few rich Igorot Christians in other communities is that they received heavenly favor through the actions of their Pagan relatives, if not through their own secret Pagan rites. A case often cited pertains to the Dangwa family of Kapangan. Buguias Pagans insist that the Dangwas continue to honor the ancestors despite their professed Christianity. The wealth of non-Igorot Christians, in contrast, is not considered problematic; lowlanders and westerners merely follow their own customs by adhering to the Christian faith—precisely the goal of the Buguias Pagans in cleaving to their own traditions. Paganism clearly advances no universalistic claims; it is specific to a particular locale and to a people with a common culture and a common group of ancestors.

Pagan thinkers dismiss the allegations that they ignore their appearances and abuse their bodies by turning these supposed vices into virtues. Willingness to wear tattered clothing and to work despite illness show a lofty and spiritual attitude; only the vain spend money on appearance, which does not honor the ancestors and brings nothing to the community. They also lightly shrug off the charge of "illness transfers." One manbunung countered that neighboring communities can simply respond in kind. "I send a sickness to Kiangan and the Kiangan priest sends it back here—before long we are tossing it back and forth just like a volleyball."

Nor do Pagans apologize for refusing to permit secular perfor-mances of ritual dances. To allow this, they claim, would be to de-base their religion, offend the ancestors, and risk the well-being of Buguias. They find the prospect of turning their rituals into cul-tural shows, as has happened in tourist locations in Ifugao and Mountain Province, utterly appalling.

The charge that rituals are so expensive as to preclude education in some families is taken more seriously. The most common re-sponse is that a balance must be sought between ceremonial and educational investments. Indeed, the theme of balancing tradi-tional obligations and modern demands runs through much Pagan rhetoric. Several children from Pagan households have received college degrees, and it is difficult to argue that Christians as a group value formal learning more than do Pagans.

An empirical bent underlies both Pagan and Christian beliefs. Arguments for both religions adduce physical evidence in support of supernatural causes. But the same phenomenon may be cited as proof by both sides. In a classic case, a prominent individual on the verge of death converted to Christianity and subsequently recov-ered. Some Christians argue that conversion saved him; Pagans claim that it was the rituals they performed on his behalf that made the difference.

THE GEOGRAPHY OF RELIGION

The ideological standoff between Paganism and Christianity throughout Benguet is reflected in a patchwork pattern of religious affiliation. Most southern Cordilleran regions are of mixed Pagan and Christian population, with some dominated by the former reli-gion, others by the latter. Christianity has made more headway in southern Benguet than in the north, yet distinct pockets of Pagan-ism persist throughout the south. Significantly, several of these lie in the political and commercial core of the province. The provincial capital, La Trinidad, has an especially strong Pagan community, and its manbunungs are noted for their conservatism. Bekkel, a small village on the outskirts of Baguio, originally settled by Buguias immigrants, is also strongly Pagan. In many of the small gold-mining communities of the middle Agno Valley, miners observe both Christian and traditional rituals.[2] Catholicism, however, predominates in many of the larger but more isolated Ibaloi villages; Kabayan Central, for example, no longer even supports a single practicing manbunung.

Several remote Ibaloi communities have retained a Pagan orientation, but with markedly simplified practices. This appears to be largely a matter of economics. Throughout Benguet, the prewar bases of wealth (cattle raising, mining, and trade) never reemerged after the war, undermining the elites' ability to finance large ceremonies. Only where commercial vegetables provided wealth could the pedit persist. Many Ibaloi villages saw their last graded prestige feast shortly after the war (see, for example, Barnett 1969:292), although lesser rituals, such as the memorial service, continue to be observed. A similar movement is apparent in some Kankana-ey districts of northern Benguet, where the more isolated villages, cut off from commercial farming, have lost their ability to support large feasts. Some have turned en masse to Christianity. In Bakun Central, for instance, wholesale conversions to Protestantism and Catholicism occurred in the 1960s (Tauchmann 1974). In Kibungan Central—according to Buguias residents—Paganism remains strong, but it has been refocused on curative rituals as pedit has been abandoned. This tendency is the reverse of that present in Buguias Paganism, where it is curative rituals that are now losing favor.

Along the Mountain Trail within Buguias municipality, diverse practices coexist. Some villages have largely converted to Christianity, but most show a rough split between Pagans and Christians. Voss (1983:229), for example, found that in Buguias municipality's roadside communities some 52 percent of individuals performed Pagan rituals.

Expensive Pagan ceremonies are less frequent along the Mountain Trail than in Buguias Village. The Mountain Trail Pagans actually tease their valley coreligionists for their incessant feasts. While the Mountain Trail's economy allows lavish ceremonies, its social milieu does not encourage them to nearly the same extent as does that of the adjacent Agno Valley. The highway villages, having sprouted after the war, did not inherit the intricate religious structure that has been transferred from one generation of elders to the next in long-settled areas. Nor was the geographic structure of "ritual congregations" (traditional village units around which all large rituals are organized) reproduced fully in these new communities. To a large extent, postwar migrants to the Mountain Trail found themselves freed from the dictates of an established elite and a council of elders.

But as prosperous farmers have emerged along the Mountain Trail, many of them have desired to legitimate their wealth in the traditional manner. Thus a significant impetus to perpetuate the old system remains, despite the general relaxing of ritual standards. Indeed, some Buguias residents claim that in the past several years prestige feasts have increased along the ridge, as farmers seek confirmation of their social positions while trying to manipulate the flow of luck. But lacking the strictures of the more conservative Paganism of Buguias Village, successful Mountain Trail residents often try to skip stages in the pedit sequence so they can more quickly rise. The Buguias priests, who often officiate here, generally disapprove of such shortcuts, but sometimes countenance them under the circumstances.

THE EASTERN FRONTIER

A distinct religious character marks the villages along the vegetable frontier east of Buguias, an area not missionized until very recently. Owing to economic change, large-scale feasts, never frequent here, largely disappeared after the war. Still, most villages not yet commercialized remain primarily Pagan. With the recent arrival of roads and vegetable growing in select areas came Christian proselytizers, mostly from obscure charismatic sects, who gained numerous converts. Particularly significant is the rise of syncretic cults in this frontier zone. Although these exist elsewhere in Benguet, syncretic movements have had little chance to develop in established areas like Buguias, which are marked by both an elaborate Paganism and an orthodox Christianity. The eclectic faiths are rather concentrated where commercialization is most recent.

Several cults of uncertain lineage thrive in the villages of eastern Buguias municipality. One conspicuous group is Milagro (Spanish for "miracle"), led by a "high priest" from a small hamlet to the east of Bad-ayan. Lay members also perform the group's characteristic curative rituals, relying on crucifixes and holy water as well as animal sacrifices. Milagro, like true Paganism, emphasizes the acquisition of wealth and the honoring of the ancestors.

Perhaps the most doctrinally complex of the syncretic religions, however, the Church of the Almighty God, is centered not east of Buguias but rather in Abatan. Its tenets are eloquently displayed on a series of needlepoint tapestries. The first, a calendar, indicates the holy days; the second illustrates the "Holy Family of the Three Kings" (the topmost monarch being labeled both with the Pagan "Kabunian" and the Christian "Apo Dios"); and the third presents an unusual map of the Buguias region. Lines representing "underground rivers" form the map's basic structure; some of these are indicated as running hot, others cold. Dots symbolize "growing stones," which are said to cause earthquakes when disturbed. The whole is crowned by the following message embroidered in English: "Believe it or not it is true, but please do not say bad things about the Almighty God." That this small sect so emphasizes underground water may reflect the worsening water crisis that marks each dry season in Abatan.

BUGUIAS AS A CENTER OF MODERN PAGANISM

Buguias is now the intellectual and ritual center of southern Cordilleran Paganism. The community no longer supports a practicing spirit medium; for this particular service Buguias residents must travel to Paoay (in Atok municipality), where the southern Cordillera's most famous mansib-ok resides. But as amply attested not only by local residents but by outsiders as well, the all-important pedit feasts, as well as other ritual events, are celebrated here more frequently and by a greater proportion of the populace than in any other Benguet community (see map 10). Moreover, Pagan ideology, especially as it theorizes the relationship between wealth acquisition and propitiating the ancestors, is most explicitly and fully articulated by the mankotoms of Buguias. Indeed, even a few of the leading Christians proudly claim that only in their community does Paganism retain both its traditional spirit and its lavish forms.

Buguias's Paganism is in some respects unique, having evolved

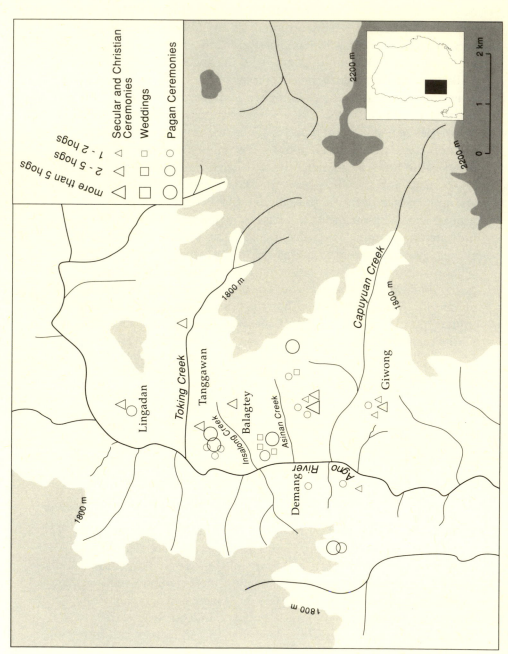

Map 10. *Prestige Feasts Held in Barangay Lubon, January and July 1986.*

Legend:

	more than 5 hogs	2 - 5 hogs	1 - 2 hogs	
△	△	△	Secular and Christian Ceremonies
□	□	□	Weddings
○	○	○	Pagan Ceremonies

Lingadan

Toking Creek

Tanggawan

Insaloing Creek

Balagtey

Asinan Creek

Demang

Agno River

Giwong

Capuyuan Creek

1800 m

1800 m

2200 m

2200 m

1800 m

0   1   2 km

in a direction independent of the traditional religious systems of other southern Cordilleran communities. Among the (once) culturally dominant Ibaloi, the graded prestige feast formerly allowed wealthy couples to legitimate their standing, but it was never viewed as an avenue along which the commoners could advance (see Pungayan 1978). The Buguias ideology, in contrast, holds that all persons may aspire to money and power so long as they are willing to follow the correct path. This tenet, which evidently emerged during the days of the trading economy, has been greatly reinforced by commercial farming. Paralleling this pseudoegalitarian bent is a decline in the position of the manbunung (priest) relative to that of the mankotom (adviser and prophet). In Buguias, the first merely performs rituals, while the latter is both the chief apologist for, and the grand strategist of, Paganism as an explicit ideology. Nowhere else in Benguet is this role so significant (see Hamada-Pawid and Bagamaspad 1985:110).

One index of Buguias's leading position in Benguet Paganism is the frequent employment of its ritual experts by residents of other communities. In June 1986, for instance, the president of the Big Wedge Igorot Mine Association in Itogon Municipality solicited the services of two Buguias manbunungs for a pedit ceremony. Buguias residents in attendance were surprised to find the Itogon youths unfamiliar with the complex procedures and in need of instruction at each step. The resident Bontoc miners were even more baffled, and they took offense on learning that they were expected to eat in village groupings. Buguias manbunungs have also officiated in Baguio City, in migrant Igorot communities in the adjacent lowlands, and on behalf of nominally Christian lowland politicians.

RELIGIOUS PLURALITY IN
PRESENT-DAY BUGUIAS

Religious Conflict

While Pagans and Christians debate fervently in Buguias, disputes seldom escalate into open confrontations. At present, leaders of both groups stress mutual respect and seek slow, deliberate change. Relations were more strained in earlier years, with tensions peaking in the 1960s after a Catholic priest hurled to the ground a sacred

Pagan marker, decrying it as the devil's sign. The incensed Pagan community responded with threats, both physical and legal. Later priests acted with more tact, and by the 1970s the two groups had reached an unsteady rapprochement. It is primarily the Jehovah's Witnesses who still occasionally infuriate Pagans, for they alone doggedly try to convert uninterested persons.

The most intense religious struggles occur upon the death of an individual survived by both Pagan and Christian offspring. Unless the deceased leaves explicit funeral instructions—and sometimes even if she or he does—the children may quarrel over the ceremony's religious content. The entire community can become involved in the ensuing arguments and intrigue. According to the resident Catholic priest, Pagan survivors have attempted on several occasions to hide death shrouds in Christian coffins.

Pagans generally respect Christian beliefs, but they nevertheless heavily pressure some converts to return to the fold, willing to accept them as fellow Pagans even if they wish to remain "part-time Christians." Elite family descendants form a particular target, since Pagans believe that even powerful ancestors may falter if denied full homage. The errant cousin or sibling may be reminded time and again of a parent's wish to be honored in the afterlife, of their family's pride and position, and of the need to follow precedent. If such entreaties are unsuccessful, relatives may threaten to deny the recalcitrant couple future business loans. As a result, even confessed Christians occasionally, if grudgingly, celebrate prestige feasts.

RECENT CHANGE AND COMPROMISE

The leaders of Buguias Paganism by no means espouse an orthodoxy. As elsewhere in the Cordillera, they not uncommonly borrow new observances from neighboring peoples and they often accept innovations in practice. Most elders do argue, however, that change should be gradual and that honoring the ancestors should remain central.

Paganism's postwar history reflects the period's economic and social transformations. A simplified prestige feast ladder now allows young couples to establish themselves more easily. Before the war, a distinct ceremony occurred before the birth of the first child;

this has now been melded with the first pedit. In earlier days, only local sacrificial hogs would do; now, lowland and "mestizo" swine are acceptable, provided they are black. Children now return to school after the first few days of their families' celebrations, whereas before they were kept home for the full duration. The Pagan funeral is also being transformed as the death chair gradually loses favor. Many Pagans now choose to be displayed in an open coffin.

Most Buguias Pagans have also changed their views on the diagnosis and treatment of disease. For a number of years a dual theory has prevailed, holding that illness may result either from natural pathogens (requiring Western medicine) or supernatural agents (calling for ritual and prayers). As late as the 1960s, most Pagans opted first for the spiritual remedy. By the 1980s, however, most had reversed the procedure, consulting the medium only if not cured first by medicine. The Pagan religious leaders see little significance here, since curing-rituals have long occupied a peripheral place in their larger ideological scheme.

A few influential Pagans now seek to establish a deeper understanding with local Christians, particularly Catholics. One Pagan elder moderates the disputes between the two groups, and he counts among his advisees several Christian leaders. He has proposed a compromise through which Pagans would more fully respect Christians while Christians would compensate by holding their own feasts (whether as secular "blow-outs" or to consecrate their own religious occasions). Conciliatory Pagans also ask their Catholic neighbors to honor Buguias's ancestors on All Soul's Day. Indeed, many Pagans acknowledge the efficacy of Christian prayer, especially as demonstrated in the "EDSA Revolution" that overthrew Marcos in February 1986.

The Catholic community, not surprisingly, is divided over the issue of socioreligious compromise. While many Catholics have recently increased their own outlays for feasts, others argue that this would only sustain an unjust economic order and penalize those who cannot afford both schooling and ceremonies.

Catholics face a greater challenge, however, from a new group of charismatic Protestant sects that are aggressively proselytizing in the Cordillera. Foremost in the Buguias region is the "Jesus Is Alive" (JIA) organization, sometimes disparagingly called *tumba*

tumba, or "falling falling," in reference to its ecstatic prayers. Although much more successful in the eastern frontier zone, JIA missionaries have converted a few Buguias Catholics, a trend worrisome to church leaders. According to one concerned man, the young are more attracted to "jolly religions," like JIA, than to the more contemplative traditional Christian churches.

TRENDS

One predicts the future of Paganism only at great risk. Most Christians believe that the old religion is in irreversible decline, for both spiritual and economic reasons. Many Pagan leaders are also worried; not only competing religions but also secular education and bachelor cynicism threaten Paganism. One manbunung foresees calamity for the community unless at least one member of each family line continues to mollify the ancestors.

For the moment, the two faiths and a variety of syncretic offshoots uneasily coexist. Despite the reiterated predictions of its demise over the last hundred years, Paganism remains the majority faith in Buguias and in many other parts of the Cordillera as well. Neither education nor economic change consistently undermines its appeal; it is an adaptable faith, which may yet convert or reconvert adherents of other religions. Indeed, a few Ilocanos, Tagalogs, and Chinese, including some wealthy and powerful individuals, have recently called on Benguet's ritual specialists to seek heavenly favor. Clearly it is too soon to say what will become of Buguias's pluralistic religious heritage when the present generation of elders passes away.

11

Conclusion:

Understanding Buguias's Aberrant Development

The central thesis of this work is threefold. First, it demonstrates that a small-scale society can become integrated into the global economic system through small-scale commodity production without necessarily experiencing a breakdown of its communitarian social order. Second, in the circumstances found here, it is not in spite of but precisely because of economic integrations that the underlying ritual system, transformed though it may be, has persisted. Finally, this unusual embrace of indigenous religion and capitalist agriculture imperils the community's ecological foundations, threatening commercial and environmental collapse.

If the environmental problems facing Buguias are painfully familiar, the peculiar linkages between economy and culture that form their social context are not. Having defied the expectations of social theory, Buguias's continued florescence of ritual practice under an essentially capitalist regime challenges us to explain why this community should so diverge from the norm.[1]

THE COMMERCIAL HISTORY OF BUGUIAS

Most small-scale societies are, or were, prior to their incorporation within the global economy, relatively equalitarian. Although often divided by rank, few were stratified by class (Fried 1967). Their economies generally relied not on monetary calculus but on reciprocal exchange, often structured through kinship. Such societies have proved highly vulnerable to the individualizing and economizing pressures inherent in a commercial order.

The villages of the southern Cordillera, by contrast, have long possessed social and economic structures that in many ways anticipated those of state-level formations. Cash-based trade formed a

significant component of their prewar economies, and class stratification was advanced. Elite couples owned the cattle herds and
the best lands, and they could pass on at least part of their wealth
to their children. Several scholars have argued that imperial machinations rather than autochthonous development produced this
elite class of "petty despots" (for example, Voss 1983:40), but while
Spanish and American authorities did bolster the indigenous elite,
I would argue that they were able to do so only because a plutoc-
racy already existed. That a baknang class, some of whose members were fabulously wealthy by later standards, predated Spanish
rule is quite clear in the historical record (Scott 1974).

The commercialized economy and stratified society of prewar
Buguias should not be overemphasized. Some goods were bartered, labor could still be mobilized cooperatively, and the bonds of
kinship and community moderated individualizing tendencies.
Moreover, the elite did not monopolize power, as most male elders
held important places in the tong tongan jury. But such qualifications notwithstanding, the socioeconomic system of prewar Buguias proved in many ways compatible with capitalism.

Elite dominance was underwritten by control of long-distance
trade. This was not a unique phenomenon; from the fifteenth to
the seventeenth centuries, Southeast Asia's "age of commerce"
(Reid 1988), commercial exchange was widespread throughout this
part of the globe. In northern Luzon, a trade originating in this period between the gold-producing uplands and ceramics- and iron-
bearing Chinese vessels had important ramifications for the Cordilleran hinterland. Supplying hogs to the gold miners allowed
highland merchants to accumulate considerable wealth, stimulated
the development of an integrated regional economy, and exposed
highland traders to the cash-based exchange system of the lowland
towns. Buguias's ultimately pivotal position between the consumption centers of the mines and the hog-producing oak-woodland nurtured in the community at large an entrepreneurial ethos. Without
the early experience in gold, the southern Cordillera in general and
Buguias in particular would have developed along very different
lines.

Since a finely stratified society and a highly commercialized
economy were firmly in place prior to the Japanese invasion, the
major transformations of the postwar period must be located in

other realms of social life. The most fundamental change during this era was the repositioning of the southern Cordillera within the global economy. Whereas Benguet's tenuous economic connection to the prewar international order was through the gold trade, the growth of a chemical-intensive temperate vegetable industry in the postwar era bound the area much more closely to national and international circuits.

The Buguias people entered these wider markets readily. They did not "resist" the new order in any of the common senses of the term. While protesting "alien" (resident Chinese) domination, they embraced the vegetable industry as a whole, including the accompanying extension and intensification of commercial exchange, the final privatization of land, the commoditization of labor, and the institutionalization of usury. Moreover, the community applauded the investment activities of its "progresso" accumulators. Voss (1983), on the basis of work among the nearby Northern Kankana-ey of Sagada, argues that despite having adopted certain forms of capitalistic relations, villagers have done so on their own terms and are thus still "resisting capital." In Buguias, such an interpretation is difficult to support. The Buguias people certainly did "accept capital" on their own cultural terms, but their local economy serves the multinational agrochemical companies as well as any.

GEOGRAPHICAL PATTERNS

The relationship between religion and economic change varies significantly across the southern Cordillera along three main axes. Foremost is the survival of ritual feasting in areas of commercial agriculture, generally those along the Mountain Trail and in the upper Agno Valley. Further, within those areas, it is the older valley settlements that retain the most elaborate ritual forms. Finally, a third crosscutting areal pattern follows cultural groupings: villages inhabited by the Southern Kankana-ey tend to be both more "progressive" economically and more conservative religiously than their Ibaloi neighbors. Let us take up each of these patterns in turn.

The survival of prestige feasting in commercialized areas is at one level a simple matter of resources. Before the war, low population densities allowed extensive pastoralism, providing abundant meat for ritual feasts throughout the area. With rapid demographic growth in Benguet during the late prewar and postwar periods, the ratio of stock to humans declined dramatically, with the consequence that sacrificial animals increasingly had to be imported from the lowlands. Only those villages able to parlay cash crops for meat could continue to celebrate lavish feasts after the war.

The eastern cloud-forest villages, however, many of which have yet to recover their prewar populations, were battered by the long-term depression of the highland gold industry. When the miners of Suyoc could no longer afford prodigious quantities of pork, the oak-woodland dwellers lost their main outlet for hogs and hence their essential source of cash. The increasing availability of cheap manufactured goods administered another blow, destroying the copper-ware industry and impoverishing the iron workshops. The final assault on the old economy was the privatization of village hinterlands; this, coupled with the ban on the open pasturage of hogs, made local meat production much more difficult than it had been.

Given, then, that for economic and ecological reasons prestige feasts persisted only in areas of commercial farming, it remains to be explained why the more elaborate forms survived only in the older villages of the Agno Valley—poor cousins, in fact, to the prosperous Mountain Trail vegetable districts. The answer lies in the local configurations of social power. Whereas the latter communities emerged wholly new after the war, social arrangements in the valley towns carried over from prewar times. Entrenched elders, who benefitted most from the traditional system, used their power to lobby for retention of the old ways. Also significant was the fact that Buguias farmlands never became concentrated in the hands of a few wealthy growers. Here dramatic individual changes of fortune have continued to occur, and ascension into the elite, while increasingly difficult, is still possible. This social and economic fluidity has supported the elders' arguments that anyone can prosper through appropriate ritual observances.

Finally, there is a persistent difference in entrepreneurial ethos between the two dominant peoples of the southern Cordillera: the Ibaloi and the Southern Kankana-ey. Although commercial farms dominate several Ibaloi districts, most continue to produce primarily for subsistence.[2] In Kabayan, an Ibaloi village directly south of Buguias, vegetables have been grown as cash crops for a number of years, but poor returns during the 1970s and 1980s persuaded many Kabayan residents to abandon market gardening altogether (Wiber 1985:428)—a response unthinkable in Buguias. Even in the commercialized (and traditionalist) Ibaloi community of Trinidad, graded prestige feasts have declined, although curing and death rituals have persisted. Moreover, the wealthiest farmers here *have* been able to stint on their ceremonial expenditures (Russell 1989*b*).

The key to this widespread difference in commercial attitudes appears to lie in the two peoples' strikingly different histories of class formation. As the onetime premier gold producers of the southern Cordillera, the Ibaloi baknangs sustained a rigidly stratified society, closing their ranks to upward mobility. Marriages did not cross the class divide, and commoners had virtually no hope of reaching elite status. This distinct socioeconomic evolution had repercussions for both commercial attitudes and ritual practices. The relative fixity of hereditary status discouraged commercial risk-taking—on the part of aristocrats as well as commoners. This in turn reduced the economic incentive for holding ceremonies, which among the Southern Kankana-ey were often undertaken to ensure business success. The Ibaloi elite of Kabayan had once used the feast system to acquire the rice terraces of their less-wealthy co-villagers, but with the decline of their economic hegemony after the war they began to abandon the prestige feast altogether (Wiber 1989). Yet at the same time, the Buguias elders were reforming their pedit into the centerpiece of a grand conceptual tableau, one encompassing both a modernizing economy and an age-old cosmos and one that explicitly posits a central role for social mobility.

The emergence of Buguias Central as a center of modern Paganism is thus a product both of the community's economic position in past generations and of its recent development. In particular, all three of the criteria that perpetuate redistributive rituals in the postwar era—the development of commercial agriculture, the existence of a long-settled community run by tradition-minded elders, and dominance by Southern Kankana-ey rather than Ibaloi cultural elements—have converged in Buguias Central, boosting this community to prominence as the center of modern Cordilleran Paganism. By the late 1980s, followers of the leading mankotom of Buguias, the community's prophet and premier adviser, could call him simply "the number one Pagan."

THE IDEOLOGY OF PAGAN ECONOMICS

The outsider may marvel at the persistence of redistribution in this commercialized economy, but Buguias Pagans view the redistributive aspect of feasting as secondary. Major rituals are above all an investment in future productivity, an indispensable step toward well-being in an undivided economic-social-cosmic totality. Understanding the economic logic embodied in these observances is critical for grasping how this community can at once embrace capitalism and retain its indigenous practices.

Buguias Pagans view ritual expenditures and wealth accumulation as positively linked, holding ritual as the bridge to the ancestral spirits who control each individual's fate. A married couple must work hard to earn the money necessary to honor the ancestors of both spouses, the ultimate fonts of their good fortune. Although an observer might predict that financing repeated banquets would counter capital accumulation, believers are convinced that heavenly favor will ratchet the devoted practitioners continually upward.

Pagans thus incorporate a spiritual element into their understanding of the economy. Where Western capitalists posit a two-stage cycle of accumulation and investment, Buguias entrepreneurs believe in three-stage cycle of accumulation, ritual, and investment. Baldly self-interested acts must alternate with feasting, for only by giving back a part of one's earnings to the ancestors (and, hence, to the community) can one hope to incur their good will. This is presented not as a sacred postulate, but as an inductive observation, to be debated on the basis of empirical findings. Of course, the actual evidence is ambiguous; most celebrants do not particularly prosper, and for those who do, other explanations could be invoked. But to date, no Buguias couples who have shirked major rituals altogether have prospered, giving Pagan apologists their most compelling line of evidence.

The manipulation of fortune is an ancient aspect of Cordilleran religion whose importance has only been enhanced with the move to commercial agriculture. In modern vegetable farming, beset as it is by extraordinary price volatility and frequent natural disasters, every couple's success clearly hinges in part on elements beyond their control. The belief that fate may be managed encourages people to plunge into this risk-fraught environment—to do such things as plant lettuce in the typhoon season or start a new bus line. The greater the risk, the stronger must be the anticipation of success; major business ventures are usually foreshadowed by signs of prosperity (sangbo). Omen interpreters readily counsel risky strategies, an index of their confidence in divining the flow of future luck, since their own fortunes ride with those of their advisees.

Buguias Pagans do not equate luck with windfall profit. Success is offered but not guaranteed; it must be captured through sincere effort. Earnest work may also help unlock ancient promises delivered to one's forebears. Such sangbo are numerous, providing many households with personal motivations to labor arduously. Operating at multiple levels, such beliefs inculcate a work ethic that far surpasses anything held by Buguias Christians.

Contention, Rhetoric, and Power

Pagan ideology is far from a single orthodoxy. Theories of reality and notions of proper conduct vary considerably; continual debate on such questions creates a shared field of discourse more than a unified body of ideas. Since whole groups of individuals have rejected the ideology of their parents for Christianity, that field of discourse has been widened and partially rent in the postwar period.

Inequalities of power color ideological discussions. Wealthy individuals seek to maintain their positions by manipulating the religious order, while less powerful groups try to counter the status quo or at least to effect compromises. In Buguias the elite cling fervently to Paganism. The richest, the chrispa sycretists, espouse Christian doctrine as well, but all seek to perpetuate the feast system.

Even the elite do not comprise an entirely homogeneous group with respect to this issue. The truly wealthy, a cosmopolitan group residing in the provincial capital as often as in Buguias, can finance their required celebrations at little cost to their businesses or to their accustomed levels of consumption. For these fortunate few, Pagan ceremonies are reasonable social and political investments, yet not indispensable ones; if the feast system were to collapse, their positions would not be jeopardized.

The village-bound middle ranks of the elite have more at stake in the system's perpetuation. This group is largely comprised of elders who owe their positions more to lifelong diligence than to dramatic business successes. They live frugally, saving as much as possible to finance their own and their neighbors' observances. By their clothing one might suspect many of them to be among the poorest members of the community. But their role in Paganism brings them considerable power in the council of elders, and if the feast system were to collapse, these individuals would fall with it.

In general, ritual obligations weigh heaviest on those of intermediate wealth. The poorest can simply decline to celebrate without fear of being turned away from their neighbors' feasts. But this option is not open to the less successful members of respectable family lines, individuals who must endure the financial and social pressures of their richer relatives. If such persons announce that they cannot afford the requisite ceremonies, they are virtually cornered into joining a Christian church. Converting will not convince relatives to desist from their hounding, but it does afford an ideological stance from which to resist, as well as an alternative community. Although all Christians do not convert for economic reasons, Christian leaders recognize that initial leanings toward the church often stem from resentment against the expenses of Paganism and the relentless pressures associated with it.

New Christians in Buguias are encouraged to study the scriptures in order to derive a less worldly foundation for their beliefs. In essence, they are taught to reject the premise that material wealth reflects spiritual worth. The fully converted level the charge of materialism against Paganism, accusing traditionalists of debasing the spiritual with the economic. Pagans, who insist that it is precisely through material goods that the linkages between heaven and earth are made manifest, return the accusation, arguing that Christians prefer to squander their wealth on personal luxuries rather than to share it with the community at large.

MAX WEBER AND THE SPIRIT OF CAPITALISM

Precisely because of the prevalence of redistributive mechanisms and ideologies stressing luck or magic, "tribal" religion has often been regarded as perhaps motivating production but necessarily as restricting accumulation—hence thwarting economic development (e.g., Goode 1951:136). The same view has been promulgated with regard to Cordilleran Paganism. In the 1960s, for example, Tadaoan (1969:247) expressed the concern of the Commission on National Integration that "pagan beliefs and practices . . . were the root-cause that retarded economic and educational projects."

Specific sects of the universalizing religions, by contrast, have long been believed to inculcate the very spirit of capitalist enterprise. Observing the Protestant affiliation of most European leaders of industry at the turn of the century, Max Weber (1904 [1930]) argued that Calvinistic "worldly asceticism" had been the ideological font of capitalism itself. The Protestant businessman, he argued, would rather invest capital than squander it in sinful pleasures, thus confirming his divine election through his pecuniary success.

Weber's followers have since found a similar ethos in the faiths of other entrepreneurial groups, including Jodo and Zen Buddhism in Japan, Santri Islam in Java, and Jainism and Zoroastrianism in India (Bellah 1968:243). Yet such assertions are rarely made for any but the so-called high religions. As Eisenstadt (1968:18) writes:

> It has been claimed that the more "magical" or "discrete" a religious system is, the less it is likely to facilitate the development of more continuous secular activities. The multitude of dispersed religious rituals found in most "primitive" religions were shown to inhibit the development of such sustained effort.

Indeed, converts to universalizing religions have often formed entrepreneurial islands within "tribal" societies.[3] Legitimating their actions by reference to their new ideologies, market-oriented converts can free themselves from onerous social demands. In Kapepa, Zambia, for instance, most successful commercial farmers are Jehovah's Witnesses who use their beliefs "to justify the repudiation of certain social relationships" (Long 1968:239).

In Buguias, the situation is reversed. Here, Jehovah's Witnesses and other Christians are distinctly less entrepreneurial than are traditionalists; in Buguias it is communitarian Paganism that inculcates both a strong business drive and a remarkable work ethic.

And unlike the people of Kabylia, Algeria (Bourdieu 1977), those of Buguias do not disguise or "socially repress" the connection between social actions and economic gains. The linkage of ritual and accumulation is not only recognized but constitutes the subject of frequent debate.

The symbiosis of religion and capitalism is if anything more tightly forged in Buguias Paganism than in radical European Protestantism. Where early modern Calvinists interpreted wealth as a *sign* of election, riches for Buguias Pagans are the necessary means to *obtain* spiritual favor. Far from being fatalistic, their belief is interventionist to the last. "Worldly asceticism," however, quickly evaporates in Buguias's rituals, replaced by an otherworldly hedonism that Weber's bourgeois businessman would find utterly sinful. But the Buguias traditionalists revel in such extravagance only so long as it remains in a ritual context—and Weber may have exaggerated the asceticism of the Calvinist burgher in any case (see Schama 1988:334, and Leroi Ladurie and Ranum 1989:113,114).

RITUAL ECONOMICS
AND THE SOCIAL ORDER

The success of the Buguias people in retaining their redistributive feasts by no means generates social equality. But neither exploitation nor social stratification is new to Buguias. Both were deeply rooted in the precolonial social order, and both are perpetuated by the long-term functioning of Pagan economics.

Prestige Feasts
and Social Differentiation

Several benefits accrue to elite celebrants, most immediately the legitimation of their wealth and enhancement of their prestige. Material reward may also follow; the respected baknang can attract clients more readily than could a disparaged noncelebrant. And for a would-be political leader, winning the support of the electorate requires major ritual investments.

But the wealthy receive their most substantial long-range benefits from the feast system through financing the rituals of their poorer neighbors. True, ritual loans carry minimal interest, but weighty debts put the borrowing class in a perpetually subservient position, allowing the elite essentially to control the community. Higher rates of return might be obtained in the short run by investing elsewhere, but the long-term benefits of maintaining a large and docile clientele are significant.

Redistributive ceremonials have been seen to serve the upper strata in other places and times as well. In the chiefdoms of northwest North America, elite villagers enhanced their positions through the potlatch even as they dispensed with much of their property (Drucker and Heizer 1967). The same was once true in Toraja mortuary rites; according to Volkman (1985:6) "ritual was thought to affirm a person's 'place' as a noble, commoner or slave, distinctions based upon descent ('blood') and, at least ideally, coincident with wealth." And whereas the "cargo" feasts of syncretic Catholicism in Mesoamerica have often been analyzed as regenerating social equality (Cancian 1965:137), Cancian found their effects at least in one Chiapas district to be more ambiguous:

> Service in the cargo system legitimizes the wealth differences that do exist and this prevents disruptive envy. There is, in effect, sufficient leveling . . . to satisfy normative prescriptions, but not enough to produce an economically homogeneous community [1965:140].

Cancian's observations hold as well for Buguias. Here, too, prestige feasts function simultaneously to redistribute riches and to reconstitute a hierarchical social order. Celebrants transform material wealth into symbolic capital (Bourdieu 1977), and while their prestige no longer allows elite villagers to mobilize labor directly, it does bolster their power in less direct ways.

For the community at large, the survival of the redistributive complex combines with the vagaries of vegetable farming to make for complex movements across class lines. Over a single generation, certain families in every class grow richer, while others, racked by ceremonial as well as other debts, fall lower in the social order. Shanin's (1972) analysis of Russian peasant household mobility patterns—highlighting the interactions of centrifugal (differentiating), centripetal (leveling), and cyclical mobility, and giving weight to chance events in each household's trajectory—provides an apt analogue.

In contemporary Buguias, chance cannot be overemphasized,

for the incorporation of risk into the deepest level of the ideological system influences all forms of mobility. The same belief in the manipulability of luck that supports entrepreneurialism has also proved devastating on occasion by encouraging untoward gambling. When Buguias residents gamed only among themselves, money remained within the community, the luck of the cards acting as a redistributive mechanism of sorts (cf. Mitchell 1988). But gambling has become a net drain for the community since the opening of a casino in Baguio City. If it is difficult for a habitué of Las Vegas or Monte Carlo to accept the inexorability of a slot machine's take, such notions are resisted even more strongly by Buguias Pagans, long schooled to consider luck the province of the ancestors. Of the four Buguias couples to have reached metropolitan elite status in the 1960s and early 1970s, three are said to have lost their fortunes in the plush rooms of the Baguio Casino (see Finin 1990 on Igorot gambling in general).

ANALYZING THE SOCIAL FORMATION OF BUGUIAS

The resulting social and economic structure of Buguias defies all conventional categories; however, all Cordilleran peoples have long been considered "tribal," based on their indigenous small-scale social organization, successful resistance to imperialism for several hundred years, sociocultural distinctiveness from the Philippine lowlanders, and retention of indigenous religion. This categorization is far from perfect; most Cordilleran groups have long been internally stratified, all were eventually brought under American political hegemony, and a large number have for some time been Christian.

The Benguet vegetable growers exhibit "peasant" characteristics as well, and several scholars refer to them as such (Russell 1983; Solang 1984; Wiber 1985). Powerful outside groups extract a large share of the gardeners' produce; labor-exchange practices coexist with wage work; and production is both for the market and for subsistence (see Wolf 1966; Shanin 1973; Scott 1976). The Benguet people have become subject to surplus extraction by both national elites and metropolitan states—a process that many scholars argue is sufficient to turn tribal peoples into peasants (Howlett 1973; Connell 1979; Howard 1980; Grossman 1984).

But the same vegetable growers have also been termed "petty commodity producers," a category related to, but not identical with, that of the peasantry (Russell 1989*a*; see Watts 1984:20). Unlike peasants *sensu strictu*, Benguet's rural (or "simple," or "petty") commodity producers cannot retreat to subsistence cultivation in the event of poor commodity prices. Thoroughly enmeshed in commercial relations, they have little to buffer them from the brutal backwash of commodity price collapses.

And finally, Buguias cultivators may even be called "capitalist farmers" inasmuch as they depend on wage labor (at least for portaging vegetables) and exhibit a (modified) capitalist economic logic. This latter attribute may be appreciated by substituting "the Buguias vegetable garden" for "the capitalist farm" in Wolf's (1966:2) classical definition of that economic form, yielding the accurate statement that "[the Buguias vegetable garden] is primarily a business enterprise, combining factors of production purchased in the market to obtain a profit by selling advantageously in a products market."

In short, Buguias vegetable growers can reasonably be classified as tribal cultivators, as peasants, as petty commodity producers, or as capitalist farmers. Each label points to important features of the community; none fully captures its present social and economic complexity. One must thus be careful in using and in interpreting such terms, for the mere act of labeling can create a fundamentally distorted picture.

MATERIALISM AND IDEALISM

The analysis presented above accords primacy neither to ideology nor to economics. The insistence on considering equally both religious belief and social structure springs from the conviction that both the ideal and the material have irreducible roles in human history. Few benefits are to be gained from jumping on either side of this hoary divide, a leap that recent social theory shows an increasing reluctance to make. For Marcus and Fischer (1986:85), "any materialist-idealist distinction between political economy and interpretive approaches is simply not supportable"; for Mann (1986: 19), the long-standing debate between the two has become a "ritual without hope and an end" (see also Errington 1989:296). As Stephen Toulmin (1990) so brilliantly shows, the current task is precisely to rejoin such dichotomized oppositions sundered by Descartes and maintained in separation by over three hundred years of stultifying, modernist thought.

At present, most scholars interested in economic transformations on the margins of the world economy still rally to the banner of materialism. Here, at least, the heirs of Marx and Comte stand together. Even those who most insightfully probe the interactions of structures and ideas usually vow fidelity to the materialist cause, as no charge appears to be more deadly than that of idealism.[4]

But I would argue that we would be better off not merely suspending this debate, but rejecting the notion that the two terms can be separated at all. Even when confining oneself strictly to economics one must confront the ineffable and purely ideal premises and trust upon which the entire modern financial edifice rests.

So too in Buguias: ideology and economy, faith and work, discourse and production—these are terms that cannot be disentangled and assigned relative priority. To expend our energies on such futile gestures is indeed to perpetuate a ritual without hope or an end.

RITUAL SURVIVAL,
ECOLOGICAL DEVASTATION

Of numerous attempts to explain the ecological dimension of ritual, Rappaport's (1967) materialist interpretation of swine sacrifice among the Maring of New Guinea probably is the best known. For Rappaport, the periodic *kaiko* ceremony, marked by mass immolation of hogs, is a mechanism for regulating the balance between human and animal species. This socioeconomic mode of "ritual regulation" is said to contrast sharply with that of the often ecologically destructive resource allocation mechanisms of the market (Rappaport 1979:73,148).

Such a model has no currency in contemporary Buguias.[5] Although its economy has come to be regulated almost entirely by market forces in the past generation, its ritual regime has not significantly changed since prewar days. One would be hard-pressed to find any "adaptive" qualities in Buguias Paganism, which if anything has predisposed its believers to enmesh themselves in a commercial order that Rappaport deems maladaptive. While retaining its ritual forms, Buguias has served the global economic system handsomely. The profits earned by a handful of local entrepreneurs pale next to those garnered annually by the chemical and seed companies. How well it has served its own environment is another matter.

ENVIRONMENTAL THREATS

Contemporary Buguias illustrates the diverse array of causal patterns that converge in any particular instance of environmental deterioration. Within the Philippines, the village occupies a peripheral locale, long neglected and at times actively victimized by the state. Given demographic expansion, poor growers have little option but to clear new gardens on steep slopes, accelerating soil loss in a pattern common to many tropical and subtropical uplands. To this extent, the community conforms to the expectations of political-ecological theory, which emphasizes the marginalization of impoverished growers as the primary cause of ecological despoliation in the Third World (Blaikie and Brookfield 1987). Buguias's most blatant degradation, however, is directly attributable to the elite, particularly to those individuals who use bulldozers to clear carelessly new gardens in the cloud-forest highlands.

To put it most succinctly, the specific forms of environmental degradation evident in Buguias derive from the actions of a stratified, demographically dynamic community with a highly entrepreneurial ethos, engaging in chemical-intensive commercial vegetable production in typhoon-prone tropical upland with a deeply weathered bedrock mantle. Truck crops simply cannot be grown profitably here without large chemical doses, owing to the vigor of insect pests and fungal growths in the moist and mild climate. Massive soil loss is similarly inevitable where root crops are grown in the wet season, when fields must be steeply sloped to allow drainage. And expansion into the eastern cloud forest, while affording entrepreneurs rich fields and cheap labor, not only aggravates local erosion and deforestation but also creates increasingly serious water shortages at lower elevations.

The Philippine state has contributed to the problem, but its actions have been contradictory and confused. Outright government hostility has occasionally threatened the livelihood of farmers, forcing them at times to deforest their own lands. And even the state's well-intentioned environmental safeguards have proved ineffectual, as competing interests have successfully lobbied for contradictory policies. Overall, the state has influenced the vegetable economy most directly through road construction, the consequences of which have been decidedly ambiguous. Roads offer gardeners profound benefits, yet by permitting continual expansion they also further watershed denudation. And even their beneficial attributes are often the unintended byproducts of policies designed primarily to enhance central control; the major roads east of Buguias, for example, were constructed to help the Philippine military combat the New People's Army.

Similar mixed consequences accrue to local land investments. As Blaikie and Brookfield show (1987:9), cultivators can forestall— and sometimes even reverse—land degradation by building walls, terraces, and irrigation facilities. Such works are ubiquitous in Buguias, forming an essential foundation for the vegetable economy. Yet it is precisely the newest and largest of such investments, the megaterraces now being leveled by bulldozers, that cause the worst losses of soil.

The commercialization of agriculture in Buguias has greatly accelerated the pace of degradation, but we should by no means assume that the prewar environment was in any sense pristine. Over the course of several centuries, the Buguias people remolded their landscape to anthropogenic contours. Many Benguet districts were extensively deforested well before the colonial era, and the entire Agno Valley has long been cleared of a number of animal species. More importantly, prewar population growth in Buguias was generating increasing environmental strains, and while it is possible that adaptive solutions could have been devised, it is unlikely that the transition would have been entirely forgiving of the landscape.

In any case, the question is now moot; the Buguias people will not, and cannot, return to subsistence cropping. Nor can they revive old land-management techniques to make their commercial farming more sustainable; the current crop complex lies entirely outside the realm of traditional horticultural methods. More feasible would be the adoption of new, less environmentally taxing forms of commercial agriculture, such as some have suggested might be found in citrus or other fruit crops. Arboriculture would demand considerable local restructuring, as well as state (and international) assistance, but it may yet prove a way out of the dilemma.

Prospects

As distressing as forest loss, soil erosion, biocide poisoning, and wildlife extinctions are, Buguias's agricultural system is in no danger of immediate collapse. To pronounce commercial farming hopelessly unsustainable here would be premature; the present system could conceivably limp along for years, as farmers devise makeshift solutions for each new ecological impasse. But we must wonder whether they will manage to sustain their living standards while doing so, and how much trauma their lands will suffer as a result.

For the nonce, at least, it would be difficult to substantiate the view that vegetable farmers are worse off for having abandoned subsistence cultivation. Successful engagement in a commercial economy has given Benguet's highlanders a degree of power vis-à-vis the Philippine government uncommon in small-scale indigenous societies, and the Buguias people themselves voice overwhelming approval of the changes they have undergone since the war. But the Benguet vegetable industry confronts an imperiled future. Already the economy is deteriorating, and absent an unforseen miracle, it will continue to do so for some time. Encouraged by their belief in the manipulability of fate to continue pushing back the vegetable frontier, the people of Buguias are indeed wagering the land against high odds.

As a counterexample to received wisdom in much of contemporary ethnography and development studies, the story of Buguias is instructive. But the particularity of the place and time—the uniqueness of Buguias's historical geography—cannot be overemphasized. It is essential to the argument presented throughout this work, as to the theoretical framework in which it has been couched, that generalized conclusions *not* be extrapolated from this one case. Moreover, the situation described is transitory, a fleeting moment in a historical process that defies prognostication. Schumpeter (1942) insisted that destructiveness was at the heart of capitalism's creativity. Destruction is amply evident in Buguias; whether the process could ultimately prove creative is a question for later years.

Glossary

AMED: the spirits of the ancestors.

BAKNANG: member of the elite class.

BARANGAY: the village community (the smallest political-territorial unit in the Philippines).

BARCADA: voluntary youth-group.

CHRISPA: a Christian-Pagan "syncretist."

DANGAS: a traditional system of labor mobilization based on the payment of meat and alcohol "wages."

GAMBANG: traditional copper pots; also refers to copper itself.

KALASAN: the high-elevation cloud forest dominated by oak.

MANBUNUNG: a Pagan priest.

MANKOTOM: a Pagan spiritual advisor (Paganism's foremost apologist).

OGBO: traditional labor exchange.

PASTOL: the arrangement under which a poor man raises the cattle of a rich man in exchange for a share; alternatively, the cattle caretaker himself.

PEDIT: the graded prestige feast forming the core ceremony of Buguias Paganism.

PUWAL: a technique used for cultivating grasslands involving the inversion of the sod using iron-tipped bars.

SALDA: the traditional land mortgage system of the Cordillera.

SALENG: the resinous heartwood of the insular pine.

SALIW: a secular feast.

SANGBO: an omen promising economic luck.

TIMUNGAO: a water spirit.

TONG TONGAN: the traditional jury system of Buguias.

UMA: a swidden field.

Notes

1. "Paganism" is used here as the Buguias people use it: to denote a specific religious creed. It is thus capitalized to avoid impugning its legitimacy as a religion.

2. For example, Worcester (1906) placed the many villages that most Spanish and German ethnographers had classified as belonging to the separate tribal groupings of the Buriks, the Busaos, and the Itetepanes into the Tinguian category (an older division that he retained). Yet it is absolutely clear that these three tribal names had earlier referred to people belonging to the groups that Worcester himself identified as the Benguet-Lepanto Igorots (the Buriks and the Busaos) and the Bontoc Igorots (the Itetepanes).

3. Another American scholar and administrator, David Barrows, was at the same time developing a much more sophisticated view of cultural and social variation within the Cordillera based on language and, more significantly, on the indigenous peoples' own definitions of their identities and those of their neighbors. Yet Worcester (1906) cavalierly dismissed Barrows's work, and subsequently Barrows dropped out of the debate (see Barrows 1905, and especially his unpublished field notes of 1902 and 1908).

4. As Boon (1982:15) shows, "standard ethnographies" of a given group characteristically lack discussions of neighboring cultural groups. This has helped create an unfortunate blindness: cultural groups exist within the scholarly literature only if they have been anthropologically scrutinized.

1. Olofson (1984) has written at length on the door-yard gardens of the Ikalahan (Kallahan) of the southeastern margin of the Cordillera. These are structurally similar to the prewar Buguias gardens, but there are several important differences. For example, the residents of Imugan studied by Olofson do not spread hog manure in their gardens (1984:318) as did the people of Buguias.

2. Keesing and Keesing (1934) and others have hypothesized that the first Cordilleran terraces were devoted to taro, with rice a later replacement. Taro is a ritually important plant in many Cordilleran villages (including

Buguias), and it probably also predated sweet potatoes as the dry-field staple. Among one small group, the I'wak of the southeastern Cordillera, taro (both wet- and especially dry-grown) is to this day the primary crop (see Peralta 1982).

3. Tapang (1985:18) writes that branding was introduced to southern Benguet by the Spaniards. If it reached Buguias during this period, it is no longer remembered. But it may simply not have spread to Buguias until a later date, since the Spaniards exercised significantly less control in the northern part of the province than they did in the south.

4. Gohl (1981:114) claims that *Themeda triandra* has poor nutritive value, is easily overgrazed when young, is unpalatable when mature, and that *Themeda* pastures are of low carrying capacity. Purseglove (1972:128), however, describes it as a valuable fodder, although he also states that it will not support truly heavy grazing.

5. According to one story commonly told in Buguias, American authorities scattered *Eupatorium* seeds from airplanes (planes were first seen in the same year that the weed appeared). Other evidence points to a purposeful introduction by a German landscape architect named "Sankhul" employed by the Americans to help "beautify" Baguio City. Sankhul evidently wanted a plant that could outcompete the indigenous grasses, and thus lessen the dry-season fire hazard (Lizardo 1955:220). *Eupatorium* served this purpose moderately well; Sankhul presumably never considered the potential damage to cattle raising.

6. Recent Amazonian research has brought into question many common assumptions regarding swidden agriculture, especially the notion that swiddens mimic tropical forest successional patterns (see Beckerman 1983). Many Amazonian swiddens are characterized not by intercropping but rather by monocropped, albeit multivarietal, concentric rings—a pattern that also existed in modified form in prewar Buguias. Stocks (1983) and Beckerman (1984) explain such patterns largely in reference to insect and shading problems. Stocks further shows that the most nitrogen-demanding plants are typically placed on the swidden margins, while undemanding plants are typically relegated to the poorer center area. Buguias uma fields fit this model reasonably well, as center area was usually devoted to the undemanding sweet potato, while heavier feeders were more often placed along the edges.

These correlations are provocative, but the different environmental conditions of Amazonian swiddens and Buguias dry fields may indicate that such resemblances are fortuitous. According to local experts, umas were structured as they were primarily for ease of working and scheduling. Interplanting of other crops with sweet potatoes was, however, avoided for reasons of soil fertility.

7. The 1903 official census enumerates only the "civilized population," that of Buguias being counted as "1" (U.S. Bureau of the Census 1905, v. 2:144). A more legitimate figure may be obtained from the Philippine Commission Report, 1901, Appendix FF. In this tabulation the figure for Lo-o must be added to that of Buguias, as these two areas were later consoli-

dated into a single municipal district. Even these latter figures are, however, suspect. An 1896 Spanish survey (Appendix II, same volume), for example, lists Lo-o as having some 916 inhabitants (whereas an 1887 census had counted 1,105), yet the Americans in 1901 found only 315 residents (Buguias did not report in this census). Such a precipitous population drop is unlikely. The problems here are several, but especially significant were the unwillingness of the people to cooperate with the enumerators (for good reason) and the continually changing "municipal" boundaries. For the 1948 population figures, see Republic of the Philippines 1954, pt. i:53.

8. Pollisco-Botengan *et al.* (1985:16) attribute the permanence of dry fields in Ambassador (Tublay municipality) to rough topography, legal classification as critical watershed, and time constraints of local farmers. These factors are no doubt important, but in prewar Buguias ecological considerations were primary.

3: SOCIAL RELATIONS

1. The actual arrangement varied both within and among different Benguet villages. In most Ibaloi areas the wealthy had an even greater advantage than in Buguias; in these places the pastol would usually receive only one of three newborn cattle. In the more restrictive *inkatlo* system (common in the nineteenth century), the cowboy would receive *only one-third of each animal*, thus precluding the possibility of ever acquiring a herd of his own (see Tapang 1985:11, and Hamada-Pawid and Bagamaspad 1985:80–81).

2. Hamada-Pawid (1984:90) argues that in Benguet, as a rule, not even terraces were really private: "Strictly speaking, there [was] no 'ownership' of land. . . . Rather, there [was a] right to *stewardship* of land." The "private" rights to terraces were certainly more restricted than in Western tenure systems; one could not, for example, forbid others to trespass. But in all societies private land rights have some limits, and by most definitions Buguias rice terraces would be considered fully private.

3. American land-policy makers gave lip service to safeguarding indigenous land rights, but their ultimate aim was to allow efficient exploitation of Benguet resources by American nationals (see Tauli 1984, and Hamada-Pawid 1984). Public Law 235 (1902) stipulated that any grants from the "public domain" should go to the actual inhabitants, and Act 496 (1902), for example, established the registration and survey system under which Torrens Titles were to be issued. While this act sent survey teams into Buguias, another act (718) of the same year potentially undermined the claims of many Buguias residents, proclaiming in effect that all tenure claims deriving from "chiefs of non-Christian tribes" were void.

4: RELIGION

1. All Benguet peoples, whether Kankana-ey, Ibaloi, or Kalanguya speakers, shared the same general religious concepts, although details varied greatly from village to village. Pungayan and Picpican (1978) have

presented an excellent synthesis of Benguet cosmology, which is, however, substantially different from the one collected in Buguias. Sacla (1987)
offers still another picture in his detailed overview of Benguet religion,
which also show substantial discrepancies with both my presentation and
with that of Pungayan and Picpican (1978). There are several possible reasons for these differences: Buguias ideology may be distinctive from that of
other Benguet communities; the individuals from whom I gathered religious data may have idiosyncratic views; ideological change in the past
few decades may have been so rapid as to erase a previous communality of
ideas; or the cosmology offered by Pungayan and Picpican and by Sacla
may apply only to select Benguet communities, or even to specific individuals. My own view is that religous beliefs are so complex and mutable
throughout this region that no single orthodox set of beliefs may be identified. See also Moss (1920b), W. H. Scott (1969), Hamada-Pawid and Bagamaspad (1985), Picpican and Guinaran (1981), Canol (1981), Tabora (1978),
and Afable (1975).

2. It is notable, however, that the Ifugao employ a similar density of
place names (Conklin 1980); this may be a generalized Cordilleran practice, unrelated to the timungao ritual.

3. The members of all Benguet communities observed pedit (in the
Ibaloi language, *peshit*), but the sequence varied greatly. In some villages,
for example, intervals were not confined to odd numbers (Pungayan and
Picpican 1978:48).

4. Such taboo (*ngilin*) marked most ritual occasions; in general, the
higher a person's status, the more often ngilin prohibitions were observed.
Some especially devout elders habitually avoided all strong-smelling foods,
and consumed no meat other than pork and chicken. This is actually a fair
indication of the relative ages of different foods; the ancestors are a conservative lot, and they do not enjoy dietary innovations. Thus they found
beef unacceptable and water buffalo only marginally tolerable.

5. Canol (1981:58) lists these blankets in a different (ascending) order:
bandala, bayaong, pinagpagan, kwabao, dil-li, and *alladang.* Although some
variation is expected, the discrepancies here—especially the relative positions of "dil-li" and "pinagpagan"—are so great as to indicate a recording
error on the part of one of the researchers. In Buguias, "bayaong" was not
a funeral blanket proper, but rather an intermediate blanket-accessory
combination.

6. According to Pungayan (1978:102), some Ibaloi baknangs were able
to "emancipate" themselves from the redistributive requirements of their
rank by performing the ritual of *aetong,* in which they would divest themselves of their social status. Evidently some were successful. In Buguias
this was not possible.

5: COMMERCIAL AND POLITICAL RELATIONS

1. The desire for cash in the remote Kalanguya villages did not reflect
tax requirements. As late as the 1930s, even such relatively accessible Ka-

languya communities as Kayapa (in western Nueva Vizcaya) did not render taxes (Light 1934).

2. According to Worcester's report (1903), largely culled from legal proceedings, most slaves sold in Nueva Vizcaya went for 80 to 120 pesos. Governor Pack (Philippine Commission 1903, v. 1:153) reported meanwhile that a cow would sell in Benguet for 80 to 100 pesos. Most slaves purchased by the Buguias traders were debtors, thieves, or captives from other Ifugao regions.

3. Some locally minted coins passed as "legitimate" (i.e., imperial). At least one observer (Lander 1904:513) took this "counterfeiting" as proof that the local people were becoming civilized! Buguias residents, however, remember their copper coins as having been struck on one side only, indicating that they were intended strictly for local use. (On American efforts to suppress Cordilleran minting, see File 1468, Record Group 350, The National Archives, Washington D.C.)

4. It must be noted that the lowland Filipino elite generally despised the sometimes close association between the Americans and the Igorots. This sentiment is clearly evident in a translated newspaper editorial from 1913:

> Notwithstanding the propinquity of the powers that be, who . . . are people ever disposed to sacrifice all on the alters of civilization and the progress of humanity, the Igorots of Baguio remain in the same state morally as when they were beside the Spanish, dirty, indecently clad, without any idea of what is required to keep up with the onward procession of humanity. And the worst of the thing is that those who should educate them and direct their intelligence along the roads of progress, take advantage of their state of ignorance to amuse themselves to the full, by their presence countenancing their feasts that the unfortunate people organize of a decidedly savage character. Before us we have a report that tells us recently there was held on these heights a canao (Igorot festival where they eat heartily of dogflesh and drink basi and dance frantically around the fires) and that at the feast all of the most prominent members of the administration in the locality put in an appearance. [From *La Democracia* March 25, 1913, held in The National Archives, Record Group 350, file 2388.]

6: THE ESTABLISHMENT OF COMMERCIAL VEGETABLE AGRICULTURE

1. The word "strategy" entered the English language through military science. The Oxford English Dictionary still gives its primary definition as the "art of the commander in chief." It is reasonable to extend the use of the term to cover other competitive occasions (such as games), in which, through the use of clever tactics, one party may win and thus cause the other to lose. But to consider all decisions made in the course of procuring a livelihood "strategic," as does Jochim (1981), is to demean life into a narrow struggle for survival. In the more circumscribed world of Benguet vegetable culture, however, the strategy metaphor is apposite.

2. The postwar retrenchment of the Suyoc mines was caused both by the poor performance of gold on the world market and by changes in the

relative value of the Philippine currency. The prewar depression years had been a boomtime for gold producers the world over (Kemmerer 1975:115); in the 1930s the value of the precious metal rose, on average "70 per cent in terms of depreciated currencies" (Palyi 1972:332). But wartime brought a near universal inflation, while the price of gold remained fixed in dollar terms. From 1940 to 1951 "the purchasing power of gold suffered continuous erosion" (Jastram 1977:167); in the postwar period, the United States held it at the increasingly artificial price of 35.0875 dollars per ounce. In the early 1960s, gold began to creep upward on the London Free Market, but a group of central banks intervened to bring it back to the desired price level (see Jastram 1977:52).

In the Philippines this situation was exacerbated by an over-valued currency. Inflation had been fierce during the mid-1940s; at the end of the war prices were approximately eight times higher than they had been five years earlier (Golay 1961:60). Furthermore, inflation persisted for some time as the U.S. government shipped in more currency than goods (see D. Bernstein 1947:218). Although the late 1940s witnessed a slight deflation (Golay 1961:74), the peso was never readjusted to the dollar, which had retained much more of its prewar value. The U.S. government actually insisted, in the notorious "Bell Trade Act," that the peso remain valued at fifty American cents. This enforced currency overvaluation made it difficult for the Philippines to export anything at all, including mineral resources (Valdepenas and Bautista 1977:161; Baldwin 1975:19).

The combination of underpricing gold while overpricing the peso made gold mining, whether by modern or traditional methods, a marginal endeavor. The Philippines' yearly production had been as high as 1,012,000 fine ounces in the late 1930s; in 1947 it totaled 65,000 fine ounces (Golay 1961:43). Although the industry began a slow recovery in the late 1940s, it lagged for many years. The Suyoc people continued to dig, but no longer could they afford to celebrate large feasts.

3. Officially, cabbage plantings increased from 1,137 hectares to 7,650 hectares (Republic of the Philippines 1954, v. 3, pt. ii:2944, and *ibid.* 1960b:76,77). For figures on potato production, see Republic of the Philippines 1954, v. 3, pt. ii:2955, and *ibid.* 1972:110.

4. Many such famines have been reported in the *Baguio Midland Courier*. See, for example, Oct. 10, 1949; May 30, 1965; June 27, 1965; December 4, 1966; and April 22, 1967.

8: ECONOMIC AND ECOLOGICAL CRISIS

1. Most recent experimental efforts at FORI have concentrated on nonagricultural issues, such as streambank stabilization and the reclamation of toxic mine tailings. FORI researchers have also cultivated test plots of a rather remarkable cloud-forest plant, the so-called petroleum shrub (*Pitasporum resiniforum*). Its highly flammable seeds contain a high-quality fuel, and foresters hope that one day commercial plantings may be feasible.

2. Bulldozer owners derive income from government road-building contracts, from clearing their own new garden plots, and from clearing the plots of other farmers in exchange for either cash or a section of land.

9: SOCIAL CONFLICT AND POLITICAL STRUGGLE

1. Although the American government recognized the land rights of the Benguet peoples, they did so only in the context of individual property. In a celebrated case, Cariño vs. Insular Government, the United States Supreme Court overruled the Philippine Supreme Court to uphold the land claims of the Ibaloi baknang Cariño (see Lynch 1984). Parpan-Pagusara (1984), however, argues powerfully, if vindictively, that this decision was more a defeat than a victory for indigenous land rights, since Cariño's 146-hectare plot had originally been a communal parcel that he had privatized under a title.

2. In 1962, Republic Act 782 granted ownership rights to farmers who had occupied public lands since 1945, offering in essence a reinterpretation of the Magsaysay policy. The more far-reaching Manahan amendments, passed in 1964 (Republic Act 3872), were designed to protect the land rights of "national cultural minorities," again by allowing individuals to acquire public lands provided they had been in residence for some years. Almost immediately after this act was passed, natural-resource interests clamored for its repeal, or at least for a strengthening of the mandatory screening process (*Baguio Midland Courier* Feb. 20 and 27, 1966). A high court soon ruled that *reserved* land was exempt from titling, effectively excluding Benguet farmers (*Baguio Midland Courier* July 29, 1966). This ruling in turn was challenged, but since the constitutionality of the original law has yet to be decided in court, the whole issue has quietly subsided (Tauli 1984).

3. Many parcels in Buguias and Lo-o were never titled even though they had been classified since the first land survey as "alienable and disposable." To obtain title to such a plot, the resident farmer must first get a court order, a cumbersome and expensive procedure. In the 1980s, however, a charitable association connected with the Catholic Church began to help farmers in selected communities gain titles.

One problem facing Cordilleran farmers who wished to gain title was the provision that no lands of slope greater than 18 percent could be classified as alienable and disposable. Benguet was exempted from this ruling on November 8, 1985, when Marcos signed Presidential Decree 1998. This infuriated many residents of the other Cordilleran provinces, whose lands were still covered by the original provision. Some claimed that the move was a ploy by Marcos to gain support in Benguet for the February 1986 election (*Baguio Midland Courier* May 25, 1986).

4. The old Mountain Province was divided in 1966 into four new provinces: Benguet, Bontoc, Ifugao, and Kalinga-Apayao. The first three had previously been subprovinces, as had both Kalinga and Apayao.

10: RELIGION IN MODERN BUGIAS

1. On February 21, 1960, *The Dynamo* (official publication of the student body of the Baguio Technical and Commercial College) ran an editorial urging Cordillerans to discard the feast system. It argued that "money [that] should be invested in the education of children or in some worthwhile pursuit is lost in one or two days of festive but meaningless revelry."

2. Several of the small-scale gold-mining communities in the Itogon area (of the middle Agno Valley) are populated primarily by Kankana-ey speakers from Suyoc. These villages therefore have a close relationship with Buguias. Information on the religious practices of Kankana-ey miners in the middle Agno was supplied by Evelyn Caballero, Ph.D. candidate, University of Hawaii.

11: CONCLUSION

1. Several scholars, overgeneralizing the notion that economic change brings cultural ruin, have misrepresented the linkages between redistribution and commercialization in Luzon's Cordillera. Solang (1984:163), for example, argues:

> While lavish feasts and *canaos* are held up to now, these, however, occur less frequently and still under a subsistent economic structure. . . . The level of surplus [necessary to hold them] is that associated with a subsistence economy. . . . With the entry of cash and other factors the Cordillera economy is getting marginalized.

Solang's argument is perhaps correct for the central and northern Cordillera, areas with which he is more familiar. It should also be noted that Eder (1982:111) has found that in Banaue (Ifugao) increasing commercialization is connected with a decline in ceremonial redistribution, while Pertierra (1988) correlates commercialization with the acceptance of Ilocano (Christian) identity in a community in the Cordillera's western foothills.

In the Philippines, and more broadly throughout Southeast Asia, redistributive ceremonies are widespread, having survived easily the spread of universalizing religions in many lowland areas (see, for example, Griffiths 1988; J. Scott 1988; von der Mehden 1986). Yet many such rituals *are* presently disappearing. James Scott (1988), for example, finds many redistributive devices, including feasts, threatened with extinction in Sungai Bujur, Malaysia. This is so, he argues, because the mechanization of agriculture has now obviated the need for labor control, formerly achieved through redistribution. This pattern is perhaps widely spread in lowland Southeast Asia, but clearly not in highland zones.

Among the Toraja of highland Sulawesi, however, the feast system seems to be endangered because formerly low-class individuals can now finance high-class funerals for their poor relatives with money earned as wage migrants, leading many persons to doubt the whole system's authenticity (Volkman 1984). Clearly, the relationship between redistribution and commercialization varies greatly from region to region.

2. Russell (1983:261–263) attributes the perceived anticommercial attitude of the Ibaloi in part to an "ethnic rhetoric" perpetuating stereotypes that she believes "distinguish between the qualifications of workers, and allow entrepreneurs not only to exploit a cheap labor force, but also to justify and legitimize their right to do so." She says further: "The result is to create a situation that perpetuates and restricts Ibaloi from expanding into . . . commercial roles."

The Buguias perspective is markedly different. Wealthy farmers along the Mountain Trail, in Bad-ayan, and in Bot-oan, do hire workers from other cultural groups (Kalanguya, Northern Kankana-ey, and Ilocano—almost never Ibaloi), but their rationale in doing so is strictly economic, never ethnic. Russell (1983) also shows, however, that certain Ibaloi individuals, and even villages, are marked by a strongly commercial orientation.

3. Sheldon Annis (1987) discovered in one region of Guatemala that individuals economically marginalized through poverty and those socially marginalized through entrepreneurial activities were inclined to leave syncretic Catholicism for Protestantism. Protestants overall tend to perform better economically than their Catholic peers, but they do so at the price of risking their cultural identity. The contrast with Buguias could hardly be more marked.

4. For example, E. P. Thompson (1978:4, 12) excoriates the self-proclaimed materialist Althusser for expounding an idealism comparable to theology if not astrology, yet Thompson himself has been accused of "swerv[ing] too far toward idealism and voluntarism while giving short shrift to material and structural analysis" (Trimberger 1984:221).

5. The Buid of Mindoro also offer swine to their ancestors, and their ceremonies also seem to lack an ecological dimension (Gibson 1986). Here the contrast with Buguias lies in the social realm. Buid individuals gain no prestige when they sacrifice to their ancestors; indeed, their whole social order prevents anyone from enhancing his or her own status. Furthermore, the ancestors here stand in a completely different position vis-à-vis human society. They are provided their (insubstantial) shares only to keep them quiet, for they are regarded as aggressive, stupid, and entirely unwelcome intruders. Buid ancestors are "bought-off" rather than beseeched, as are those of Buguias. And as a final contrast, Buid rituals function to decompose the household in recreating the larger community (Gibson 1986:177), where Buguias rituals unite households as they demonstrate divisions (as well as bonds) inherent in lineages, classes, and especially hamlets and villages. (See J. DeRaedt [1964] for an ecological theory of variations within the Cordillera in regard to the status of ancestors.)

Bibliography

Afable, Patricia. 1975. "Mortuary Rituals among the Ibaluy (Philippines)." *Asian Folklore Studies* 34(2): 103–126.

———. 1989. "Language, Culture, and Society in a Kallahan Community, Northern Luzon, Philippines." Ph.D. Dissertation, Department of Anthropology, Yale University, New Haven.

Anderson, James. 1969. "Buy-and-Sell and Economic Personalism: Foundations for Philippine Entrepreneurship." *Asian Survey* 9(9): 641–668.

Annis, Sheldon. 1987. *God and Production in a Guatemala Town*. Austin: University of Texas Press.

Anti-Slavery Society. 1983. *The Philippines: Authoritarian Government, Multinationals, and Ancestral Land*. London: Anti-Slavery Society (Indigenous Peoples and Development Series).

Antolin, Francisco. 1789 [1970]. "Notices of the Pagan Igorots in 1789." *Asian Folklore Studies* 29:177–253. (Translated and edited by William Henry Scott.)

Arenal-Sereno, L., and R. Libarios. 1983. "The Interface Between National Land Law and Kalinga Land Law." In *Human Rights and Ancestral Land: A Sourcebook*. Diliman, Quezon City. (Prepared for the *National Congress on Human Rights and Ancestral Land*, Dec. 8–9, 1983.)

Bahatan, Fernando, Henry Bahingawan, Peter Cosalan, and Alberto Tejano. 1970. "An Analysis of the Programming Behavior of Vegetable Farmers in the Province of Benguet." Unpublished Master's Thesis, Saint Louis University, Baguio.

Baldwin, Robert. 1975. *Foreign Trade Relations and Economic Development: The Philippines*. New York: National Bureau of Economic Research. (Distributed by Columbia University Press.)

Barnett, Milton. 1969. "Subsistence and Transition in Agricultural Development among the Ibaloi in the Philippines." *In* C. R. Wharton, ed., *Subsistence Agriculture and Economic Development*. Chicago: Aldine.

Barrows, David. 1902. *Benguet and the Cordillera of Luzon*. Unpublished Field Notes, Bancroft Library, University of California, Berkeley.

———. 1905. "Population." *Census of the Philippine Islands, 1903*. Washington: Government Printing Office.

———. 1908. *Trip Through Benguet*. Unpublished Field Notes, Bancroft Library, University of California, Berkeley.

Barton, Roy F. 1930. *The Halfway Sun*. New York: Brewer and Warren.

Bassett, Thomas. 1988. "The Political Ecology of Peasant-Herder Conflicts in the Northern Ivory Coast." *Annals of the Association of American Geographers* 78(3): 453–472.

Beckerman, Stephan. 1983. "Does the Swidden Ape the Jungle?" *Human Ecology* 11(1): 1–11.

———. 1984. "A Note on Ringed Fields." *Human Ecology* 12(2): 203–206.

Bellah, Robert. 1968. "Reflections on the Protestant Ethic Analogy in Asia." *In* S. N. Eisenstadt, ed., *The Protestant Ethic and Modernization*. New York: Basic Books. 243–251.

Belshaw, Cyril. 1965. *Traditional Exchange and Modern Markets*. Englewood Cliffs, New Jersey: Prentice Hall.

Bernstein, David. 1947. *The Philippine Story*. New York: Farrar, Straus and Company.

Bernstein, Henry. 1977. "Notes on Capital and Peasantry." *Review of African Political Economics* 10:660–73.

Blaikie, Piers. 1985. *The Political Economy of Soil Erosion in Developing Countries*. London and New York: Longman.

———, and Harold Brookfield. 1987. *Land Degradation and Society*. London: Methuen.

Bodley, John. 1975. *Victims of Progress*. Menlo Park, California: Benjamin/Cummings.

Boon, James. 1982. *Other Tribes, Other Scribes*. Cambridge: Cambridge University Press.

Boserup, Ester. 1965. *The Conditions of Agricultural Growth*. Chicago: Aldine.

Bourdieu, Pierre. 1977. *Outline of a Theory of Practice*. Cambridge: Cambridge University Press.

Brookfield, H. C. 1972. "Intensification and Disintensification in Pacific Agriculture: A Theoretical Perspective." *Pacific Viewpoint* 13(1): 30–48.

Buasen, Carlos. 1981. "Repayment Deficiencies of Agricultural Loans among Farmers in the Mountain Provinces." *Mountain State Agricultural College Research Journal* 8:1–24.

Buguias Municipality. 1983. "A Study of the Public Market and Slaughterhouse of the Municipality of Buguias." Benguet Province.

Cain, Mead. 1981. "Risk and Insurance." *Population and Development Review* 7(3): 435–474.

Calanog, Lope. N.d. "Ethnographic Reseach on the Mount Pulog Region with Emphasis on Shifting Cultivation." *Forestry Research Institute Report*. Baguio City.

Caldwell, J. C. 1978. "A Theory of Fertility: From High Plateau to Destabilization." *Population and Development Review* 4(4): 553–577.

Cancian, Frank. 1965. *Economics and Prestige in a Maya Community*. Stanford: Stanford University Press.

Canol, Lilia. 1981. "Death Rituals among Benguet Kankanaeys." *Saint Louis Research Journal* 12(1): 37–72.

Clarke, William. 1988. "Comment (in Reply to Dennett and Connell 1988)." *Current Anthropology* 29(2): 283.

Clifford, James. 1986. "On Ethographic Allegory." *In* J. Clifford and

G. Marcus, eds., *Writing Culture*. Berkeley, Los Angeles, London: University of California Press. 99–121.

Conklin, Harold. 1980. *Ethnographic Atlas of Ifugao*. New Haven: Yale University Press.

Connell, John. 1979. "The Emergence of a Peasantry in Papua New Guinea." *Peasant Studies* 8(2): 103–137.

Corbridge, Stuart. 1986. *Capitalist World Development: A Critique of Radical Development Geography*. London: MacMillan.

Cordillera Consultative Committee. 1984. *Dakami Ya Nan Dagami: Papers and Proceedings of the First Cordillera Multi-Sectoral Land Congress*. Baguio: Cordillera Consultative Committee.

CPA (Cordillera People's Alliance). 1984. "Papers and Documents from the First Cordillera People's Congress." June 1–3, Bontoc, Mountain Province.

Crowder, L. V., and H. R. Chheda. 1982. *Tropical Grassland Husbandry*. London: Longman.

Dar, William. 1985. "Intensification of Highland Fruit Culture." *The Highland Express* 5(2): 1–4.

Davis, William. 1973. *Social Relations in a Philippine Market*. Berkeley, Los Angeles, London: University of California Press.

Dennett, Glenn, and John Connell. 1988. "Acculturation and Health in the Highlands of Papua New Guinea." *Current Anthropology* 29(2): 273–299.

DeRaedt, Carol. 1983. "Resource Flow in the Development of an Upland Commercial Farming Village." Research Paper presented at EAPI-SUAN Symposium on Research and Impact of Development on Human Activity Systems in Southeast Asia, Institute of Ecology, Padjadjaran University, Bandung, Indonesia. (Mimeographed copy, Cordilleran Studies Center Library, Baguio City.)

DeRaedt, Jules. 1964. "Religious Representation in Northern Luzon." *Saint Louis Quarterly* 2(3): 245–348.

de Souza, Anthony, and Philip Porter. 1974. *The Underdevelopment and Modernization of the Third World*. Washington, D.C.: Association of American Geographers. (Commission on College Geography, Resource Paper No. 23.)

Drucker, P., and R. Heizer. 1967. *To Make My Name Good*. Berkeley, Los Angeles, London: University of California Press.

Duhaylungsod, Noel. N.d. "The Cropping Systems in the Lo-o Watershed." Unpublished Research Paper, Lo-o Valley Project Series, Cordilleran Studies Center Library, Baguio City.

Duncan, James. 1980. "The Superorganic in American Cultural Geography." *Annals of the Association of American Geographers* 70(2): 181–198.

Early, John. 1931. "Reminiscences." Unpublished Manuscript, John Early Files, Bentley Historical Library, University of Michigan, Ann Arbor.

Eder, James. 1982. "No Water in the Terrace: Agricultural Stagnation and Social Change at Banaue, Ifugao." *Philippine Quarterly of Culture and Society* 10(3): 101–116.

Eisenstadt, S. N. 1968. "The Protestant Ethic in an Analytical and Comparative Framework." *In* S. N. Eisenstadt, ed., *The Protestant Ethic and Modernization*. New York: Basic Books. 3–45.

Errington, Shelly. 1989. *Meaning and Power in a Southeast Asian Realm*. Princeton: Princeton University Press.

FAO. 1984. *Sociological Annex* (Benguet Agriculture). Rome: United Nations Food and Agriculture Organization.

Figoy, Geraldine. 1984. "Tradition and Change in Loo Valley." *Cordillera Studies Center, Monograph Series 3, Folio Issue* 1:33–37.

———. N.d. "The Loo Valley Vegetable Industry: A Research Agenda for Social Science Agricultural Development." Unpublished Paper, Loo Valley Project Series, Cordillera Studies Center Library, Baguio City.

Finin, Gerard. 1990. "Regional Consciousness and Administrative Grids: Understanding the Role of Planning in the Philippines' Grand Cordillera Central." Unpublished Ph.D. Dissertation, Department of City and Regional Planning, Cornell University, Ithaca, New York.

Fisher, James. 1986. *Trans-Himalayan Traders: Economy, Society and Culture in Northwest Nepal*. Berkeley, Los Angeles, London: University of California Press.

Fried, Morton. 1967. *The Evolution of Political Society*. New York: Random House.

Fry, Howard. 1983. "A History of the Mountain Province." Quezon City: New Day.

Gibson, Thomas. 1986. *Sacrifice and Sharing in the Philippine Highlands*. London: Althone.

Gohl, Bo. 1981. *Tropical Feeds*. Rome: FAO.

Golay, Frank. 1961. *The Philippines: Public Policy and National Economic Development*. Ithaca, New York: Cornell University Press.

Goode, William. 1951. *Religion among the Primitives*. Glencoe, Illinois: The Free Press.

Goodstein, Marvin. 1962. "The Pace and Pattern of Philippine Economic Growth." *Data Paper Number 48*, Southeast Asia Program, Department of Asian Studies, Cornell University, Ithaca, New York.

Goodway, Martha, and Harold Conklin. 1987. "Quenched High-Tin Bronzes from the Philippines." *Archeomaterials* 2(1): 1–27.

Grant, Jill. 1987. "The Impacts of Dependent Development on Community and Resources in Kilenge, Papua New Guinea." *Human Ecology* 15(2): 243–260.

Griffiths, Stephen. 1988. *Emigrants, Entrepreneurs, and Evil Spirits*. Honolulu: University of Hawaii Press.

Grossman, Larry (Lawrence). 1981. "The Cultural Ecology of Economic Development." *Annals of the Association of American Geographers* 71(2): 220–236.

———. 1984. *Peasants, Subsistence Ecology, and Development in the Highlands of New Guinea*. Princeton, New Jersey: Princeton University Press.

Hamada, Sinai. 1960. "Nationalizing the Local Vegetable Industry." *Baguio Midland Courier* 13(37): 1 (Feb. 28, 1960).

Hamada-Pawid, Zenaida. 1984. "Indigenous Patterns of Land Use and Public Policy in Benguet." In *Dakami Ya Nan Dagami: Papers and Proceedings of the First Cordillera Multi-Sectoral Land Congress*. Baguio, the Philippines: Cordillera Consultative Committee. 89–98.

———, and Anavic Bagamaspad. 1985. *A Peoples' History of Benguet*. Baguio, the Philippines: Baguio Printing and Publishing (Copyright by Benguet Province).

Harkins, Philip. 1955. *Blackburn's Headhunters*. New York: W. W. Norton.

Harris, Marvin. 1979. *Cultural Materialism: The Struggle for a Science of Culture*. New York: Random House.

Hartendorp, A. V. 1967. *The Japanese Occupation of the Philippines*. Manila: Bookmark.

Hecht, Susanna, and Alexander Cockburn. 1989. *The Fate of the Forest: Developers, Destroyers, and Defenders of the Amazon*. London: Verso.

Hefner, Robert. 1983. "The Problem of Preference: Economic and Ritual Change in Highlands Java." *Man* 18:669–689.

Howard, Rhoda. 1980. "Formation and Stratification of the Peasantry in Colonial Ghana." *Journal of Peasant Studies* 8(1): 61–80.

Howlett, Diana. 1973. "Terminal Development: From Tribalism to Peasantry." *In* Harold Brookfield, ed., *The Pacific in Transition: Geographical Perspectives on Adaptation and Change*. New York, St. Martin's Press. 249–273.

Hutterer, Karl. 1978. "Dean C. Worcester and Philippine Anthropology." *Philippine Quarterly of Culture and Society* 6:125–156.

Jacobs, M. 1972. *The Plant World on Luzon's Highest Mountain*. Leiden: Rijksherbarium.

Jastram, Roy. 1977. *The Golden Constant*. New York: John Wiley and Sons.

Jenista, Frank. 1978. "The White Apo: Ifugao and American Perceptions of Colonial Rule." Unpublished Ph.D. Dissertation, Department of History, University of Michigan, Ann Arbor.

Jenks, A. E. 1905. "The Bontoc Igorot." *Department of the Interior Ethnological Survey Publications* (1): 1–266.

Jochim, Michael. 1981. *Strategies for Survival*. New York: Academic Press.

Keesing, Felix. 1962. *The Ethnohistory of Northern Luzon*. Stanford: Stanford University Press.

———, and Marie Keesing. 1934. *Taming Philippine Headhunters*. Stanford: Stanford University Press.

Kemmerer, Donald. 1975. "The Role of Gold in the Past Century." *In* Hans Sennholz, ed., *Gold is Money*. Westport, Connecticut, and London: Greenwood Press. 104–122.

Kowal, Norman. 1966. "Shifting Cultivation, Fire and Pine Forests in the Cordillera Central, Luzon, Philippines." *Ecological Monographs* 36(4): 389–419.

Lander, A. Henry Savage. 1904. *The Gems of the East*. New York: Harper Brothers.

LeBar, Frank. 1975. *Ethnic Groups of Insular Southeast Asia: Volume 2, Philippines and Formosa*. New Haven: Human Relations Area Files Press.

Lednicky, 1916. "The Palidan Slide Mine." *Philippine Journal of Science* 11-A, 5:241–249.

Lehlbach, Leonard. 1907. "The Mancayan Copper Deposits in the Philippine Islands." Unpublished Manuscript, file 16503, Record Group 350, The National Archives, Washington D.C.

Leroi Ladurie, Emmanuel, and Orest Ranum. 1989. "The Scribe-Ethnographer, Pierre Prion of Aubais." *In* Eugene Genovese and Leonard Hochberg, eds. *Geographical Perspectives in History*. New York: Basil Blackwell. 95–118.

Lewis, Martin. 1989. "Commercialization and Community Life: The Geography of Market Exchange in a Small-Scale Philippine Society." *Annals of the Association of American Geographers* 79(3): 390–410.

Light, J. W. 1934. "Letter to the Director of Education, Manila." Unpublished Manuscript, Bentley Historical Library, Joseph Ralston Hayden Collection, Box 28, Folder 25. University of Michigan, Ann Arbor.

Lizardo, Leonor. 1955. "Natural Regeneration in Pine Forests." *Philippine Journal of Forestry* 11(3–4): 211–226.

Lizarondo, Maura, Zenaida Dela Cruz, and Taciana Valdellon. 1979. "A Socio-Economic Study of Vegetable Farmers in Benguet." *Agricultural Marketing Report* 1(4) (Bureau of Agricultural Economics, Ministry of Agriculture, the Philippines).

Long, Norman. 1968. *Social Change and the Individual*. Manchester: Manchester University Press.

Lynch, Owen. 1984. "Native Title: The Legal Claim of Indigenous Citizens to Their Ancestral Lands." In *Dakami Ya Nan Dagami: Papers and Proceedings of the First Cordillera Multi-Sectoral Land Congress*. Baguio: Cordillera Consultative Committee. 173–182.

Magannon, Esteban. 1988. "Kalinga History and Historical Consciousness." *In* John Taylor and Andrew Turton, eds., *Sociology of "Developing Societies": Southeast Asia* (New York and London: Monthly Review Press), 241–249.

Mamdani, Mahmood. 1972. *The Myth of Population Control: Family, Caste, and Class in an Indian Village*. New York: Monthly Review Press.

Mann, Michael. 1986. *The Sources of Social Power: Volume 1, A History of Power from the Beginning to A.D. 1760*. Cambridge: Cambridge University Press.

Marche, Alfred. 1887 (1970). *Luzon and Palawan*. Manila: Filipiniana Book Guild.

Marcus, George, and Michael Fischer. 1986. *Anthropology as Cultural Critique*. Chicago: University of Chicago Press.

Medina, C. P. N.d. "Crop Protection Studies in the Vegetable Producing Loo Valley Area." Unpublished Research Paper, Loo Valley Project Series, Cordillera Studies Center, Baguio.

Meyer, Hans. 1890 [1975]. "A Trip to the Igorots" and "The Igorots." *In* William Henry Scott, ed., *German Travelers on the Cordillera*. Manila: Filipiniana Book Guild. 104–128.

Mitchel, William. 1988. "The Defeat of Hierarchy: Gambling as Exchange in a Sepik Society." *American Ethnologist* 15(4): 638–657.

Moss, Claude. 1920a. "Nabaloi Law and Ritual." *University of California Publications in American Archeology and Ethnology* 15:207–342.

———. 1920b. "Kankanay Ceremonies." *University of California Publications in Archeology and Ethnology* 15(4): 343–384.

MPDA (Mountain Province Development Authority). 1964. "Preliminary and Economic Survey Report." Unpublished Paper, Cordillera Studies Center Library, Baguio.

Nietschmann, Bernard. 1979. "Ecological Change, Inflation, and Migration in the Far West Caribbean." *The Geographical Review* 69:1–24.

Numata, M. 1974. *The Flora and Vegetation of Japan.* Tokyo: Kodansha (and New York: Elsevier).

Ogawa, Tetsuro. 1972. *Terraced Hell: A Japanese Memoir of Defeat and Death in Northern Luzon.* Rutland, Vermont (and Tokyo: Charles E. Tuttle).

Olofson, Harold. 1984. "Toward a Cultural Ecology of Ikalahan Dooryards: A Perspective for Development." *Philippine Quarterly of Culture and Society* 12:306–325.

Palyi, Melchior. 1972. *The Twilight of Gold.* Chicago: Henry Regnery.

Parker, Barbara. 1988. "Moral Economy, Political Economy, and the Culture of Entrepreneurship in Highland Nepal." *Ethnology* 27(2): 181–194.

Parpan-Pagusara, Mariflor. 1984. "The Kalinga Ili: Cultural-Ecological Reflections on Indigenous Theoria and Praxis of Man-Nature Relationships." In *Dakami Ya Nan Dagami: Papers and Proceedings of the First Cordillera Multi-Sectoral Land Congress.* Baguio: Cordillera Consultative Committee. 30–65.

Penafiel, Samuel. 1979. "Net Primary Productivity and Vegetation Characteristics of a *Pinus*-Grass Community." *Sylvatrop* 4(3): 167–177.

Peralta, Jesus. 1982. *I'wak.* Manila: National Museum Anthropological Paper Number 11.

Perez, Angel. 1902. *Igorotes, Estudio Geografico y Ethnographico sobre algunos Distritos del Norte de Luzon.* Manila: El Mercantil.

———. 1904. *Relaciones Augustinianas de las Razas del Norte de Luzon.* Ethnological Survey, Publication Volume 3. Manila: Bureau of Printing.

Pertierra, Raul. 1988. *Religion, Politics, and Rationality in a Philippine Community.* Honolulu: University of Hawaii Press.

Philippine Commission. 1900–1915. *Reports of the Philippine Commission,* 32 vols. Washington D.C.: U.S. War Department, Government Printing Office.

Picpican, Isikias, and Ermelinda Guinaran. 1981. "Folk Medicine among Benguet Igorots." *Saint Louis University Research Journal* 12(1): 93–123.

Polanyi, Karl. 1957. "The Economy as as Instituted Process." *In* K. Polanyi, C. Arensburg, and H. Pearson, eds., *Trade and Market in Early Empires.* Glencoe: The Free Press. 243–270.

Pollisco-Botengan, M. A., C. G. Dawang, H. J. Folosco, and A. B. Galuba. 1985. "Conditions for Participation in an Integrated Social Forestry Program." *In* P. Sajise and A. T. Rambo, eds., *Agroecosystems Research in Rural Resource Management and Development*. Los Baños, The Philippines: University of the Philippines Program in Environmental Science and Management.

Potts, M. J. 1983. "Potato Production in Benguet, Philippines." *In* M. J. Potts, ed., *On Farm Potato Research in the Philippines*. Manila: International Potato Center with the Republic of the Philippines Ministry of Agriculture.

Preston, David. 1985. "Society, Household, and Environment: The Process of Proletarianization in the Cordillera of Luzon, Philippines." Unpublished Seminar Paper, Department of Human Geography, Research School of Pacific Studies, The Australian National University.

Pungayan, Eufronio. 1978. "A Sociolinguistic Analysis of Kinship Structure among Benguet Ibalois in the Philippines." Unpublished Master's Thesis, Saint Louis University, Baguio, the Philippines.

————, and Isikias Picpican. 1978. "Ritual and Worship among the Benguet Igorot." *Saint Louis University Research Journal* 9(3–4): 460–493.

Purseglove, J. W. 1968. *Tropical Crops: Dicotyledons*. London: Longmans.

————. 1972. *Tropical Crops: Monocotyledons*. New York: John Wiley and Sons.

Rappaport, Roy. 1967. *Pigs for the Ancestors*. New Haven: Yale University Press.

————. 1979. *Ecology, Meaning, and Religion*. Berkeley: North Atlantic Books.

Reed, Robert. 1976. *City of Pines: The Origins of Baguio as a Colonial Hill Station and Regional Capital*. Berkeley: Center for South and Southeast Asian Studies Research Monograph No. 13.

Reid, Anthony. 1988. *Southeast Asia in the Age of Commerce: Volume One, The Lands Below the Winds*. New Haven: Yale University Press.

Republic of the Philippines. 1954. *Census of the Philippines: 1948*. Manila: Bureau of Printing.

————. 1960a. *Census of the Philippines*. Manila: Bureau of Census and Statistics.

————. 1960b. *Journal of Philippine Statistics* 13(1–3). Manila: Bureau of Census and Statistics.

————. 1970. *Census of the Philippines*. Manila: National Census and Statistics Office.

————. 1972. *Journal of Philippine Statistics* 25(4). Manila: Bureau of Census and Statistics.

Richards, Paul. 1983. "Ecological Change and the Politics of African Land Use." *African Studies Review* 26(2): 1–71.

Robertson, J. A. 1914. "The Igorots of Lepanto." *Philippine Journal of Science* 9:465–529.

Roccamora, J. 1979. "The Political Uses of PANAMIN." *Southeast Asia Chronicle* 67:11–21.

Rosaldo, Renato. 1980. *Ilongot Headhunting 1883–1974*. Stanford: Stanford University Press.

Ruppert, David. 1979. "Marketing at the Crossroads: Ethnic Diversity in a Periodic Market in the Highland Philippines." Unpublished Ph.D. Dissertation, Department of Anthopology, University of Arizona, Tuscon.

Russell, Susan. 1983. "Entrepreneurs, Ethnic Rhetoric, and Economic Integration in Benguet Province, Highland Luzon, Philippines." Unpublished Ph.D. Dissertation, Department of Anthropology, University of Illinois, Urbana-Champaign.

———. 1987. "Middlemen and Moneylending: Relations of Exchange in a Highland Philippine Economy." *Journal of Anthropological Research* 43(2): 139–161.

———. 1989a. "Simple Commodity Production and Class Formation in the Southern Cordillera of Luzon." Unpublished Paper presented at the 1989 Annual Meeting of the Association for Asian Studies, Washington D.C.

———. 1989b. "Ritual Persistence and the Ancestral Cult among the Ibaloi of the Luzon Highlands. *In* Susan Russell and Clark Cunningham, eds., *Changing Lives, Changing Rites: Ritual and Social Dynamics in the Philippine and Indonesian Uplands* (Ann Arbor: Michigan Studies of South and Southeast Asia, Number 1), 17–44.

Sacla, Wasing. 1987. *Treasury of Beliefs and Home Rituals of Benguet.* Baguio: Published by the Author.

Sahlins, Marshall. 1972. *Stone Age Economics.* New York: Aldine.

Schama, Simon. 1988. *The Embarrassment of Riches.* Berkeley, Los Angeles, and London: University of California Press.

Scheerer, Otto. 1932 (1975). "On Baguio's Past." *In* William Henry Scott, ed., *German Travelers on the Cordillera* (Manila: Filipiniana Book Guild), 173–218.

Sheridan, Thomas. 1988. *Where the Dove Calls: The Political Ecology of a Peasant Corporate Community in Northwestern Mexico.* University of Arizona Press: Tuscon.

Schmink, Marianne, and Charles Wood. 1987. "The 'Political Ecology' of Amazonia." *In* Peter Little and Michael Horowitz, eds., *Lands at Risk in the Third World* (Boulder, Colorado: Westview), 38–57.

Schumpeter, Joseph. 1942. *Capitalism, Socialism and Democracy.* New York: Harper Brothers.

Scott, James. 1976. *The Moral Economy of the Peasant: Rebellion and Subsistence in Southeast Asia.* New Haven: Yale University Press.

———. 1988. "Rituals of Compassion and Social Control." *In* John Taylor and Andrew Turton, eds., *Sociology of "Developing Societies": Southeast Asia.* New York and London: Monthly Review Press. 200–206.

Scott, William Henry. 1960 (1969). "The *Apo-Dios* Concept in Northern Luzon." *In* William Henry Scott, *On the Cordillera.* Manila: MCS. 123–142 (originally published in *Philippine Studies* 8[4]).

———. 1974. *The Discovery of the Igorots.* Quezon City, the Philippines: New Day.

Scott, William Henry. 1986. *Ilocano Responses to American Aggression 1900– 1901*. Quezon City, the Philippines: New Day.

Semper, Carl. 1862 (1975). "Trip through the Northern Provinces of Luzon." *In* William Henry Scott, ed., *German Travelers on the Cordillera* (Manila: Filipiniana Book Guild), 17–34.

Shanin, Teodor. 1972. *The Awkward Class: Political Sociology of Peasantry in a Developing Society: Russia 1913–1925*. London: Oxford University Press.

———. 1973. "The Nature and Logic of the Peasant Economy: A Generalization." *Journal of Peasant Studies* 1(1): 63–80.

Simms, S. C. 1906a. "Letter: Simms to Dorsey." Unpublished Manuscript, Field Museum of Natural History, Department of Anthropology, Expedition Files for R. F. Cummings, Philippine Expedition 1906–1909. Chicago.

———. 1906b. "Rainy Season Route to Quiangan." Unpublished Manuscript, Field Museum of Natural History, Department of Anthropology; Expedition Files for R. F. Cummings, Philippine Expedition 1906–1909. Chicago.

Smith, Carol. 1976. *Regional Analysis*. New York: Academic Press.

Smith, Robert. 1963. *Triumph in the Philippines*. Washington D.C.: Office of the Chief of Military History, Department of the Army.

Solang, Benedict. 1984. "The Marginalization of the Cordillera Interior." In *Dakami Ya Nan Dagami: Papers and Proceedings of the First Cordillera Multi-Sectoral Land Congress*. Baguio: Cordillera Consultative Committee. 140–162.

Stocks, A. 1983. "Candoshi and Cocamilla Swiddens in Eastern Peru." *Human Ecology* 11(1): 69–84.

Tabora, Flora. 1978. "Some Folk Beliefs and Practices among the Mountain People of Northern Luzon. Peshit: A Feast among Rich Ibalois." *Saint Louis University Research Journal* 9(3–4): 494–499.

Tadaoan, Pio. 1969. "An Appraisal of the Economic, Political, Social, and Religious Practices of the Cultures of the Mountain Province in Light of the Objectives of the Commission on National Integration and the Community School." Unpublished Thesis, Saint Louis University, Baguio.

Tapang, B. P. 1985. *The Ibaloi Cattle Enterprise in Benguet*. Baguio, the Philippines: Cordillera Studies Center (Social Science Monograph Series 5).

Tauchmann, Kurt. 1974. "Socio-economic Developments and Their Relationship to Multidenominational Missions in a Benguet Community." *Philippine Journal of Culture and Society* 2(1–2): 61–71.

Tauli, Anne. 1984. "Historical Background to the Land Problem in the Cordillera." In *Dakami Ya Nan Dagami: Papers and Proceedings of the First Cordillera Multi-Sectoral Land Congress*. Baguio, Cordillera Consultative Committee. 66–88.

Thomas, William, ed. 1956. *Man's Role in Changing the Face of the Earth*. Chicago: University of Chicago Press.

Thompson, E. P. 1978. *The Poverty of Theory and Other Essays*. New York and London: Monthly Review Press.

Toulmin, Stephen. 1990. *Cosmopolis: The Hidden Agenda of Modernity*. New York: The Free Press.

Trimberger, Ellen Kay. 1984. "E. P. Thompson: Understanding the Process of History." *In* Theda Skocpol, ed., *Vision and Method in Historical Sociology*. Cambridge: Cambridge University Press. 211–243.

Turner, B. L. 1989. "The Specialist-Synthesis Approach to the Revival of Geography: The Case of Cultural Ecology." *Annals of the Association of American Geographers* 79(1): 88–100.

United States Bureau of the Census. 1905. *Census of the Philippine Islands*. Washington D.C.: Government Printing Office.

Valdepenas, Vicente, and Gemelino Bautista. 1977. *The Emergence of the Philippine Economy*. Manila: Papyrus.

Veracion, V. P. 1077. "Diameter Growth of Tapped Benguet Pines." *Sylvatrop* 2(2): 127–130.

Volckmann, R. W. 1954. *We Remained: Three Years Behind the Enemy Lines in the Philippines*. New York: W. W. Norton.

Volkman, Toby. 1984. "Great Performances: Toraja Cultural Identity in the 1970s." *American Ethnologist* 11(1).

———. 1985. *Feasts of Honor: Ritual and Change in the Toraja Highlands*. Urbana and Chicago: University of Illinois Press.

von der Mehden, Fred. 1986. *Religion and Modernization in Southeast Asia*. Syracuse: Syracuse University Press.

Voss, Joachim. 1980. "Cooperation and Market Penetration: Indigenous and Institutional Forms of Cooperation in the Cordillera Central of Northern Luzon." *VRF Series* 75. Tokyo: Institute of Developing Economies.

———. 1983. "Capitalist Penetration and Local Resistance: Continuity and Transformations of the Social Relations of Production of the Sagada Igorots of Northern Luzon." Unpublished Ph.D. Dissertation, Department of Anthropology, University of Toronto, Toronto.

Wadell, Eric. 1972. "Agricultural Evolution in the New Guinea Highlands." *Pacific Viewpoint* 13(1): 18–29.

Watts, Michael. 1983. *Silent Violence: Food, Famine, and Peasantry in Northern Nigeria*. Berkeley, Los Angeles, London: University of California Press.

Weber, Max. 1904 (1930). *The Protestant Ethic and the Spirit of Capitalism*. New York: Charles Scribner's and Sons.

White, Leslie. 1959. *The Evolution of Culture: Civilization to the Fall of Rome*. New York: McGraw-Hill.

Wiber, Melanie. 1985. "Dynamics of the Peasant Household Economy: Labor Recruitment and Allocation in an Upland Philippine Community." *Journal of Anthropological Research* 41(4): 427–441.

———. 1986. "Communal, Corporate and Cooperative: Property Relations of the Ibaloi of Northern Luzon, Philippines." Unpublished Ph.D. Dissertation, Department of Anthropology, University of Alberta, Edmonton.

———. 1989. "'The Canao Imperative': Changes in Resource Control,

Stratification and the Economy of Ritual among the Ibaloi of Northern Luzon. *In* Susan Russell and Clark Cunningham, eds., *Changing Lives, Changing Rites: Ritual and Social Dynamics in Philippine and Indonesian Uplands*. Ann Arbor: Michigan Studies in South and Southeast Asian Studies, Number 1. 45–62.

Wilson, L. L. 1947. *Igorot Mining Methods and Legends*. Baguio: Published by the Author.

Wolf, Eric. 1966. *Peasants*. Englewood Cliffs, New Jersey: Prentice-Hall.

———. 1982. *Europe and the People Without History*. Berkeley, Los Angeles, London: University of California Press.

Worcester, Dean C. N.d. "The Government of the Philippines under American Rule" and "What the United States Has Done for the Non-Christian Tribes of the Philippine Islands." Unpublished Manuscripts, Bentley Historical Library, Worcester Collection, Box 1, Folders 20 and 21: University of Michigan, Ann Arbor.

———. 1903. *Slavery and Peonage in the Philippine Islands*. Manila: Bureau of Printing.

———. 1906. "The Non-Christian Tribes of Northern Luzon." *Philippine Journal of Science* 1:791–887.

———. 1930. *The Philippines Past and Present*. New York: Macmillan.

Wurm, S. A. and S. Hattori, eds. 1983. *Language Atlas of the Pacific: Volume 2, Japan Area, Taiwan (Formosa), the Philippines, Mainland and Insular Southeast Asia*. Canberra: Australian Academy of the Humanities.

Zimmerer, Karl. 1988. "Seeds of Peasant Subsistence: Agrarian Structure, Crop Ecology, and Quechua Agricultural Knowledge with Special Reference to the Loss of Biological Diversity in the Southern Peruvian Andes." Unpublished Ph.D. Dissertation, Department of Geography, University of California, Berkeley.

ARCHIVAL SOURCES

The Bancroft Historical Library, Berkeley.
The Bentley Historical Library, Ann Arbor.
The Cordilleran Studies Center Library, Baguio, the Philippines.
The Field Museum of Natural History, Chicago.
The National Archives, Washington, D.C. (Record Group 350).

NEWSPAPERS

Baguio Midland Courier, Baguio, the Philippines.

Index

Abatan, 1, 15, 90, 141–142, 205, 227
Abra River, 1, 175
ACCFA (Agricultural Credit and Co-operative Financing Administration), 128
Accounting, indigenous, 91
Agno River, 1, 24, 28, 175, 180
Agricultural chemicals, 2, 122, 130, 135, 143–144, 164, 169, 172
Agricultural intensification, 38, 41–44, 172
Agriculture. *See* Animal husbandry; Subsistence cropping; Swidden; Vegetable cultivation
Alcohol problems, 191, 203. *See also* Rice beer
Alnus japonica, 179
American colonialists: administrative system, 15; encouragement of vegetable growing, 96; ethnographic conceptions, 12; failure to provide relief after war, 110; forestry policy, 174; impressions of Cordilleran peoples, 103–104; interference with rituals, 100; land policies, 56, 196, 198; political regime, 99–101; public works, 102; racism, 103; and social stratification, 234; visions of future, 104–105
Ancestor worship, 1, 59, 61, 66–67, 173
Ancestral lands, 196–197
Ancestral spirits (*amed*), 59; and control of luck, 3; communications with, 74. *See also* Prestige feast; Rituals
Andropogon annulatus, 32
Animal husbandry: damage during the war, 110; decline, 117; interference by American authorities, 100; and land tenure, 55; prewar patterns, 30–31; and social relations, 46–47; and trade, 85–86
Animal sacrifice: changes in, 231; and Christianity, 221; and curing rituals, 60; and jury deliberations, 76; prewar patterns, 65–67. *See also* Paganism; Prestige feast; Rituals

Antolin, Francisco, 83
Aquino, Benigno, 169
Aquino, Corazon, 211
Atok, 96, 101, 121, 227
Autonomy, Cordilleran, 210–211

Bad-ayan, 108, 141–142, 155, 159, 188, 227
Baguio, 1, 3, 79, 88, 96, 138, 142–143, 154, 189, 229, 244; vegetable market in, 15, 140
Bakun, 186, 225
Balweg, Conrado, 211
Banditry (the "*busol* problem"), 50, 100
Banking. *See* Capital
Barrows, David, 95
Beans, 126, 133
Beets, 166
Bell peppers, 126, 133
Bidens pilosa, 36
Blackburn, Don, 107–108
Blaikie, Piers, 8
Blankets, ritual, 71–72, 88, 222
Bodley, John, 5
Bontoc: agricultural patterns, 43; animosity toward, 88; diet, 65; religion, 229
Boserup, Ester, 41
Brookfield, Harold, 8
Bulldozers, 4, 183, 192, 214

Caballero, Evelyn, 260
Cabbage, 95, 119–120, 123, 125, 132, 136, 139, 159, 170, 184
Cajanus cajanus, 24
Calvinism, 241
Cancian, Frank, 243
Capital: and agricultural cooperatives, 128; bank loans, 163; bank loans and class, 155; bank loans and delinquency, 165; cultural acceptance, 235; financing from vegetable traders, 168; postwar sources, 151–152; and religious expectations, 207, 219, 238; shortages in frontier zones, 186;

Designer: U. C. Press Staff
Compositor: G&S Typesetters, Inc.
Text: 10/13 Palatino
Display: Palatino
Printer: Braun-Brumfield, Inc.
Binder: Braun-Brumfield, Inc.